Cambridge Studies in the History and Theory of Politics

EDITORS

MAURICE COWLING   J. G. A. POCOCK
G. R. ELTON   J. R. POLE
E. KEDOURIE   WALTER ULLMANN

A MACHIAVELLIAN TREATISE
by
STEPHEN GARDINER

A MACHIAVELLIAN TREATISE

BY STEPHEN GARDINER

EDITED AND TRANSLATED BY
PETER SAMUEL DONALDSON

CAMBRIDGE UNIVERSITY PRESS

CAMBRIDGE

LONDON · NEW YORK · MELBOURNE

Published by the Syndics of the Cambridge University Press
The Pitt Building, Trumpington Street, Cambridge CB2 1RP
Bentley House, 200 Euston Road, London NW1 2DB
32 East 57th Street, New York, NY 10022, USA
296 Beaconsfield Parade, Middle Park, Melbourne 3206, Australia

© Cambridge University Press 1975

Library of Congress catalogue card number: 74-12963

hard covers ISBN: 0 521 20593X

First published 1975

Printed in Great Britain
at the
University Printing House, Cambridge
(Euan Phillips, University Printer)

Library of Congress cataloguing in publication data

Gardiner, Stephen, Bp. of Winchester, 1483?-1555.
  A Machiavellian treatise.
  (Cambridge studies in the history and theory of politics)
  Translation of Ragionamento dell'advenimento delli inglesi et normanni in
Britannia, a 16th century ms. that was originally written in English.
  Originated from the editor's thesis, Columbia. Includes bibliographical references
and index. 1. Political science—Early works to 1700. 2. Machiavelli, Niccolò,
1469-1527—Influence.
I. Donaldson, Peter Samuel, 1942-   II. Title.
JC137.G37 1975   320.1   74-12963

ISBN 0-521-20593-X

CONTENTS

PREFACE

The text edited and translated here is the last work of Stephen Gardiner, Bishop of Winchester, a leading statesman in the reign of Henry VIII and Lord Chancellor under Philip and Mary. It is entitled, in the Italian version of George Rainsford which is the only form in which it has survived, *Ragionamento dell' advenimento delli inglesi et normanni in Britannia*. There are two manuscripts, Escorial I. III. 17 and Besançon 1169, and these have been almost totally ignored by previous scholars. In fact, apart from the several catalogue references, there is only one previous notice of the existence of the work. In 1933, in an introduction to his edition of Gardiner's letters, James Arthur Muller cited a reference to the text in the *Catalogue général des manuscrits des Bibliothèques Publiques de France*. Muller, Gardiner's ablest biographer, had not been aware of the existence of the work previously. He asked Pierre Janelle, another leading Gardiner specialist who had not known of the treatise before, to examine it, but apparently this was not done, and the business of following up Muller's valuable lead has gone unattended until now. The present edition owes its existence to the suggestion of Professor Paul Oskar Kristeller: he examined the Besançon manuscript in 1966 and recognized the need for an edition. When work on that manuscript was nearly complete, Professor Kristeller found a reference to the second manuscript in a catalogue of Italian MSS at the library of El Escorial. This manuscript proved to be the one sent to Philip II to whom the Italian translation is dedicated, and it has served as the copy text for this edition.

According to the translator (fol. I^r) Gardiner's original text was in English. No copy of an English version has been found, and this is not surprising, for Gardiner's posture in the work is far more pro-Spanish than he would have wished to appear to his countrymen. It is unlikely that Gardiner wanted an audience much larger than the two men to whom the surviving MSS were sent (Philip II and Antoine Perrenot, Bishop of Arras and later Cardinal Granvelle, Charles V's chief diplomatic minister), and when Elizabeth became queen the translator or anyone else who had a copy of the work would have had little reason to retain it, much less make it public, for Gardiner's work, though nominally historical, offers political counsel to Philip of Spain designed to perpetuate Habsburg rule in England. The work does treat the Norman and Anglo-Saxon conquests, as the title says, but the purpose was not solely historical. The dynastic changes in England's past are presented as parallels to the coming of Philip, and the historical examples are explored for the sake of practical political counsel: how can a foreign prince rule England effectively and pass it on to his heirs?

In turning history into political advice, Gardiner drew upon the greatest political writer of the time: though the debt is never acknowledged, Gardiner borrows some 3,000 words directly from *The Prince* and *The Discourses*. Gardiner's relation to Machiavelli was, like his relation to the Habsburgs, more intimate than scholars have thus far been able to demonstrate, and the Elizabethan polemicists who pictured him as a Machiavellian schemer determined to betray poor England to the Spaniard were, despite their simplifications, not altogether mistaken. In fact, a fresh and thorough examination of Gardiner's whole career, rich in contradictions, is now in order; not only because Gardiner was, literally, a Machiavellian, but also because the present work clarifies his position on many important issues of the day, and, above all, affords an unequalled opportunity to study the way in which he looked to history and to political theory for the solution of practical political problems.

Gardiner's treatise is also an essential document in the wider history of European Machiavellism, and should be studied in that context: there were others, like Nifo, who quoted Machiavelli at length without attribution or otherwise covertly transmitted his works and ideas. There were others, too, like William Thomas, who tried to influence the policies of their sovereigns by offering analyses of current affairs drawn from Machiavelli. Gardiner's case is perhaps the most interesting and new work is called for in this field also. The present introduction cannot adequately explore either Gardiner's career or sixteenth-century Machiavellism in the light of the new evidence, and full treatment of these questions must be reserved for another occasion. This introduction is confined to the manuscript tradition, textual questions, the biography of the translator, a brief account of the sources, and the placing of the treatise in its immediate historical context in the reign of Mary.

Also, the present edition is of Gardiner's text and Rainsford's dedication only: the MSS include an appendix by Rainsford entitled *Ritratto d'Inghilterra*. This work was intended to supplement what Gardiner had done, to complete his analysis of English history and politics with the kind of formal description of the country that the Venetian ambassadors customarily sent home at the end of their service. It is usefully studied together with Gardiner's text, particularly as Rainsford's opinions on a number of issues are different from those of Gardiner. However, it has been decided to publish Rainsford's text separately in a forthcoming volume of the *Camden Miscellany* series. The limitation of space has made this necessary: his work, particularly his economic analysis of English society, raises issues of its own impossible to treat fully here.

I should like to thank Professor Kristeller for his generous help at every stage. Professor William Nelson, Professor G. R. Elton, Professor Richard Koffler and my wife Alice Donaldson also gave me the kind of assistance without which I could not have finished the job. I received valuable aid also from Professor Joseph Mazzeo, Professor Eugene Rice, Professor Daniel Javitch, Professor William Watson, Professor Paolo Valesio, Miss Judith Shenfield, Mrs Anne Rourke, Michael Moore, Craig Karpel, David Miller, John Muller IV, and my parents John J. and Constance Donaldson. I wish to thank the libraries of Besançon and El Escorial for permission to use their manuscripts, and the Old Dominion Fund of MIT for financial support.

This project, which began as a PhD dissertation at Columbia, has been long in preparation, and the present volume is not the end of it. The words of William Watts, Augustine's seventeenth century translator, seem relevant to my own experience, as they have seemed to other translators since his time: 'This translation I began for the exercise of my Lenten Devotions; but I quickly found it to exercise more than my Devotions: it exercised my skill (all I had); it exercised my Patience, it exercised my Friends too (for it is incomparably the hardest task that ever I yet undertook).'

Cambridge, Mass.　　　　　　　　　　　　　　PETER S. DONALDSON
May 1974

RAGIONAMENTO

DELL' ADVENIMENTO DELLI INGLESI
ET NORMANNI IN BRITANNIA .

STEPHANO . ALPHONSO ·

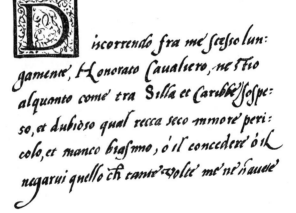

iscorrendo fra me stesso lun:
gamente, Honorato Caualiero, ne stio
alquanto come tra Silla et Caribbe)sospe:
so, et dubioso qual recca seco mmore peri:
colo, et manco biasmo, ò il concedere ò il
negarui quello ch tante volte me ne hauete

INTRODUCTION

THE MANUSCRIPTS

There are two extant manuscripts of Stephen Gardiner's *Ragionamento dell'advenimento delli inglesi et normanni in Britannia*.
(I) Escorial MS I. III. 17 (cited as E). A manuscript of 197 leaves numbered I–IV, 1–189 with two blank leaves at the beginning and two at the end, parchment, 214 × 159 mm. The cover, which is not original, is red silk. The title page has gilt lettering on a red ground as does the salutation (fol. II^r) which is also ornamented in gilt. There are gilt borders on the title page and throughout the dedication (fols. I^r–IV^r). The text is in a careful Italic hand with corrections in several places in the same hand. The margins are very wide, ruled, and contain many notes in the same hand as the text. Gardiner's treatise occupies fols. 1^r–140^r: the remainder of the MS is devoted to Rainsford's appendix, *Ritratto d'Ingliterra*.

The formal appearance of the manuscript suggests that it was the presentation copy prepared for Philip II to whom the translation is dedicated, and this is confirmed by its inclusion in the *Catalogo de los libros de su Magestad* of 1574.[1] The MS was described in Jole Ruggieri's 'Manoscritti italiani nella Biblioteca dell'Escuriale', *La bibliofilia*, XXXIII (1931), 148, and is listed in P. Gregorio de Andrés' *Documentos para la historia del monasterio de San Lorenzo de el Escorial*, Vol. 7 (Madrid, 1964), p. 197.

(II) Besançon MS 1169 (cited as B). This manuscript was described by Castan as follows:

MS 1169: 1556. Ecriture penchée, de fort calibre, très soignée, d'un copiste italien. Papier – 93 feuillets, 290 sur 210 millim. Manchettes. Rel. originale, en carton, couvert de veau; fleurons d'or dans les compartiments du dos et aux angles, ainsi qu'au milieu des filets qui encadrent les plats. Sur la principale tranche, l'inscription suivante est peinte transversalement, au vermillon: RAGIONAMENTO–DELLE–COSE–D'ANGLITERRA.[2]

This copy is in ink throughout, lacking the gilt lettering and other formalities of presentation of E. The copyist may have been Italian,

---

[1] Entries of books in Italian from this catalog are printed by Jole Ruggieri in *La bibliofilia*, XXXII (1930). From the Gardiner entry we learn that the MS was formerly covered in crimson velvet embroidered with the royal arms in gold (pp. 422–3).
[2] *Catalogue général des manuscrits des Bibliothèques Publiques de France – Départements*, Vol. 32, Besançon, ed. Auguste Castan (Paris, 1897), I, 823.

I

as Castan states, but 1556 was not too early to find good professional Italic handwriting in England. The hand had been in limited use in England since the end of the fifteenth century: Linacre used it customarily, as did Leland, and by the 1550s it was common for educated people and professional scribes to learn it. The first Italic signature in the Common Paper of the Scriveners' Company appears in 1554[1].

The MS is listed in an undated (late sixteenth or early seventeenth century) inventory of the books of Cardinal Granvelle.[2] It is absent from the inventory of 1607[3] but appears in the first inventory of the library founded by Abbé Boisot at Besançon in 1694 and also in the inventory of 1764.[4] Muller's notice appears in *The Letters of Stephen Gardiner* (Cambridge, 1933), p. xxxv.

A microfilm copy of this MS has been used in preparing this edition.

DATE OF COMPOSITION

Gardiner's treatise is in the form of a dialogue between Stephano (a character based on the author) and Alphonso, who has come to England in search of knowledge of affairs of state. The discussion takes place at the English court, which is referred to as the court of Philip, King of England (fol. 7^v). Philip came to England in the summer of 1554 and began to hold court in late August. But since the dialogue is a fictional one, there is no reason to exclude the possibility that work on it began earlier, in the expectation that there would soon be a court of Philip in England. The Queen announced her intention of marrying Philip in November 1553, and work on the treatise could have begun no earlier, for not only does the dialogue take place at Philip's court, but the political questions that occupy the interlocutors, especially those concerning the behavior of a foreign prince in a new possession in which he intends to found a dynasty, assume the Spanish marriage.

1 Hilary Jenkinson, *The Later Court Hands in England* (Cambridge, 1927), p. 63; see also Alfred Fairbank and Bruce Dickins, *The Italic Hand in Tudor Cambridge* (London, 1962).
2 *Catalogus mss. codicum bibliothecae Granvellanae*, Papiers de Philibert de la Mare, recueillis par Fontette, Bib. Nat. coll. Moreau, vol. 849, fols. 180–3 – as cited by Castan, p. xvi.
3 Castan examined one copy of this inventory, and L. P. Gachard printed another in *Inventaire des papiers laissés par le cardinal de Granvelle à Madrid en 1586. Inventaire des archives trouvées au Palais de Granvelle, à Besançon, en 1607. Histoire d'un procès célèbre à propos de ce dernier inventaire* (Brussels, 1862).
4 Castan, p. 822.

But while the treatise could have been started before August 1554, it is doubtful whether it could have been finished before Philip actually arrived, bringing the political problems of the new reign into sharper focus. At the close of the treatise, Stephano hears the six o'clock bells, and takes his guest to dinner with the Duke of Norfolk. This suggests a date after August 1554 for Thomas Howard, Duke of Norfolk, died on 25 August and his grandson, a boy of nineteen, inherited his title on that date. The old duke was never at court during the period in question. He fled before Wyatt's forces in January 1554 and retired to Norfolk on 30 January.[1] The new duke had been at court since Mary's coronation. When Philip came to England, he was appointed first gentleman of the chamber and became a great favorite of the King, who stood godfather to his first son in 1557.[2] Thus the duke referred to in the treatise is probably the younger.

Also, the closing pages of the book, in which Philip is called upon to bring peace to Europe, make best sense if a date after 25 October 1555 is assumed. On that day Charles V yielded the sovereignty of the Netherlands to Philip, who thus became the leader of the Habsburg side in the dynastic struggles against the Valois, and hopes for European peace briefly turned to him.[3] In the last pages of Gardiner's work, Philip is addressed in terms which would have been inappropriate while his father retained his full power: in particular, Gardiner says that by the English marriage 'his kingdoms and his power in these parts are now consolidated, and he has become without dispute the arbiter of peace and war of all Christendom' (fol. 139ᵛ). Both the joining of the kingdoms (the Netherlands and England) and Philip's role as arbiter of all Christendom argue the late date. It is not likely that Gardiner was here indulging in careless inflation: he was a leading proponent of peace between Habsburg and Valois, and is here addressing a serious plea for peace to the man now in a position to bring it about. If so, Gardiner worked on the treatise during the very last weeks of his life while confined, for the most part, to his bed.[4] He died on 12 November 1555. Thus the

[1] *Chronicle of Queen Jane*, ed. J. G. Nichols, Camden Soc. (London, 1850), pp. 37–40.
[2] Mandell Creighton in *DNB* s.v. 'Howard, Thomas II', 'Howard, Thomas III'.
[3] Cf. E. H. Harbison, *Rival Ambassadors at the Court of Queen Mary* (Princeton, 1940), p. 255: 'How would the Emperor's coming abdication of his sovereignty in the Low Countries affect the international situation? Would Philip listen more readily than his father to overtures of peace? Such questions as these had first to be answered before the peace of Europe could be settled.'
[4] James Arthur Muller, *Stephen Gardiner and the Tudor Reaction* (London, 1926), chapter xxxiv.

treatise was written between November 1553 and November 1555, and probably not finished until very near the end of that period.

GEORGE RAINSFORD AND THE RAINSFORDS

Rainsford dated his translation of Gardiner's work 16 March 1556 (fol. IV[r]), four months after Gardiner's death. Thus before the story of the transmission of the text can be told, it will be necessary to ask who Rainsford was, what his connection to Gardiner may have been, and how he may have obtained a copy of Gardiner's treatise.

It is possible to identify the translator with confidence: there were several Rainsford families in sixteenth century England, but only one George Rainsford is recorded, and though information about the man himself is scant, there is ample indication that several members of his family must have known Gardiner: one brother had been gentleman usher to Henry VIII during Gardiner's years at court, and another brother and a nephew served Lord and Lady Lisle, Gardiner's close friends and hosts during his years in France.

George Rainsford was descended from the Rainsfords of Rainsford Hall in Lancaster. His great-grandfather acquired the manor of Great Tew or Twe Magna in the county of Oxford in the middle of the fifteenth century. George was the third son of John Rainsford, who died in 1551. As a younger brother he did not inherit Great Tew: in fact, according to his father's will he inherited only a gold ring, a chamblet gown, a satin doublet, and forty shillings.[1]

As the son of a prosperous country gentleman he was probably educated at the university or at the Inns of Court, though it has been impossible to find him in the surviving records.[2] He probably travelled as well, almost certainly to Italy, for his Italian is quite fluent,[3]

---

[1] *The Visitations of the County of Oxford*, ed. William Turner (London, 1871), pp. 165–70; *The Visitation of the County of Warwick*, ed. John Fetherston (London, 1877), pp. 48–9; *Oxfordshire Record Society*, XVII (1935), 60; Bodleian MS Wills Oxon., Ser. I, Vol. III, fol. 66[r].

[2] University records for the period are far from complete (see *Book of Matriculations and Degrees 1544–1659*, ed. John and J. A. Venn [Cambridge, 1913], introduction, for an account of how records were kept). Rainsford's descendants are listed in the records of Lincoln's Inn from 1586 onward, and a Thomas Rainsford, possibly a relative, was admitted in 1568. See *Records of the Honourable Society of Lincoln's Inn, Vol. 1: Admissions from A.D. 1420 to A.D. 1799*, pp. 76, 105, 198, 276, 294, 315.

[3] William Thomas published his *Italian Grammar* in 1550, and after that it was increasingly common for Englishmen to learn some Italian at home: but Rainsford's proficiency suggests travel. He makes many grammatical errors (or his scribe does) but the prose is fluid and idiomatic.

4

but no record of his travels has come down to us.[1] We know
from the heralds' accounts that he married Katherine Taverner, the
daughter of a prosperous farmer in Theydon Garnon, Essex, and
in 1552 he appears as a complainant before the Court of Requests
in a dispute concerning the administration of his deceased father-
in-law's property. The estate was large: it is reckoned in the de-
positions at £300 plus the leasehold of Garnon Mill Farm. The
farmhouse, which stood until 1950, was a substantial one, described
in the reign of Edward IV as 'anothyr costlewe byldyng at a ferme
callyd Garnouns myll, new byldyd'.[2]

Taverner had left

To my godson, John Rainsford, 20s ... To my daughter, Katherine, £20
on the day of her marriage, willing my brother George Rainsford to have
the guardianship of my daughter, and to convert such £20 for her benefit,
with 50s for his trouble ... I give to my said son Christopher my leasehold
farm of Garnish mill, with stock and stores ... My brothers Maynard and
Glastock are to have the keeping of the farm until he attains twenty one
years, and to render their accounts to Rainsford and my neighbor Thos.
Shingleby ... Executors Wybred, Rainsford, Glastock, Maynard.[3]

Within a year of Taverner's death Rainsford and Wybred were
charging that the estate had been mismanaged, and the property
converted to the use of Maynard and Glascock. The award of the
court is not recorded.

Taverner's will was made in 1552, and it indicates that George
Rainsford had not yet married Katherine Taverner at that time.
Rainsford's own will, made on 23 March 1559 and proved at the
Court of the Archdeacon of Essex, makes it clear that at that time
he had six children, only two of whom were minors. Thus he
must have been married before, and must have been in his forties,
at least, when he worked on Gardiner's treatise. Styling himself
George Rainsford, gentleman, he left a total of £90 'in money and

---

[1] He is not listed in Io[hannes] Aloys[ius] Andrich, *De natione Anglica et Scota iuristarum
universitatis Patavinae* (Padua, 1892), and is absent from the careful lists compiled by
George B. Parks, *The English Traveler to Italy* (Stanford, 1954) as well as from the
supplement to Parks, Edward John Baskerville, 'The English Traveller to Italy
1547–1560' (unpub. diss. Columbia 1967).

[2] Documents of the case are in the Record Office, R.O. Req.2/1/57, Req.2/2/125 and
Req.2/18/77 and are listed in *List of Proceedings in the Court of Requests, Vol. 1*,
Public Record Office Lists and Indexes, No. 21 (New York, 1963). On the farm see
Transactions of the Essex Archaeological Society, N.S., v (1895), 28 and *Victoria History
of Essex*, iv, 260.

[3] *Calendar of State Papers, Domestic, Elizabeth, with Addenda 1547–65*, VI, 413–14. The
will is dated 16 August 1552.

money worth' to his six children and his son-in-law, Andrew Larder, who was to get his cloak and a coat of buff leather as well. Whatever was left after these bequests was to go to Richard, the eldest son, who was also to receive the farm and the lease of the park ground for four years, after which the farm would go to the son-in-law. Rainsford bequeathed the care of his soul to 'almightye god to our Lady Saynt Mary and all the celestiall company',[1] a dedication perhaps suggestive of a preference for the older religious forms. George Rainsford was buried on 27 March 1559 in the parish of North Weald Bassett, which adjoins the parish of Theydon Garnon in which his father-in-law's farm was located.[2]

George Rainsford was a younger brother, obliged to seek his fortune. It does not seem that he succeeded very well. His marriage to Katherine Taverner brought him something, which he tried to increase through litigation. We do not know how his translation was received by Philip II, but it did not earn him a pension or a place at court. In his *Ritratto d'Ingliterra* he complains of the fate of younger brothers in England. He paints a glowing picture of the life of the gentry, with its hospitality, independence and local loyalty. The gentry

rarely come to court, and they do not seek offices, honors or dignities; except for the younger brothers, who do not inherit in England . . . they do not divide estates and patrimonies among survivors as is done in Germany and Italy, but only the first born is the heir. The other brothers must be patient and attend the kindness of the first born. Therefore all the younger sons become soldiers or serve at court, so that by those means they may gradually acquire a living comparable to that of their elder brothers (fols. 155^v–156^v).[3]

His own eldest brother was a very successful man, and George never attained a standard of living comparable to his.

William Rainsford was a gentleman usher to Henry VIII from 1516 until the end of the reign. He was a daily waiter, a steward, and toward the end of the reign he was the man responsible for

---

[1] Essex Record Office D/AEW/3/321. Mr K. C. Newton, County Archivist, supplied a photocopy of the will, which is listed in *Wills at Chelmsford (Essex and East Hertfordshire)*, Vol. 1 (*1440–1690*), British Record Society, No. 78 (London, 1958), p. 339.

[2] The burial is recorded in the parish register at the Essex Record Office (D/P 84/1/1).

[3] 'Vengono rare volte à la corte, non circanno ne officii, honori, ne dignitade (eccetti i fratelli minori i quali non hereditanno in Ingliterra). . . . Non dividono i stati et patrimonii tra gli figlioli, come si fa in Alemagna et in Italia, anzi il primogenito solo è herede; li altri fratelli stanno pacienti, et à la cortesia del primogenito. Pero si danno tutti a l'armi et di servire nella corte, accioche per quel mezo vengino à gradi di comperarsi un stato di vivere à pari di lor fratelli.'

preparing various apartments for the royal presence, supervising
the preparation of the parliament chamber at Westminster, 'making
ready' at Grafton, Dover and Sittingbourne. In this work he was
assisted by three yeomen and three grooms (listed in the royal
household expenses as 'Mr Rainsford's servants' along with the
amount of their 'reward', usually 6s 8d). Rainsford's own wages
for the period 1526–45 were £20 per annum in addition to 'bouch
of court' and stabling for three horses. When Henry died he left
£200 to be divided between Rainsford, Blunt and Norris, gentlemen ushers.[1]

But the chief reward for service to the King was, at that time, land,
and Rainsford was able to obtain a number of valuable grants and
leases. In 1531 he was given custody of the person and lands of
Edward Hall, lunatic. With the fall of the monasteries, his property
increased greatly. He received a grant of the priory and lands of
Wroxton in Oxfordshire in 1537, and thereafter an interest in the
lands of Combe Abbey, Warwickshire. He obtained a lease for
Ellingspittel Priory and lands at Peterchurch, Warwickshire from
the Duchess of Somerset, and was granted the rectory and advowson
of the vicarage of Michell Tewe and the chapel of Netherworton.[2]
A letter relating to his negotiations for land is preserved, and it
shows that Rainsford was not only a suitor for land himself, but
was in a position to help others obtain it. Dated 8 December 1539,
the letter, from Richard Androys [Andrews] is calendared thus:

Is sorry that he put him to so much pain and begs him to regard no letter
but this. Has tried all day the truth for Water Eton ferm and Cuttislo close.
The former is gone by convent seal three years ago to a neighbour of the
writer's. The latter was also granted by convent seal which is now in the
keeping of the lord Privy Seal [Thomas Cromwell], as Dr London can
inform him. It was he caused all the seals granted under colour to come to
my lord's hands. Begs him to speak to my lord for the said seal, which is
£6 yearly. Will give my lord £20 for it. Reynesford may obtain Sandford
and little Tewe in his own name. Will give him 20 mks if he obtains
Cuttislo for 40 years. Would not sue for it, but that it lies next his own
ground. Hears that Dr London is now with my lord. Will help Reynesford
to some pasture about Combe Abbey, if possible.[3]

[1] *Letters and Papers, Foreign and Domestic, of the Reign of Henry VIII* (London, 1862–
1932), hereafter cited as L.P., II, 872; XIII, Pt. II, 499, 537; XIV, Pt. II, 313; XVI, 180;
XX, Pt. II, 550; *The Genealogist*, N.S., XXX (1914), 20; *A Collection of Ordinances
for the Government of the Royal Household* . . . , Society of Antiquaries (London,
1790), p. 169; *Acts of the Privy Council of England*, ed. John Roche Dasent, N.S. II, 186.
[2] L.P., V, 103; XII, Pt. I, 251; XIV, Pt. I, 4; XVI, 276; XXI, Pt. I, 353.
[3] L.P., XIV, Pt. II, 239.

The relationship between Andrews and Rainsford was a mutually profitable one, and was cemented by the marriage of Rainsford's heir to Andrews' daughter.[1] The letter suggests that Rainsford had influence with Cromwell. What the precise relationship was is not clear, but among Cromwell's papers is 'a bill of Mr Raynsford for the room of a sewer',[2] and in 1532 Thomas Elyot wrote to Cromwell, thanking him for his letters by Mr Rainsford and asking him to 'continue yor favor toward Mr Raynford whome ye shall fynde as honist and faithful as any'.[3] The Rainsford referred to is probably John, William's younger (and George's elder) brother, who will be discussed below. William seems to have used his influence with Cromwell, with Elyot, and with others to help several members of his family to find employment.

When not at court, Rainsford served as justice of the peace in Oxfordshire, and in that capacity participated in the process of the dissolution of the monasteries from which he profited as a courtier, for we find him the recipient of commissions of inquiry into Church holdings in Henry's reign as well as in Edward's. After Henry's death William no longer appears at court, and it is only in his local offices of justice of the peace and, after 1549 (the year in which he is first referred to as Sir William) as high sheriff that he appears in the record thereafter. He died in 1555 and was buried in the chapel at Great Tew.[4]

Gardiner must have known him: we cannot say how well or whether as friend, ally[5] or mere acquaintance, but Gardiner had

---

[1] D. Royce, 'History of Great Tew and South Newington', Arch. Soc. of North Oxfordshire, *Reports and Transactions*, XIII (1875), 7.

[2] *L.P.*, VI, 132.

[3] B.M. Cotton. MS Titus B.I., fol. 372. The summary in *L.P.*, V, 674 omits this reference to Rainsford.

[4] *Calendar of Patent Rolls, Edward VI*, I, 88, V, 339, 415; *L.P.*, VIII, 50; XI, 491, XII, Pt. II, 52; XX, Pt. I, 323; *List of Sheriffs for England and Wales*, PRO Lists and Indexes, No. 9, p. 109; *Acts of the Privy Council*, N.S., III, 181; IV, 116; V, 30; Royce, p. 7.

[5] There is an item in *L.P.* that may imply that William Rainsford was a conservative in religion like Gardiner: 'Gilbert Whetell came to Raynsford and Sir John of Powell who were together and twice or thrice spoke of "a pair of sheets", and said "he that lodgeth a priest overnight on the morning he shall find him a knave". Sir John replied "knave to thee again". Whetell then said "Priest, I counsel thee to bear a longer dagger for thou shalt have need thereof", and other "opprobrious words" at which all the folks in the church wondered' (*L.P.*, *Addenda*, Pt. II, 508). John and Thomas Rainford (see below) were members of the household of the conservative Lord and Lady Lisle, and may have shared their views. But only George Rainsford can be shown (on the evidence of his preface to Gardiner's work) definitely to have taken a Catholic position: there is not enough evidence to assess the religious views of the rest of the family.

first come to court in 1529 and was, after Cromwell's fall, perhaps Henry's closest adviser: he could scarcely have avoided meeting a man who had been gentleman usher to the King for all those years. Members of the Rainsford family could also have met Gardiner at the house of Lord and Lady Lisle at Calais, where Gardiner often stayed during his diplomatic missions in France. John, the brother intermediate in age between William and George Rainsford, was in their service for a time, as was his son Thomas.

In an interesting letter, Sir Thomas Elyot wrote to Lady Lisle to ask her to forgive her servant, Thomas Rainsford, for his gambling habits. Sir Thomas assured her that Rainsford repented dicing. Elyot considered the boy's uncle, the gentleman usher, his 'long approved friend', and promised that if the nephew is forgiven, the father and uncle 'will be bound to pray for her'.[1] This was in 1533. The following year the Duke of Suffolk recommended John Rainsford, Thomas' father, for a place in the Lisle household. After that the Rainsfords are frequently referred to as the carriers of letters between Lord and Lady Lisle and their correspondents.[2]

The Lisles were friends and allies of Gardiner's: in 1540, at the height of the struggle between Gardiner and Cromwell, Lisle was imprisoned in the Tower on a charge of having plotted to deliver Calais to Cardinal Pole. The shock of this episode drove Lady Lisle mad, and she remained mad for many years. In 1538 or 1539 Gardiner took James Basset, her son by a former marriage, into his service, and he became Gardiner's closest friend: Basset lived with Gardiner in the Tower during the Edwardian years, waited upon him day and night while he was dying, and was one of the executors of his will.[3]

Thus George Rainsford was connected, through his family, both to the court at which Gardiner served, and to members of the inner circle of Gardiner's acquaintants, the Lisles and Bassets.

TRANSMISSION OF THE TEXT

One may safely assume that the original English version never circulated widely because of its sensitive (Machiavellian, pro-Spanish) nature, and that Rainsford received the text from Gardiner himself or from someone with access to the Chancellor's papers

---

[1] L.P., VI, 605.
[2] L.P., VI, 146; VII, 153; XII, Pt. II, 430, 434, 445.
[3] Muller, *Stephen Gardiner*, 51, 69, 72, 90, 289, 291, 292.

after his death. The second possibility is the more likely, for if the translation had been commissioned, Rainsford would have wanted to say so in order to lend authority to his project. Instead, he dedicates the book to Philip and to the memory of Gardiner, and states that he has added his own description of England 'so that nothing might be lacking in this little book that might contribute to an understanding of the laws, procedures, customs, nature and humor of the people of Britain' (fol. IV^r). Thus he assumes Gardiner's purpose was to instruct Philip, and regards his own efforts as complementary to that intention, but he does not say that Gardiner asked him to translate the work nor otherwise give indication of how he received the text.

An attractive conjecture is that James Basset had a hand in the matter: on the one hand he knew the Rainsfords, for John and Thomas had served his family during his childhood. On the other hand, he was Gardiner's closest friend in the last years, and his executor. Gardiner's will makes no mention of manuscripts or private papers,[1] but no one was in a better position to have access to such material than Basset, who had been in continuous attendance on Gardiner in his final days. Basset was also Mary's Chamberlain and was fast becoming one of Philip's closest English associates:[2] he was thus in an excellent position to grasp the relevance of the late Chancellor's work to the immediate situation.

In the spring of 1556 Philip was in Brussels. Mary wanted him to return and was making diplomatic efforts to convince him that he could rule England effectively. A treatise such as Gardiner's, showing how foreign princes had succeeded in establishing themselves in England, could not have failed to interest her, and in fact the translation of the treatise may have been undertaken for diplomatic reasons. It is necessary to examine the circumstances in detail.

Mary's false pregnancy terminated in the spring of 1555, and by summer it was common knowledge that Philip would leave and that he was unlikely to return. Mary seems not to have known

---

[1] *Wills from Doctors' Commons*, ed. John Gough Nichols and John Bruce, Camden Soc. (London, 1863). The will does give the name of the man to whom Gardiner left his 'humanitie and lawe books' (Thomas Worliche).

[2] Basset received one of the largest pensions from Philip (300 crowns in 1557, 1300 crowns in 1558, see *Calendar of State Papers, Spanish*, XIII, 374, 405). Basset was entrusted with a number of diplomatic missions, and was active in planning strategy for the war with France: on 18 January 1558, Philip recommended that the Duke of Savoy follow Basset's suggestions for the prosecution of the war, and later Gomez wrote to Philip that 'if the English are to go overseas, measures should be taken in time to deal with the points raised by Basset', *Span. Cal.* XIII, 334, 345.

it, but it was the common gossip of the court, as in this anonymous note, written in August:

Some say that when he retires the Emperor will be in Brussels and that the King will go to see him on such pretext as may be devised, that he will not return here [i.e. to England] again, and that if the Queen wishes to stay with him, she will have to go and join him, and provide otherwise than heretofore for order in England.[1]

Order in England had not been provided for to his liking. He himself told Mary he considered his small role in the governing of the kingdom unbecoming to his dignity, and made his return conditional upon sharing the government with her.[2]

In her letters to the Emperor Mary pleads for the return of Philip. Here is one from April, when she had sent Lord Paget on a mission to Brussels:

Now that the abdication is over and the truce concluded, and the arrival of the King of Bohemia should contribute to permit the King, my husband, to return, I implore your Majesty most humbly, for the love of God, to do all that is possible to permit it. I see every day that the end of one negotiation is the beginning of another. I beg your Majesty to forgive my boldness, and to remember the unspeakable sadness I experience because of the absence of the King.[3]

In May, she writes that her Vice-Chamberlain, Jerningham, has returned from Brussels with hope that Philip would soon return: 'As your Majesty well knows, he is the chief joy and comfort I have in this world.'[4] And in July, she writes that she has waited long for Philip, 'however, as your Majesty has been pleased to break your promise in this connection, a promise you made to me regarding the return of the King, my husband, I must perforce be satisfied, although to my unspeakable regret'.[5] The editor, Royall Tyler, adds: 'written in a trembling hand'.

In April she dispatched Lord Paget to Brussels, bearing with him, possibly, Stephen Gardiner's political dialogue in George Rainsford's translation. Here is the Venetian ambassador's account of Paget's mission:

Her Majesty is determined to send this very day to the Imperial Court Lord Paget, now Lord Privy Seal . . . under pretence of congratulating the Emperor and the King on the truce, and in order that with this opportunity

---

[1] *Span. Cal.*, XIII, 247.   [2] *Calendar of State Papers, Venetian*, VI, Pt. I, 212.
[3] *Span. Cal.*, XIII, 259.   [4] *Ibid.*, 267.
[5] *Span. Cal.*, XIII, 271.

he may perform such office as was announced in my foregoing letters with regard to the King's return, reminding him as impressively as possible not only of the desire of the most Serene Queen and of the entire kingdom, but also of the need and necessity for compliance by reason of her Majesty's age, which does not admit of delay; and as told me by Cardinal Pole, Lord Paget will request the King, should he be delayed with the wish to wait for the King of Bohemia, or any other impediment, as his Bohemian majesty has come so far to let him proceed even to England, where the King and he can treat and decide all that and other business as conveniently as in Flanders, her consort being no less at home here than there; and in the meanwhile the most Serene Queen will not distress herself.

With the opportunity afforded by this commission, Lord Paget will be enabled to discover the inmost determination of the King and of the Emperor, and being deep in the confidence of both the one and the other, ascertain whether the delay is caused by any hidden motive; or because the King wishes for greater authority, and greater public marks of respect; or greater convenience and scope for availing himself of the revenues of the realm than he has had hitherto.[1]

Mary, in other words ('the need and necessity for compliance by reason of her Majesty's age') had not yet given up hope of producing an heir, despite the disappointment of her long false pregnancy, and she was ready to offer Philip increased authority if he would return. The Venetian ambassador at Brussels reported on Paget's mission from that court, and his account is more specific concerning the lengths to which Mary would go to have Philip return.

On the 13th instant Lord Paget arrived here, who had audience of the King of Spain immediately, and has returned to his Majesty every day, holding long conversations with him, and I understand that the chief object of his discourse was to inspire the King with that hope, on his return to England, of his being crowned, which has never yet been given by the Queen his consort; and besides performing this office in her name, he, of himself, as it were, proposed various means for adoption whereby to obtain the desired result, with the consent of those who can be induced to give it, and without risk from those who might choose to oppose the measure. He also communicated to him several things which it is necessary to do in that kingdom at present, and to provide for there, hereafter.[2]

In Mary's Council it had been Paget who was closest to Imperial interests, ever since her accession. He had suggested to Charles as early as 12 November 1554 that Philip take over the actual governing of England, with a reduced Privy Council which would exclude Bishop Gardiner, whom he characterized as inimical to the Empire.[3]

[1] *Ven. Cal.*, VI, Pt. I, 399.   [2] *Ibid.*, 415.   [3] *Span. Cal.*, XIII, 87–92.

Charles agreed in principle that Philip should begin to govern, 'for the object of the marriage is that he should do so', but took exception to dropping Gardiner from the Council and to other of Paget's specific suggestions, proposing the rule of Philip's great-grandfather Ferdinand of Aragon as a model. As Ferdinand with Isabella, so Philip should proceed with Mary so 'that while he in reality does everything, the initiative should always seem to proceed from the Queen and her Council'.[1]

While Paget had been friendly to the Empire, Gardiner had originally opposed the Spanish marriage, and had often opposed Paget on the question of Spanish control of England: but in the last months of his life he seemed to change course, favoring increased powers for Philip,[2] and it was said that he died reconciled to Paget.[3] Now it appeared that he had died leaving a manuscript of a work showing how England could be successfully ruled by a foreign prince, and those, like Mary and Paget, who wished to convince Philip to return could have found no more impressive demonstration that Gardiner would have agreed with their views. Philip, who was an avid reader of works on statecraft, had always admired Gardiner's political sense. For Paget to be able to enlist the implied support of the late Chancellor would have been a telling addition to the other persuasions he brought to Brussels. The translation is dated 16 March 1556, and thus it was ready by the time that Paget left in April.

Thus the Brussels mission was a politically appropriate occasion for the gift to Philip of a treatise such as Gardiner's, and the likelihood that the treatise was presented then seems increased by the fact that James Basset, Gardiner's executor, played a part in the negotiations for Philip's return. When Paget was in Brussels, it was Basset, not Mary, who wrote to him. The Queen was not well enough to write to the King, and thought it unsuitable to write to anyone else if not to him, and therefore employed Basset to make her pleasure known to Paget. The correspondence between the two men on the subject of the King's return continued even after Paget's return from Brussels, with an exchange of several letters in November and December 1556.[4]

---

[1] *Span. Cal.*, XIII, 90–1.

[2] Gardiner's attitude to Habsburg rule will be discussed more fully below: even when he opposed the marriage he was not as inimical to the Empire as he appeared.

[3] *Calendar of State Papers, Domestic (1547–1580)*, 72.

[4] Plas Newydd Papers, Early Paget Correspondence, Series 1, Box 2, fols. 35–44 (nos. 23–7). C. J. Harrison is currently engaged in making a calendar of the Early

Before Gardiner's treatise was sent to Philip, an appendix was added to it (Rainsford's *Ritratto d'Ingliterra*), and it is interesting that Rainsford's views on a number of issues differ from Gardiner's in ways that suggest the policies, dominant after Gardiner's death, of Paget.[1] Thus Gardiner argues for peace and blames the French–Imperial war entirely upon the Italian refugees (fols. 96^v–97^r). Rainsford celebrates the military might of England, recounts the litany of English victories over France, and recites the claim of the English sovereign to the crown of France (fols. 174^r–185^v). Rainsford, like Paget, also differed from Gardiner in his attitude toward the property confiscated from the Church by Henry VIII. For Gardiner, Henry 'gave his people great opportunity to conspire against him when he began the rape of the spiritual property' (fol. 127^v). Rainsford admits Henry usurped ecclesiastical powers in taking the land, but his main emphasis is upon the inestimable wealth Henry's action brought to the Crown (fol. 173^r) and upon the productive use to which the former monastic lands had been put (fols. 162^r–162^v). Under Mary, Paget was a firm supporter of the large landholders in their insistence upon confirmation of their title to the lands they had received in Henry's time. This issue is related to the wider issue of class relations: Gardiner's treatise is strongly biased against the large landholding gentry and nobility, and he blames them for the revolts that were so frequent in England (fol. 57^r). Rainsford's pro-gentry, pro-mercantile analysis of the English economy (fols. 161^v ff.) and his harsh opinion of the laboring class (fol. 152^r) balances Gardiner's tendency, and here, as in the other matters, brings the work of the late Chancellor into closer harmony with the policies of Paget. These convergences do not necessarily indicate direct influence: the opinions Rainsford expresses may have been his own, or they may have been calculated to please Philip; but whatever forces shaped the *Ritratto*, its inclusion made the book a more apt vehicle for the kind of diplomacy in which Paget was engaged. Gardiner provided essential support on the main issue – whether Philip could rule and where his views on

Paget Correspondence. The letters from Paget to Basset (fols. 41–4) will be printed in a forthcoming volume of the *Camden* series edited by Barrett L. Beer and Sybill Jack. I am grateful to the Marquess of Anglesey and Mr Harrison for this information and for photocopies of the letters.

[1] Harbison's account (pp. 216 ff. and *passim*) of Paget's positions is still useful, but see also S. R. Gammon [III], *Statesman and Schemer: William Lord Paget – Tudor Minister* (Hamden, Conn., 1973), and G. A. Lemasters, 'The Privy Council in the Reign of Queen Mary I' (unpub. diss. Cambridge, 1971) for later work on Paget.

other issues diverged most sharply from Paget, their impact was moderated by the inclusion of Rainsford's remarks to the contrary. The differences between Gardiner and Rainsford are important in another way as well – as evidence that Rainsford chose an honest way of expressing disagreement with his author. Since the English original has not been found it is fortunate that Rainsford reveals his own biases in the *Ritratto*, and the fact that he allows Gardiner's opinions to stand even though they differ from his own is a valuable indication of his reliability in transmitting what Gardiner had written.

Thus we have a likely sequence of events: Basset came into possession of the manuscript and, perhaps after consultation with Paget or Mary, it was translated into Italian so that Philip could read it.[1] Because the work was favorable to Spanish rule in England, discretion was called for, and a translator close to Basset's family was chosen. The finished book was taken to Brussels by Paget and presented to Philip with a copy for Antoine Perrenot de Granvelle, Charles V's chief diplomatic minister. The copy given to Philip found its way to the Escorial with the rest of Philip's books, and the copy given to Granvelle was taken to Besançon with the rest of his papers and became part of the library founded by Abbé Boisot in 1594.[2]

---

[1] The fact that the treatise was translated into Italian rather than Spanish is interesting. Philip's English was notoriously poor, and he had been tutored in Italian from a very early age (see C. Bratli, *Felipe, Rey de España*, trans. P. Angel C. Vega [Madrid, n.d.], p. 68). Correspondence in Italian was often addressed to him, for example that of the Duchess of Parma (see *Papiers d'état du cardinal de Granvelle d'après les manuscrits de la Bibliothèque de Besançon* [Paris, 1841–52], v, 32). The choice of Italian made the translator's work easier, for the long passages quoted from Machiavelli could be quoted in the original language. Italian may have seemed the proper medium for political discourse, and it may also have been the modern language most easily understood by educated Englishmen, Spaniards and Franc-Comtois alike.

[2] Castan (p. 823) offered a different explanation of how the Besançon MS reached Granvelle: 'La présente copie est vraisemblablement celle que le traducteur avait offerte à Simon Renard en souvenir de ses relations avec Gardiner au sujet du mariage de la reine Marie et de Philippe d'Espagne.' But Renard, the Imperial ambassador, had left England long before the translation was finished (September 1555, see Harbison, p. 259) and by December 1555 his reputation was seriously compromised by the arrest of his maître d'hôtel, Etienne Quiclet, on a charge of high treason (see Mathieu Tridon, 'Simon Renard: ses ambassades, ses négociations, sa lutte avec le cardinal de Granvelle', *Mém. de la Soc. d'Emulation du Doubs*, 5th Series, vi (1881), 107–376). There is no need to imagine Rainsford sending a copy to Renard, then suspected of French sympathies, on the strength of his previous relationship with Gardiner, which had not been a wholly friendly one in any case.

SOURCES

A. Machiavelli

Approximately 3,000 words of Gardiner's text are quoted from *The Prince* and *The Discourses* with only minor changes. The passages borrowed vary in length from a dozen words to three quarters of one of Machiavelli's chapters (fols. 120ʳ–121ᵛ; *Disc.* III: 20), but the debt is not to be gauged by quantity alone: many of Gardiner's main arguments are borrowed entirely from Machiavelli, and the material borrowed represents a generous selection from Machiavelli at his most distinctive and controversial. The danger of mercenaries, the role of fortune in human affairs, the horror of wars of migration, the prince's responsibility for the defects of his people, the need to show respect for old laws (even if one breaks them), the folly of trusting exiles, the relative merits of cruelty and kindness, the special position of the new prince, the necessity of seeming virtuous while employing the politically useful vices, and, above all, the princely imperative of staying in office ('keeping one's state') by any means necessary: all these are issues on which Gardiner not only takes a Machiavellian position but also borrows Machiavelli's words in formulating the position.[1]

[1] Gardiner quotes from Machiavelli on the following subjects: how reputation is acquired (fols. 16ʳ–17ᵛ, *Disc.* III: 34); the need for military self-sufficiency and the danger of mercenaries (fols. 23ᵛ–24ʳ, 41ᵛ–43ᵛ, *Prince* XII, XIII, XIV); fortune (fols. 29ʳ⁻ᵛ, *Disc.* II: 29); wars caused by migration, how countries lose their names (fols. 32ᵛ, 34ʳ–35ʳ, 36ʳ–37ᵛ, *Disc.* II: 8); that the defects of a people are due to the prince (fol. 61ᵛ, *Disc.* III: 29); the folly of insult (fols. 73ʳ–74ʳ, *Disc.* II: 26); respect for law (fols. 77ᵛ–78ʳ, 79ᵛ–80ʳ, *Disc.* I: 45, III: 5); the folly of trusting exiles (fol. 96ʳ⁻ᵛ, *Disc.* II: 31); that men forget the death of their father sooner than the loss of their patrimony (fol. 81ʳ, *Prince* XVII); new princes must be cruel (fol. 101ʳ, *Prince* XVII); new favors do not cancel old injuries (fol. 101ᵛ, *Disc.* III: 4); the need to eliminate rivals and extinguish the former royal line (fols. 102ᵛ, 103ᵛ, 104ʳ, 124ʳ, *Prince* III, *Disc.* III: 4); relative claims of cruelty and kindness (fols. 109ʳ, 111ᵛ–112ʳ, 113ʳ–114ʳ, 115ʳ–116ʳ, 120ʳ–121ᵛ, *Disc.* I: 26, III: 19, 20, *Prince* XVII); a new prince should live in his new state (fol. 125ʳ⁻ᵛ, *Prince* III); that it suffices to avoid those vices which result in loss of a state (fols. 132ᵛ–133ʳ, *Prince* XV); the need to seem virtuous while being otherwise, the example of Pope Alexander VI (fols. 133ʳ–134ᵛ, *Prince* XVIII). In addition, Gardiner paraphrases Machiavelli on: fortune (fol. 18ᵛ, *Prince* XXV); Henry VIII in France (fol. 50ʳ⁻ᵛ, *Disc.* I: 21); respect for law (fol. 76ᵛ, *Prince* I, II, III, *Disc.* III: 5); discord among allies (fols. 90ʳ–93ᵛ, *Prince* XII, XIII); and disagrees with Machiavelli on the following points: the constancy of the populace contrasted with that of the prince (fol. 61ᵛ, *Disc.* I: 58); the utility of fortresses (fol. 109ʳ, *Prince* XX). The parallels are set forth fully in the notes. A great deal could be said about such an extensive list of borrowings and my remarks here are introductory rather than exhaustive: a more detailed analysis of the relation between Machiavelli and Gardiner appears in my forthcoming monograph.

This is not to imply that Machiavelli is all there is to Gardiner, nor that Gardiner always agrees with his source. While he quotes Machiavelli for the most part approvingly, there are cases in which the two differ; Gardiner takes a contrary position on the utility of fortresses (fol. 109^r, *Prince* xx) and dissents from the view that the people are more constant and knowing than princes (fol. 61^v, *Disc.* I: 58). Gardiner blames the errors of the people on the mistakes of their princes, as does Machiavelli, but he was nothing if not a monarchist, and insists (as he had previously in *De Vera Obedientia*) that the faults of the prince never justify rebellion (fols. 62^r ff.): he never follows Machiavelli into republicanism.

There is, moreover, an important rhetorical difference between the two: Machiavelli has a tendency to stress the novelty of his views, and to underscore their divergence from common opinion. In fact he often seems to put things as shockingly as possible. Gardiner, on the other hand, makes an effort (though not, I think, at the expense of the coherence of Machiavelli's thought) to present Machiavelli's views in a way that makes them seen consonant with traditional or orthodox opinion. To this end, he makes use of the traditional dichotomy between reason and appetite, lending the sanction of rationality to strategies for which Machiavelli had claimed only effectiveness. Thus Gardiner's subtitle ('how princes have succeeded or failed depending upon whether they ruled according to reason or appetite') strikes a moralizing, un-Machiavellian note: successful political strategies are presented as rational (those of Hengest, King Stephen, William the Conqueror) while unsuccessful ones are evidence of the sway of appetite over the mind of the prince, as in the case of Vortigerius, Edward II, Henry VI. The appeal to proverbial wisdom is another way Gardiner has of making his Machiavellian politics seem more traditional: defending the use of cruelty, he uses the simile of the good surgeon, who must use the knife and the fire when gentler measures fail (fol. 110^r). When Alphonso (who is usually the one to raise objections to Machiavelli's ideas) objects to Stephano's view that the people should be armed, the objection is met by a series of adages: there are dangers in arming the populace, but the good prince must learn to pluck the rose among the thorns, and like the bee make honey from the same flower from which the frog draws only poison (fols. 49^{r-v}). Gardiner uses an animal fable to illustrate the folly of calling in auxiliary troops (fols. 21^v–22^v), and in one case in which Machiavelli cites Livy as his own source, Gardiner ignores the attribution and calls his own version a proverb (fol. 29ʳ, *Disc.* II: 29).

The differences are minor, and the debt is major: Gardiner follows Machiavelli closely in essentials and even borrows many of the passages which were under attack by the Church. Machiavelli's works were not yet on the Papal Index, for this was not prepared until 1557 and was published only in 1559,[1] but they had incurred the censure of important clerics, and when Gardiner wrote the movement for condemnation was well advanced. Reginald Pole had been among the first to attack Machiavelli, and his criticisms, made in a preface written in 1539 (the 'Apologia ad Carolum Quintum') were influential though they were not published during his life. The Portuguese bishop Osorio attacked Machiavelli in his *De Nobilitate Christiana* (1542), the sale of Machiavelli's books was banned in Rome in 1549, and Ambrogio Caterino Politi, probably influenced by Pole, attacked Machiavelli's works in his *De libris a Christiano detestandis* (1552). Among the charges against Machiavelli were that he treated Moses as a secular prince, ignoring his divine mission; that he compared Christianity unfavorably with paganism; and, above all, that his advice to princes (particularly that offered in *Prince* XVIII) justified deceit, hypocrisy and nearly every other kind of immorality in the name of security and efficiency.[2] Gardiner does not follow Machiavelli's praise of pagan religion (*Disc.* II: 2), but he does treat Moses as a secular conqueror (fols. 36ʳ–37ᵛ, *Disc.* II: 8), and, more importantly, he quotes large portions of *Prince* III, XV, and XVIII and *Disc.* III: 4 in which Machiavelli most uncompromisingly subordinates religious and moral values to political considerations (fols. 102ᵛ, 103ᵛ, 104ʳ, 124ʳ, 132ᵛ–134ᵛ), arguing that a new prince must eliminate those of royal blood, that of the vices it is sufficient to avoid those which result in the loss of one's state, and that seeming virtuous is more important than being virtuous in fact. The conflict between religion and politics is inescapable in Gardiner's version of *Prince* XVIII – 'a

[1] Fr. Heinrich Reusch, *Die indices librorum prohibitorum des sechzehnten Jahrhunderts* (Tübingen, 1886, repr. Nieukoop, 1970), p. 198.

[2] See Antonio Panella, *Gli antimachiavellici* (Florence, 1943), pp. 24 ff.; Giuseppe Prezzolini, *Machiavelli anticristo* (Rome, 1954), pp. 295–6; Hardin Craig, *Machiavelli's 'The Prince': an Elizabethan Translation* (Chapel Hill, 1944), p. xiv; Reginald Pole, *Epistolae*, ed. Quirini (Brescia, 1744–57), I, 137 ff.; Hieronymus Osorius, *De Nobilitate Christiana* (Lisbon, 1542), fols. 98–9. L. Firpo prints Italian translations of the pertinent documents in his *Il pensiero politico del Rinascimento e della controriforma* (Milan, 1966), pp. 591–621.

new prince especially cannot observe all the things by which men are
held good, even if he wants to, since it is often necessary, to maintain
his state, to act contrary to mercy, religion, and faith' (fol. 134ʳ). In
another place, Gardiner states the principle of separation between
political and religious questions directly (Machiavelli himself never
makes it quite this explicit): when Alphonso points out that
William the Conqueror's elimination of rivals was contrary to
divine law, Stephano replies, 'our purpose at present is not to show
what a prince is permitted to do and what he is not permitted to do,
but only to show by what ways and means a prince can maintain
or lose his state' (fol. 103ʳ). We do not know whether Gardiner
knew of the clerical criticism of Machiavelli or not: if he did know
of it he ignored it.

Was Machiavelli readily available in Gardiner's time? Cardinal
Pole, who attacked him, certainly knew him in the 1530s. William
Thomas had used Machiavelli in a series of papers of advice to
Edward VI. Ascham and Morison had also read him and refer to
him.[1] It is still unfortunately a common view that real knowledge
of Machiavelli did not exist in England in the sixteenth century, and
that what knowledge there was came late in the century through the
distorting medium of Gentillet's Contre-machiavel. This view is
no longer tenable: on the one hand Machiavelli was read in the early
Tudor period, and on the other the English translation of Gentillet
has now been shown to be a seventeenth century work.[2] In fact,
Gardiner's treatise itself is the most impressive evidence to date of
Machiavelli's penetration of England in the sixteenth century.
We do not know how early on in his career Gardiner read Machiavelli, or where he got his copy, but he quotes so much and so
directly that there is no doubt concerning his access to the original.

Gardiner himself says nothing about Machiavelli that might help
to date his first encounter with this author: in fact Gardiner says
nothing about Machiavelli at all; though he uses him constantly he
never reveals his source, and may even have wished to conceal it.

[1] See John Wesley Horrocks, 'Machiavelli in Tudor Opinion and Discussion',
unpub. D. Lit. thesis, University of London, 1908, passim and the opening chapters
of Felix Raab, The English Face of Machiavelli (London, 1964).
[2] The old view was put forth in Edward Meyer's influential book Machiavelli and the
Elizabethan Drama (Weimar, 1897). Horrocks and Raab offer evidence of the early
dissemination of Machiavelli's ideas, and Antonio D'Andrea has shown that the
dating of the English Gentillet to 1577 was mistaken, 'Studies on Machiavelli and
his Reputation in the Sixteenth Century', Medieval and Renaissance Studies, v (1960),
247–8; 'Machiavelli, Satan, and the Gospel', Yearbook of Italian Studies, I (1971),
156–77.

Sixteenth century practice was lax in the matter of citing source material, but in several cases Gardiner gives references which are actually misleading, perhaps intentionally so. He introduces the story of Camillus and the schoolmaster of the Faliscans thus: 'And Camillus attained a similar reputation for his kindness, as anyone who has read Livy knows' (fol. 120^r). The story is based, ultimately, on Livy v: 27 – but Gardiner follows *Disc.* III: 20, not Livy, quoting three quarters of Machiavelli's chapter (including material not in Livy's passage) verbatim. In another case, Paul the Deacon is credited with the saying that Rome fought all others for dominion, but the Gauls for survival. This occurs in a long passage (fol. 34^r–35^r) which follows *Disc.* II: 8 nearly verbatim. In Machiavelli, the remark is attributed to Sallust, in whose *Jugurtha* the saying actually appears. Paul the Deacon (d. 797) did write on the Roman wars (*Historia Romana*, ed. Crivellucci [Rome, 1914]) but he does not make the point Sallust made concerning the difference between wars of conquest and wars of necessity. In any case, Gardiner's source is neither Paul nor Sallust; he takes the quotation from Machiavelli, following it with a discussion of the flight of the Moors before Moses, which appears in neither Paul nor Sallust, but which is next in order in Machiavelli's chapter.

Two final points concerning Gardiner's Machiavelli must conclude this discussion. First, Gardiner uses both *The Prince* and *The Discourses*, and when they differ, as they sometimes do, he attempts synthesis. In his discussion of the relative merits of cruelty and kindness, for example, Gardiner collects widely scattered passages from both of Machiavelli's major works. Those from *The Discourses* seem to counsel mildness in contrast to those from *The Prince*, but Gardiner tries to resolve the disparity by developing Machiavelli's notion that different circumstances require different tactics (fol. 117^v). In another case Gardiner brings Machiavelli's discussion of mercenaries into useful conjunction with his discussion of migrations (fols. 23^v–37^v, *Prince* XII, XIII, *Disc.* II: 8). Gardiner's historical source (Polydore Vergil) offered two explanations for the coming of the Anglo-Saxons, and Machiavelli showed that in either case it was a mistake to admit them, for foreigners can threaten the state whether they come as soldiers or settlers. As an implicit commentator on Machiavelli we must place Gardiner among the 'unifiers', for he looked for the continuities between *The Prince* and *The Discourses* and uses both works to illustrate his points.

Gardiner's use of Machiavelli cannot be assessed solely in terms of literary influence; he borrowed much, and absorbed many of Machiavelli's central ideas; but he also applied those ideas to the current political situation. That situation will be discussed in the next section, in order to show that Gardiner borrowed from Machiavelli not merely as one writer borrows from another, but as a statesman, attempting to create a theoretical basis for what he thought would be the new dynasty, the Habsburg dynasty in England.

B. Polydore Vergil

Polydore Vergil's *Anglica Historia* is Gardiner's regular authority for English history prior to the reign of Henry VIII. He quotes from this source at length on the coming of the Saxons (fols. 14^r–31^r), on the Peasants' Revolt (fols. 60^r–61^r) and on the uprising in York (fols. 53^r–54^r). In other cases he follows his source less closely, paraphrasing Book XVIII on the reign of Edward II (fols. 67^v ff.), borrowing bits and pieces for his account of the conflict between Harold and Tostig (fols. 95^r–96^r), and echoing Polydore's phrasing in his treatment of Rufus (fols. 81^v–82^r), John (fols. 82^r–83^r), James III of Scots (fols. 78^r–79^r) and elsewhere; full parallels are given in the notes.

Gardiner handles material from Polydore differently from material from Machiavelli, paraphrasing more and quoting less. On the other hand, what is quoted directly from Polydore is sometimes identified as quotation, whereas quotation from Machiavelli never is. Gardiner introduces the story of the election of Vortigerius (fol. 14^r ff.) with the words, 'the text says . . .' clearly indicating quotation. In addition, this passage is given in Latin, and there are inverted commas in the margin beside it (though these may be Rainsford's or the scribe's). The story of the calling in of the Saxons is likewise given in Latin, and introduced by 'as the history says . . .' (fol. 19^r). It is true that Gardiner does not name Polydore as the author of 'the history', but he does make it quite clear he is following another writer. In other passages he does not repeat these relatively careful introductory formulas; nevertheless he is more open concerning his use of Polydore than he is about Machiavelli, from whom he borrowed a great deal more.

Gardiner's use of this author, like his use of Machiavelli, is judicious; he chooses from Polydore principally those reigns in which a major dynastic change was effected (Vortigerius, William) or in which the sovereign lost his power (John, Edward II, Richard II). He often combines material in Polydore with material from Machiavelli and weaves them together with care, without subordinating one to the other; Machiavelli is not used merely to gloss Polydore, nor Polydore to provide examples of Machiavelli's precepts. Gardiner tries to adapt Machiavelli's principles to the English historical experience, and for this purpose the *Anglica Historia* was well suited; like Machiavelli, Polydore emphasized the character of the prince and the means by which states are kept or lost.

There are several errors in Gardiner's use of Polydore; he thoroughly confuses the revolt of the Duke of York against Henry VI with the revolt of the Earl of Warwick against Edward IV (fols. 53^r ff.) and places the battle in which Richard III was defeated by Henry VII at Barnet rather than Bosworth (fol. 94^r), an odd slip for a Tudor statesman. There are also several deliberate alterations; Polydore's adaptation of Eusebius is followed for the pre-Roman period (fols. 10–14), but Gardiner ignores Polydore's skepticism concerning Brutus, the supposed ancestor of the Britons. Polydore considered Brutus mythical, Gardiner presents him as an historical personage. Gardiner's alterations of the account of the decision to call in the Saxons (fol. 19^r) are also deliberate; he cuts and alters Polydore to imply that the King was solely responsible for the decision, and invents a long speech in which the barons try to dissuade the King from calling in auxiliary troops. In Polydore's version, the decision was jointly taken by the King and the barons.

Polydore's history was widely available. A first edition was published in 1534, and a second, revised edition in 1546. A third was published at Basel in the year of Gardiner's death (1555). He could have used any of these, though the third edition may have reached England too late. Also, the earlier editions cover events to 1509[1] and the third continues to 1538, but when Gardiner refers to events that occurred between 1509 and 1538 he does not use Polydore. If he knew the third edition he regularly ignores it in favor of his own version of events within his memory.

The treatment of events in the reigns of Henry VIII and Edward VI for which Gardiner used no source requires comment here. The story about Edward VI's law against insult, a law allegedly designed to protect former rebels from the taunts of their countrymen (fols.

[1] See Denys Hay, *Polydore Vergil: Renaissance Historian and Man of Letters* (Oxford, 1952) for a full account of the publishing history.

74^r–75^v) is an invention; there is no such statute, in fact no record whatever of Edward's having protected rebels in this way. There is also no record of the mutilations Gardiner describes in fols. 130^r–131^v. It is true that some of those who had been too assiduous in collecting the exactions of Henry VII (including Empson and Dudley, the masters of the forfeits) were executed when Henry VIII came to the throne. But the several mutilations Gardiner describes would have been contrary to law, and are quite possibly exaggerated, perhaps even wholly invented. Similarly, we have no way of knowing whether Henry VIII actually met a poor man who had been mistreated by the gentry in the North and promised him redress (fols. 128 ff.) but it is clear that Henry had no power to hang the offending gentlemen at their own gates, as is alleged. These passages remain puzzling; possibly Gardiner felt free to invent *exempla* for his purpose.

C. Paolo Giovio

Gardiner's source for Turkish history was Paolo Giovio, whose *Commentario de le cose de' Turchi* was published in Rome (Blado) in 1535. This was translated into Latin by Franciscus Niger Bassinates and that version translated into English by Peter Ashton, whose book *A Shorte Treatise upon the Turkes Chronicles* appeared in 1546. Gardiner's short account of the Turkish conquest of Greece can be found in Giovio (Gardiner fols. 92^r–93^r; Ashton fols. iii^r–vi^r). Gardiner's version is condensed, and where Giovio gives the number of troops sent by the Turk to aid the Emperor of Constantinople as 15,000, Giovio has 12,000. But Gardiner is usually inaccurate when it comes to numbers, erring also in regard to the number of insurgents at York (fols. 54^v–55^r: Gardiner has 10,000, Polydore 15,000) and the number of ships William of Normandy brought to Hastings (fol. 98^v: Gardiner 50, Polydore 30). Gardiner also uses Giovio for his account of the rise to power of Selym (fols. 105^v–108^v, Ashton liii^r–lxxvii^r). Again, there are minor numerical differences and Gardiner's version is condensed.

POLITICAL CONTEXT (1553–5)

The purpose of this section is to show that Gardiner's treatise provided a detailed (though for the most part implicit) analysis of the political situation under Philip and Mary, and that in it Gardiner offered Philip suggestions for dealing with many of the difficulties of the reign. The implicit parallels to Philip's situations are many and will be discussed below; in several cases the treatise refers to public issues directly. In one case Gardiner warns that the Spanish rule in Milan and Naples is too harsh, and that the Spaniards there may end as did the Danes in England (they were slaughtered without mercy when the native population regained the upper hand [fol. 88^v]). In another case 'the present wars in Tuscany' are attributed to the folly of Henry II of France who too readily trusted the promises of Italian exiles (fols. 96^v–97^r) and the wise prince (Philip had his own Italian suitors urging war) is admonished not to believe such promises. Later (fol. 138^r) Philip is called upon directly to make peace with France. In most cases, however, Gardiner stops just short of direct comment on current affairs; he cites an historical example, draws from it a general political principle, and leaves the application to his reader; but there nearly always is an immediate parallel – his historical material is selected with the contemporary situation always in mind.

The most important political fact of Mary's reign was of course her marriage to Philip of Spain, a marriage which had been conceived from the very outset as the conquest of England for the Habsburg dynasty. Queen Dowager Mary of Hungary had written to the Bishop of Arras on the subject as early as 1551: 'Many people are of the opinion that the kingdom of England would not be impossible to conquer, and especially now that it is a prey to discord and poverty.' She recommended that an able ambassador such as Renard be sent there, and suggested that a Habsburg wishing to conquer England could do no better than to marry Princess Mary to secure his power.[1] Once Mary came to the throne, Charles did send Renard, and on 5 November 1553 he visited Gardiner, now Chancellor, and solicited his opinion on the subject of the Queen's marriage.

Gardiner was widely thought to favor Edward Courtenay as a match, and his reply was that if asked he would recommend the Queen to marry an Englishman. Her people hated foreigners, particularly Spaniards, whose inability to get along with other nationals was well-known. If the Queen should marry a Spaniard, she would be entangled in wars with France. England would either be put to the expense of aiding the Spanish against the French in Europe, or, worse, if Spain lost there, England would fall to France, which already claimed the throne through Mary Stuart. If Mary

[1] *Span. Cal.*, x, 376–80.

were to marry Philip, a dispensation would be needed because of their kinship. If such a dispensation were made public, the people would resent the implication of Papal authority. If it were secret, the succession would be questioned. Heretics in England would use a foreign marriage as evidence that religious restoration meant foreign domination. The people would doubt Philip's intentions to adapt himself to English ways – 'and for the people, fearing and believing were the same'. Moreover, since Philip and his attendants couldn't speak the language, 'there would be a great confusion among a rough, fickle and proud people, who could neither understand nor make themselves understood in the requisite manner'. There would even be personal danger to Philip from the unruly English.[1]

This analysis is not as negative as it first appears. Gardiner made it clear he opposed the match – but most of his objections were either bargaining points or indications of areas in which sensitivity would be needed to make the plan work, hints that Philip would have to *learn* to rule England. Many of these points were met by clauses in the treaty. Others, such as Philip's lack of knowledge about England, were met by the manual on ruling England that Gardiner wrote: the *Discourse on the Coming of the English and Normans to Britain*, our present work. A word is in order at this point concerning Gardiner's public image at the time, for most previous commentators have not seen beyond it and have misinterpreted Gardiner's resistance to the match as narrow patriotism. Gardiner may have sincerely believed that Courtenay would have been a better match; but his objections served another purpose as well: they gave him great bargaining power in setting the final terms of the treaty. Gardiner had developed a reputation as a patriotic Englishman, extreme in religious matters, but opposed to the Spanish marriage and to the foreign influences feared as a consequence of that marriage and Paget, long associated with Charles V, was commonly thought to stand for Spanish influence in England. E. H. Harbison expresses the traditional view, which derives from Pollard. He describes the two factions of Mary's Privy Council. On one side, there was Gardiner and Mary's household,

most of them devoted Catholics and few of them possessed of any political experience. Gardiner's zealous interest in restoring the old religion, his narrow legalism, and his honest patriotism were characteristic of the group, as also his lack of finesse and flexibility in political matters. The other faction,

[1] *Span. Cal.*, XI, 338–9.

led by William, Lord Paget, a shrewd and supple *homme nouveau* who managed to get on well with four successive sovereigns, consisted of the nobles and civil servants who felt that they had a natural or acquired right to govern the country. In Pollard's comparison, they were like the French *politiques* of a later day who preferred political sanity to spiritual salvation...
Gardiner's party looked to Rome, Paget's to Brussels. The Catholic patriots believed that a reconverted and regenerated England could and should stand upon her own feet. They feared and hated the political – though not the religious – influence of the foreigner, whether it came from Paris, Brussels or Madrid, and looked to a religious restoration as the solution of all the country's ills.[1]

But Gardiner's resistance to the foreign marriage cannot be explained in this way, for his objections to it were political ones, and the problems he saw turned out to be very real ones. Further, by stating his views thus strongly he was able to exert a powerful influence upon the drafting of the treaty. Renard was soon to assure him, on Charles V's authority, that his objections would be met. He promised that

his Highness [Philip] would adapt himself to English ways and laws, leave the government to the Chancellor and other faithful Councillors who should be chosen, have English servants, and rule in a manner that, far from dissatisfying the people or anybody, would prove profitable to all. England would not be dragged into a war with France, for your Majesty [Charles V] and his Highness would promise nothing that they did not intend to keep. He knew your Majesty's integrity and good faith, *and besides the foregoing every condition that seemed to him useful would be passed.*[2]

Gardiner was well-pleased with the results, exclaiming, when he saw a draft of the treaty, 'that the match is more advantageous than any other in all Christendom could be'.[3] This is not the grudging acceptance of a foreigner Harbison's picture of a myopically patriotic Gardiner would suggest. Gardiner gained a great deal by his resistance – he got a marriage treaty that would calm English fears and insure the national integrity of England. As Machiavelli taught, a new prince had to take account of the governed, unless he destroyed them. The treaty gave the assurances Gardiner wanted, and his *Discourse on the Coming of the English and Normans to Britain* explained and justified the need for the concessions made in the treaty with examples from English history and quotation from *The Prince* and *The Discourses*.

[1] Harbison, pp. 61–2. But see also G. A. Lemasters, 'The Privy Council in the Reign of Queen Mary I', unpub. diss. Cambridge, 1971 and S. R. Gammon [III], *op. cit.*
[2] *Span. Cal.*, XI, 347 (emphasis added).   [3] *Span. Cal.*, XI, 416.

After this success, Gardiner became an active supporter of the match, arguing forcefully for it in the inner circle of the Privy Council on 3 December, and before the whole Council on 7 December. He also sought support among the leading nobles in early December.[1] On the twenty-first, Charles V wrote to Gardiner thanking him for 'the pertinent arguments you lately employed in persuading the assembly to which the Queen communicated this affair'.[2] In April of the following year, Gardiner was to argue before Parliament, as Renard recounts to Charles, that whereas the rebels against the marriage, led by Sir Thomas Wyatt, 'had said that his Highness wished to conquer the kingdom, in reality the kingdom was conquering your Majesty, his Highness and your realms and dominions'.[3] This is polite exaggeration, but it shows how eagerly Gardiner supported the match he had before opposed.

The treaty itself seemed extremely favorable to England. Philip and Mary were to enjoy their titles jointly. Philip was to 'ayde her Highnes being his Wyef, in the happy administration of her Graces Realmes and Dominions',[4] but Mary alone was to have the power of dispensing offices and grants, which would go only to Englishmen. All business was to be transacted in the languages traditionally used (not Spanish), and Mary was to receive a considerable dowry. As to the succession, the heir of the marriage was to inherit England and Lower Germany and Burgundy unless the issue was female and married a foreigner without Don Carlos' consent, in which case Don Carlos would inherit Lower Germany and Burgundy. Don Carlos was to inherit Spain, with the reversion in case his line failed to the issue of Philip and Mary. England, on the other hand, was not to revert to Don Carlos under any circumstances. There was to be between the realms 'entier and sincere fraternitee unitee and most streight Confederacye...so as thei shall mutuallye...ayde another in all thinges'.[5]

In addition to the marriage articles, there was a second treaty, containing many of the concessions most embarrassing to Philip's dignity. These articles were also the ones most reassuring to popular fears, and they were among the things Gardiner had argued strongly for. He wanted them included in the marriage treaty itself, which wasn't done[6] – his only failure in the matter, and a very slight one.

---

[1] Harbison, pp. 100–3.   [2] *Span. Cal.*, XI, 447.
[3] *Span. Cal.*, XII, 201.
[4] *Foedera*, ed. Thomas Rymer (London, 1728), XV, 377–81 and *Statutes of the Realm*, IV, 222–6 for text. I quote the English version of the *Statutes*.
[5] *Statutes*, IV, 224.   [6] *Span. Cal.*, XII, 12.

According to this second treaty, aliens were not to hold office in England, Philip was to be served by Englishmen, he was to make no innovations in the laws of England, he was not to compel the Queen to leave the realm or take the jewels out of the kingdom, or attempt to succeed her himself. England was not to be involved in Spanish wars with France, and the Queen alone was to enjoy the revenue of Crown property.[1]

Severe limitations, but necessary if Spanish rule was to be accepted by the English; they would resent Philip, and he would be most effective if his involvement appeared minimal. Philip had every intention of ruling, of course. Immediately after signing the treaty, Philip foreswore it before witnesses, claiming that he had signed it in order that the marriage might take place, 'but by no means in order to bind himself or his heirs to observe the articles, especially any that might burden his conscience'.[2] This is astonishing, but not really out of character. There is even some evidence that Mary herself may have consented to some of Philip's attempts to evade the treaty, for, in a letter of 21 January 1554, Charles tells Philip of the English Council's desire to have Philip swear to the treaty and the laws of England at the time of his marriage, but 'the Queen, however, assures us that in secret it shall be done according to your desire and we trust her word'.[3]

Philip was unhappy with the treaty from the outset, and Gardiner's treatise was in part an attempt to explain some of the principles upon which the treaty was based, for in the book Gardiner takes up a number of the issues raised by the treaty – the question of the war with France, the problem of the succession, the fear of Spanish domination, the need to respect English laws – and offers Philip counsel based on Machiavelli and English history. In addition, Gardiner deals with a number of other issues in the treatise (the problem of insulting behavior, the need of the prince to ally with the poorer classes) which are not mentioned in the marriage pact, but which had special relevance to Philip's situation nonetheless. The following represent the major topics on which he counsels the new sovereign.

A. War and Peace

Gardiner was a firm and consistent advocate of peace – not only did he favor keeping England out of war with France, but he favored mending the breach between Habsburg and Valois

---

[1] *Statutes*, IV, 224.   [2] *Span. Cal.*, XII, 5.   [3] *Span. Cal.*, XII, 36.

altogether. He was the leader of the opposition to England's entry into war at Mary's third Parliament,[1] but even before the Spanish marriage had made the possibility of England's involvement so vivid, Gardiner had proposed English mediation between Habsburg and Valois (1553), and was active between August 1554 and June 1555 in arranging and then participating in the peace conference at Marcq.[2] In the first reference to peace in the treatise, Alphonso draws a distinction between conquerors like Alexander on the one hand and Christian princes on the other – Christian wars ought to be wholly defensive and aimed at the establishment of a lasting peace (fol. 45^v). But much more to the point is Gardiner's discussion of Tostig's calling in of Harold of Norway against King Harold of England on the promise that Tostig would provide a considerable army and that England could be easily taken. This leads to a speech on the folly of trusting the words of exiles

who very often speak things remote from the truth to return to their country or to avenge themselves on their enemies...they often fill ambitious princes with hope of undertaking exploits which later make them consume a treasury in vain, or even bring about their own downfall.

Of this old books are full of examples, and there are also many modern examples before our eyes. He who considers the present wars in Tuscany will see that they do not proceed from anything but the industry of the exiles of Florence, Salerno, Naples, and the other cities of Italy. They have convinced the Most Christian King that by means of them and their friends they could take possession of Tuscany, and then in time of all Italy. The valorous and magnanimous prince believed them because men easily believe that which they desire, and he also had reason for hope because of the division among the princes of Italy, so that he made a very great expenditure and the final result of it will be as God wills (fols. 96^r–97^r, cf. *Disc.*, II: 31).

The prince referred to is Henry II of France, who had been goaded into aggression by the Italian *fuorusciti*. But the lesson was applicable to Philip of Spain as well at this time, for it was not merely the exiles at the French court who were stirring up the flames of war, but also those at the English court, such as Emmanuel Philibert of Savoy. According to Harbison, in the winter of 1554–5, 'François de Noailles [the French ambassador] found London swarming with Flemish and Italian nobles, all asking the King for money or for protection of their estates from the French "so that one need only

[1] Harbison, p. 216.
[2] Harbison, Chapter ix ('The Quest for European Peace').

come to London to see all of Europe"'.[1] Not only does Gardiner speak respectfully of Henry, but he blames the war on the Italians and warns against the very real danger of Philip's listening too eagerly to his own Italian suitors.

And, further, the document ends with a long praise of peace and of Philip as (Gardiner hopes) the bringer of peace: he was 'brought forth in this age...so that Christianity after such dark clouds would have the bright light of the sun, and the Christian people, after such long and cruel wars, would enjoy the precious and inestimable joy of peace' (fol. 138^r). Gardiner goes on to contrast Philip with the warmongers: 'he who takes peace from men takes the sun from the world and life from the creatures. But Philip is the man who is ordained to restore the one and the other' (fol. 138^v). The challenge is quite pointed, for Philip was in fact waging war at the time.

B. *The succession*

Gardiner deals with this question in the treatise in two ways: he implies that the Habsburg dynasty has come to England to stay, and he counsels the elimination of possible rivals to the throne. Gardiner's stated subject in the treatise is political transition: the coming of the Anglo-Saxons and Normans, and the means by which princes keep or lose their states. The subject on which Alphonso asks Stephano to discourse is the great 'alterations' that have occurred in English history: these include the Anglo-Saxon and Norman invasions, but the coming of Brutus, the Roman conquest and the Danish rule are also discussed, so that the treatise includes all the great dynastic changes. The coming of Philip is placed in this context:

After thirty years of rule they [the Danes] were driven out by the English, who were subjugated after 22 years by the Norman, whose successors ruled securely until the death of Edward VI. Since he had no bodily heir the kingdom passed to his sister Mary, who with the consent of the lords and in accordance with the procedures of the kingdom took for husband and king Philip, son of the Emperor Charles V, for the common good of the kingdom and for the good (as will afterwards be said) of all Christendom.

I wished to list these alterations in brief, so that you would be better able to understand what I have to say concerning specific details. (fols. 13^r–14^r)

The pro-Habsburg stance of the treatise is quite striking. Both Rainsford (in his dedication) and Gardiner leave Mary pointedly and

[1] Harbison, p. 239.

almost completely out of account, in contrast to the marriage treaty, partly framed by Gardiner, in which it was Philip whose role was minimized. Rainsford refers to Philip's having restored religion 'with the help of the most Serene Mary'. That is his only reference to her in his elaborate praise of Philip. Gardiner mentions her once – in the passage quoted above – but the context links her marriage to other great transitions. Her reign is presented as the beginning of the Habsburg dynasty.

In the final pages of his work, the coming of Philip is again placed in the context of dynastic succession, and its legitimacy is argued:

Now nothing remains for me to say on this subject, having shown how William subjugated the realm of England and left it in trust to his successors until the coming of the powerful and most merciful Philip, son of the Emperor Charles V. This I do not call change or alteration in the kingdom, but legitimate succession, confirmed by all orders, for the restoration of religion, the honor of the kingdom and benefit of the people. (fol. 135^{r-v})

In these references to Philip's succession, Mary's role is understated, and the contingent nature of the Habsburg succession is completely ignored. The implication is that if Philip rules wisely, he will, like the Anglo-Saxons and Normans, found a lasting dynasty in England.

All of this, of course, is in contrast to the severe restrictions on Habsburg succession in England under the treaty: all depended upon Mary's producing an heir, and this could not be taken for granted. Mary was thought to be pregnant in the fall of 1554 and spring of 1555, and that was reason to hope but no guarantee that a child would be born who would live to rule, especially in view of the family history. After April 1555 (and the evidence suggests Gardiner worked on the treatise after that time) there was no reason whatever to expect Mary would bear a child: her age, health and false pregnancy indicated the contrary.

Gardiner never mentions the need for an heir in the treatise, and there is evidence that he tried, as Chancellor, to strengthen Philip's claim to the throne so that he could succeed the Queen himself if he survived her. In a dispatch Renard tells the Emperor: 'I am sending your Majesty a genealogical tree that has been published here to show that his Highness is no foreigner, but an offshoot of the House of Lancaster. When Paget heard that the Chancellor had devised it, he said it was being done to give his Highness a right to the throne.'[1] This was in the summer of 1554. By the time winter came, and Mary's third Parliament convened, a movement for Philip's rights had won sympathizers in the lower House, and 'Some private members proposed that in case of the Queen's death without issue the King should remain absolute sovereign for life, but this was not adopted.'[2] The aims of the faction that introduced this bill have puzzled previous commentators, as has the support they received from Gardiner. The faction was led by Sir John Pollard, who, like Gardiner, had originally opposed the marriage, and had in fact been the member who presented the petition against the marriage to Mary in her first Parliament. The movement for the Habsburg succession seemed to draw its supporters from the poorer members of the House. Why did they ally with Gardiner, and why did he support them?[3] With Gardiner's treatise in hand, some of the mystery evaporates, for Gardiner now appears far more pro-Habsburg in his sympathies than recent commentators have recognized.[4] The treatise sheds light on why Gardiner aligned himself with the poor members of the Commons against the Lords: Gardiner roundly condemns the nobility for their factionalism, and the wise prince is counseled to ally with the common people against them.[5]

The second way in which Gardiner addresses the question of succession is by offering advice, based on Machiavelli, concerning the elimination of rivals to the throne. Gardiner adjusts Machiavelli's categories carefully in order to make the principle of the elimination of rivals specifically applicable to Philip's situation: a prince who has come to power through favor of friends, hereditary laws, or by *matrimony* should use kindness rather than cruelty in his administration. However, that kindness must not extend to those of royal blood, who must be eliminated (fols. 102^v–104^r, 123^v–124^r, cf. *Prince* III, *Disc.* III: 4). Gardiner adds to Machiavelli's division of the subject the category of the matrimonial prince, pointing the moral.

[1] *Span. Cal.*, XII, 242.   [2] *Span. Cal.*, XIII, 125 (Renard to Charles V).
[3] Harbison discusses the movement, pp. 216–18, but finds no real explanation for it.
[4] Late sixteenth century Protestant polemicists, on the other hand, had no doubt of Gardiner's sympathies. Here is Sir Francis Hastings' charge: 'I affirme, that *Gardiner* and his complices never rested until they had brought in the *Spaniard* and matched him with *Queene Marie* . . . doe all they what they could or the Queene her selfe, they could never set the Crowne of *England* upon King *Philip's* head.' (*An apologie or Defence of the Watch-word*, p. 136.) The Elizabethan view of Gardiner as a Catholic conspirator vastly oversimplified his position with respect to Philip, but was not without foundation.
[5] See below, section E.

Gardiner also approves of the execution of the Yorkist pretender by
Henry VII, giving a clear English application of the principle. He
had done no wrong, but his execution was justifiable on the grounds
of the danger he posed to Henry's security (fol. 104ᵛ). The obvious
contemporary application of Machiavelli's rule would have been
the execution of Elizabeth and Courtenay, and what Gardiner says
in the treatise seems to imply that he favored this. After Wyatt's
rebellion, Gardiner was insistent upon having Elizabeth put in the
Tower,[1] yet he was blamed for the slowness with which the case
against her and Courtenay was prosecuted and suspected of shielding
Courtenay, with whom he had spent time in the Tower under
Edward. When Renard reproached him for this, Gardiner replied
severely that 'as long as Elizabeth lived he had no hope of seeing
the kingdom in peace'.[2] But he did not secure her execution and
contented himself finally with the task of having her declared a
bastard,[3] a goal for which he and his supporters worked without
success in Mary's third parliament. Henri Griffet was the first to
point out that, though Gardiner may have wanted Elizabeth dead,
he did not think the laws could be stretched to allow her execution.[4]
He was torn, apparently, between his view that judicial process
ought not to be tampered with and his view that Elizabeth ought to
die. In the treatise, he does not resolve this particular contradiction,
but it is significant that the examples he gives of how princes rid
themselves of rivals include political assassination (Selym's murder of
his rivals, Richard III's murder of the princes) – Gardiner points
out that such methods are tyrannical, but he cannot refrain from
adding that they are also effective.

In the *Acts and Monuments* the martyrologist John Foxe presented
Gardiner as a determined plotter against Elizabeth's life.[5] According
to Foxe Gardiner actually sent an order for Elizabeth's execution
to the Tower, which the lieutenant disobeyed. When Elizabeth was
at Woodstock, Gardiner sent James Basset with twenty or thirty
men to murder her, but the party was refused access to the princess
because of the (providential) absence of the keeper. In the light of
what Gardiner says about political assassinations in his treatise, such
stories cannot be dismissed out of hand.

[1] *Span. Cal.*, xi, 335; xii, 167. [2] *Span. Cal.*, xii, 200.
[3] *Span. Cal.*, xii, 125–6.
[4] Henri Griffet, *Nouveaux éclaircissements sur l'histoire de Marie, reine d'Angleterre*
(Amsterdam, 1766), see also the anon. Eng. trans. *New Lights Thrown upon the
History of Mary Queen of England* (London, 1771), pp. 95–6 and *passim*.
[5] Ed. Townsend, vii, 592; viii, 618.

C. Fear of Spanish Domination

Gardiner gives several reasons why Vortigerius lost his crown to the Anglo-Saxons, but the principal one is that he admitted foreigners to the realm. Foreign troops are dangerous as auxiliaries (a point relevant to the military separation of England and Spain envisaged by the treaty) but even civilian settlers are dangerous,[1] and Philip was severely limited in the number of Spaniards he could bring with him to England. A nation can prosper under the rule of a foreign dynasty, but for a foreign prince to bring his own people with him and set them in power over the English would be disastrous, as Gardiner had argued in his original interview with Renard, when the question of the Spanish match was first broached. The examples he selects to illustrate this point are Stephen and the Danish kings. Stephen's policy was that in England the English would rule, and in Normandy the Normans. This strategy succeeded, 'and by this means there was a continual fraternal love between the English and Normans, and he, though he was French (the name of which is hated by the English) ruled until his natural death' (fol. 88ʳ). This passage closely echoes the very language of the marriage treaty. There was to be 'entier and sincere fraternitee' between the realms, but England was not to aid in Spanish wars, and there were to be no foreign appointments. And the following passage points the moral unmistakably, for Gardiner, in a rare criticism of Spain, warns: 'And the prince who does otherwise will find those dangers the aforesaid Canute found, unless he is continually in arms, as the Spaniard in Milan and Naples' (fol. 88ᵛ). The example of Canute is chilling in this connection, and Gardiner's boldness in introducing it is an index of the firmness with which he insists that, while Philip may rule in England, substantial limitations must be accepted. For when the English regained their freedom from the Danes, who had elevated their own people to the important offices of the land, they slaughtered them without respect to age or sex. Stephano and Alphonso both defend this slaughter:

Alph: I do not marvel at all at the cruelty of the English when the causes which moved them to it are considered, for it is an extreme grief to men of any nation or province to see other men, foreigners, possess those honors, offices and dignities which in past times their fathers or predecessors

---

[1] In developing the theme of the danger of foreign presence, Gardiner relied heavily on Machiavelli's treatment of mercenaries and migrants (fols. 23ᵛ–24ʳ, 27ʳ⁻ᵛ, 32ᵛ–42ᵛ, *Prince* XII, XIII, XIV, *Disc.* II: 8).

enjoyed, and to see their own children deprived of them without cause, as unworthy.

Steph: It is quite true, and reason supports them in such a case, for in every age some of their predecessors, their ancestors long dead, have lost life or property in the service of their country's honor, advantage or interest, and reason does not permit nor can the nature of man patiently suffer unknown foreigners to enjoy the fruits of other men's labor. (fols. 86ʳ–87ʳ)

D. *Respect for English Laws*

We have seen that Gardiner's respect for the law was a factor in his failure to prosecute Elizabeth vigorously even when he believed her a threat to the government and thought the reign in danger while she lived. A full study of Gardiner's attitude toward the law is not possible here, but one can say that Gardiner always made a distinction between transgression of the law and contempt for the law, arguing in one tract that contempt for human law was more serious and should be punished more severely than *any* transgression of divine law, apart from contempt.[1] The institution had to be preserved, even though laws were broken. This principle may help to explain how Gardiner can repeatedly (fols. 41ʳ, 77ʳ, 79ʳ) admonish the prince to respect the laws while at the same time offering political assassination and imprisonment without cause as effective ways of dealing with rivals and asserting that in order to rule a prince must often 'act contrary to mercy, religion and faith' (fol. 134ʳ).

There is a problem here, just as there is in the writings of Machiavelli, and to some such an attitude will never seem to be anything but cynicism. But if it is that, it is cynicism with a history, for Gardiner's source for the passages in which he calls for respect for law, as well as for those in which he discusses strategies that appear to be illegal, is Machiavelli (*Disc.* I: 45, III: 5, *Prince* III, XV, XVIII).

The 'clausula annexa' of the marriage treaty stipulated that Philip could make no innovation in the laws of England, and this was a case in which Machiavelli's advice to the new prince coincided with the interests of the prince's new subjects. Gardiner argues, following his source, that respect for the laws of a new possession is practical, and that it strengthens the rule of the prince in the long run.

[1] See 'Contemptum humanae legis' in *Obedience in Church and State*, ed. Pierre Janelle (Cambridge, 1930).

E. *The prince and the people*

In his treatise Gardiner is consistently, though of course paternalistically, on the side of the people. He defends the practice of arming the populace (Stephano, whose views are usually those of Stephen Gardiner, has the last word in the debate on the point, fols. 42^r–62^v) and claims that the reputation for rebelliousness of the English populace is undeserved: when they have risen they have done so because of the unfair exactions or bad example of the prince, or because of the example set by the factions among the nobility, or because they have been misled by the promises of one faction or the other (fols. 52^r–62^v). He quotes Machiavelli on the need to arm the populace and on the responsibility of the prince for the defects of the people, although his only model of government remains the monarchic one, whereas Machiavelli considered the republican form superior (*Disc.* 1: 58).

In addition, Gardiner lays great stress on the need for the prince to listen to the complaints of the poor. King Stephen (one of Gardiner's favorite examples) did so and ruled safely, though he had usurped the throne and was French 'whom the English hate', for 'among all the qualities there is none of greater force in gaining fame and reputation with a people than to listen to the complaints and supplications of the poor and avenge their injuries' (fol. 126^v). This was the strategy by which Absalom gained power in Israel, and it was effective even though it was insincere. Solomon and Augustus likewise favored the poor, and in Henry VIII's case taking the side of the poor against their immediate oppressors gave him sufficient strength to withstand even the pro-Catholic uprisings in his reign (fols. 126^v–130^r).

For Gardiner it is always wise for a prince to seek the friendship of the poor, and to beware of the factious nobility. And there is a correlation between this point of view and his political activity under Mary. In Mary's time, the main fear of the Lords and the large landholders among the Commons was that the lands which had been distributed to them under Henry VIII would be returned to religious use under the Catholic Queen. Gardiner, Cardinal Pole and Mary were on the side of returning the property to the Church;[1] Lord Paget, Simon Renard, Philip and the Emperor were against it as impolitic. Pole, as Papal Legate, had been given the authority to confirm lay owners in their title, but the vexed

[1] Harbison, pp. 199, 204–5.

question, which persisted even after lengthy negotiations before
Pole's arrival in England, was whether enough assurances had been
given that he would in fact use this power fully. As the Parliament
of winter 1554 began, an alliance began to develop between
Gardiner and some members of the Commons, as we have seen.
Their strategy was to press for Philip's rights and prerogatives as a
way of weakening the power of the Lords and those members of
the lower House who had been enriched by the dissolution.
Gardiner, like Pollard, the leader of the faction, had originally
opposed Philip. But now the suitor was king, and to strengthen the
Crown against the dissolution-enriched Lords was a logical strategy
for the Commons, because of their class interest, and for Gardiner
because of his interest in restoring property to the Church. If an
alliance could be made between Philip and Englishmen of small
property, it would be a victory for Catholicism, for the Crown,
and for domestic stability.

Thus, when the landholders introduced a bill establishing 'all
spiritual and ecclesiastical possessions and hereditaments conveyed
to the laity',[1] there was resistance. Harbison comments: 'The
landholders in both houses wanted the Papal dispensation included
in the statute itself. Pole threatened to return to Rome if this were
done, and some members of the House of Commons who owned
no abbey lands moved that no dispensation whatever should be
granted to the lay holders.'[2] The bill passed in January, over the
objections of Gardiner and his faction.

In the treatise, Gardiner does not make specific suggestions about
the restoration of Church property, but when he mentions the
dissolution of the monasteries, his attitude is clear. Of Henry VIII
he says 'Truly he gave his people great opportunity to conspire
against him when he began the rape of the spiritual property and
the overthrow of the monasteries' (fol. 127ᵛ). As we have seen, it
was only Henry's taking the side of the common people against
the gentry that saved him, in Gardiner's version. And, though the
restoration of Church lands is not raised, Gardiner offers in the
treatise a view of class relations that is consistent with his parlia-
mentary maneuverings: the prince will do better to seek strength
among the poor than among the factious and self-serving nobility.

[1] Harbison, p. 216.   [2] Ibid., pp. 216–17.

F. Philip's special problems

They were two. He was tactless, and he knew nothing of England. The treatise offers to make up for his deficiencies in the latter area. Gardiner provides an analysis of English history, and Rainsford adds a description of the country and its laws, institutions and customs.

Philip's tactlessness, which is naturally not directly referred to in the treatise, was a well-known problem. It was no minor matter, and troubled even the Emperor, who wrote to the Duke of Alva concerning Philip's coming to England thus: 'For the love of God, Duke, see to it that my son behaves in the right manner; for otherwise I tell you I would rather never have taken the matter in hand.'[1] Philip provided several examples of this failing before his arrival in England. One was that although his marriage to Mary was celebrated by proxy in March 1554, he did not write to her in his own hand until May. Another was that he signed letters to the English Council 'Philippus Rex' before he had even arrived in the land.[2] When, in his interview with Renard, Gardiner expressed doubts that the English could get along with Philip, he no doubt also had in mind the possibility that Philip's own bearing would complicate the problem.

In the treatise, Gardiner borrows a long passage from Machiavelli (fols. 73^r–74^r, *Disc.* II: 26) on the subject of the danger of insult, and he follows this with a series of English examples of kings who came to grief through their insulting behavior.

On the basis of this review of the political situation in England, Gardiner's intentions in the treatise become clear. He was trying to lay the theoretical basis for the new reign, which he saw as a new dynasty ruled by a Machiavellian new prince. Gardiner saw in Machiavelli, I think, a way of reconciling Habsburg rule with English national interests and English national integrity, for the new prince is advised by Machiavelli to reach an accommodation with his new subjects if his circumstances permit him to do so. Gardiner's treatise does explain how Philip can rule, and assumes that he will rule in his own right in a way that would have seemed treasonable to many Englishmen of the time. But how can Philip rule? Only by respecting English arms, English laws, and English

[1] Harbison, p. 184, citing *Foreign Calendar Mary*, 85, etc.
[2] Harbison, p. 188.

customs. Philip is welcomed as the founder of a new dynasty in England, but Spain and the Spaniards are excluded from influence in England in the interests of that dynasty itself. The English know the evils of foreign domination well: they know what it would mean to have Spanish troops on English soil as supposed allies. They are suspicious of foreigners, and, when they are oppressed, they are rebellious and capable of taking bloody revenge, as upon the Danes. The safe and prudent way for a new prince to rule them is to respect them.

Gardiner may well have been sincere in his early opposition to Philip: but once Philip came, Gardiner set to work (with Machiavelli's help) on an account of English history and politics that would point the way to common interests.

Study of the historical context thus indicates that Gardiner's debt to Machiavelli was practical as well as literary. Machiavelli is central to the *Ragionamento* – quotations from his works are the foundation on which Gardiner rests his interpretation of English history and his advice, implicit and explicit, to the new prince. Furthermore the strategies proposed in the treatise bear a direct and intimate relation to Gardiner's actual work as Chancellor during the last two years of his life – his Machiavellian borrowings throw light upon his role in the marriage negotiations, on his attitude toward Elizabeth, and on his belated support for Philip of Spain. It is worth insisting that Machiavelli's influence on Gardiner's practice in this period was coherent and decisive – for it has often been denied, as, for example, by J. W. Allen in his influential *History of Political Thought in the Sixteenth Century* (New York, 1960, pp. 490–1), that Machiavelli's influence on political conduct in the sixteenth century could be other than fragmentary. In Gardiner's case, at least, the evidence clearly indicates a vital connection between theory and practice.

NOTE ON THE TEXT

The copy text for the present edition is E, which, of the two extant MSS, has the greater authority: it was the copy presented to Philip II, to whom the translation is dedicated, and, while B may be an emended copy of E, E cannot be a copy of B, for B corrects many of the grammatical errors of E. We cannot imagine the scribe of E systematically introducing errors in gender and agreement for B's legible and correct readings. When the possibility of scribal error in E and the fluidity of Renaissance Italian are accounted for there remain a great many grammatical errors for which the translator himself may have been responsible. The agreement of adjectives and nouns is frequently in error, most often when the form of the noun gives no clue to gender, as in the case of nouns ending in -e. Plurals are often formed improperly, and the first person singular of verbs is often substituted for the third person singular (-o for -a, usually). The pattern of error in the vowels of grammatical endings is clear enough to suggest that Rainsford's Italian (though quite fluent) was lacking in grammatical precision; even if all the errors were scribal (which I think highly unlikely) Rainsford allowed them to stand in the copy destined for the king. The possibility that the E readings preserve linguistic errors of the translator, then, is another reason for its selection as the copy text.

The editorial procedures employed have as their aim the production of an intelligible, rather than grammatically correct text. If Rainsford's Italian is imperfect, his errors and idiosyncrasies are part of the historical evidence and the anomalies of spelling and form of the E MS have therefore been retained in the present text, which follows that MS exactly except in the case of obvious errors which seriously obscure the meaning, and in graphic matters unlikely to reflect Rainsford's knowledge of the language. Thus the word division of the MS has been respected (*iquali* does not become *i quali*) as has the use of the accent and apostrophe (*à i* does not become *ai*, nor *p'el pel*). Other punctuation has been normalized, as have the use of capital letters and the use of *u* and *v*. The combination *ij* has been rendered *ii* (as in *Maurusij* and Roman numerals). Paragraph divisions have been made by the editor, and the form of the attribution of speeches has been standardized. In the MSS a variety of abbreviations is found for Stephano and Alphonso. In this text speeches begin with paragraphic indentation and the abbreviation *Alph:* or *Steph:*. Other abbreviations have been silently expanded.

Normalization apart, the E reading has been abandoned only when illegible or clearly in error in a way that seems likely to cause real confusion. In such cases the B reading has been preferred, or, in a very few cases, an emendation has been made. In all such cases rejected readings from the MSS are preserved in the apparatus, as are all the B variants except for variants of capitalization and punctuation.

Occasionally editorial confirmation of misspellings and other anomalies is indicated in the notes. This has been done in cases of possible confusion: no attempt has been made to direct attention systematically to all of the irregularities of E's usage.

RAGIONAMENTO/ DELL'ADVENIMENTO
DELLI INGLE/ SI, ET NORMANNI IN BRITANNIA./
NEL QUALE SI TRATTA DEL FELICE ET/ INFELICE
SUCCESSO DI PRINCIPI, SECON/ DO CHELORO
GOVERNO E STATO DAL/ RAGIONE O DAL   5
APPETITO FONDATO/ COMPOSTO PER IL
MOLTO RIVRENDO/ SIGNOR STEPHANO
GARDINERO VESCOVO/ CONSIGLIERO REGIO,
GRAN CANCEL/ LIERO D'INGLITERRA, ET
CAVALIERO/ DEL SUMMO ORDINE DEL   10
REALME/ TRADOTTO DAL'INGLESI NEL ITALI/
ANA, PER GEORGIO RAINS FORDO./ CON UN
RITRATTO D'INGLITERRA/ COMPOSTO DAL
TRADOTTORE.

Ir: 5. DAL/ RAGIONE] dalla ragione B; CHELORO] che loro B
      7. RIVRENDO] Riverendo B
     12. RAINS FORDO] Rainsfordo B; NEL ITALIANA] nel'Italiana B

II^r　ALLO POTENTISSIMO ET CLEMENTISSIMO/
　　PRINCIPE, PHILIPPO, PER LA GRA-/ TIA DI
　　DIO RE DI CASTIGLIA, LEO-/ NE, ARRAGONA,
　　INGLITERRA/ FRANCIA, DUE SICILIE,/
5　HIERUSALEM, HI-/ BERNIE ARCHIDU-/ CA
　　D'AUSTRIA,* DE-/ FENSORE DE/ LA FEDE/
　　CATHO-/ LICA./ FELICITA, ET COMPIEMENTO/
　　DI SUOI DESIDERII SANCTI./ LO ETERNO
　　　　　　IDDIO.

10 Fonte purissimo di bontà ineffabile, et d'industriosa Natura Sacra
Maiesta, tra diversi intervalli di tempo produsse, p'el beneficio delli
mortali, spiriti magnanimi et in ogni sorte di virtu maravigliosi,
II^v i quali quantunque⫽per diverse strade, secondo la diversita del
humore deli celesti segni infuso, facevano un medesimo viagio
con certa emulatione caminando à quel eccelso monte di fama, à
l'eterna palma di gloria, et à que' spatiosi campi della vita beata.
5 Onde Hercoles per l'incredibile fortezza di corpo, fu da gl'antichi
sopra l'humana felicità essaltato. Alessandro contra per virtù
d'animo era nomato Magno. Cesare per l'humanità singolare,
quale in tutte le sue vittorie et triomphi che hebbe usò sempre
verso gli vitti, fu detto Clemente. Antonio,* fra l'imperatori
10 devotissimo, Pio. Tito, che iudicò la somma della humana felicità
consistere nel adiutare gli bisognosi, Liberale. Et Ottavio che
governò l'imperio in pace fu primo salutato Augusto. Se adunque
questi, per esser supremi in una virtu sola, hanno da gl'ethnici
ottenuti titoli immortali à lor virtù appropriati, con chi sopranomi
15 potron hora gli cristiani salutare il felice nome di Philippo potentissimo, defensore della fede, et re et padre di tanti varii popoli
III^r clementissimo? Che desidera non altrimente che l'ardente⫽fiamma
la sopranza delli altri elementi la perfettione di tutte le virtu.
Imperò, per la somma providentia divina, al imperio di si ampli et
potenti regni essaltato p'el beneficio della fede vera, per la concordia
5 della grege cristiana, et per l'antica gloria di Britannia. Il che fanno
chiaro testimonio al mondo l'ottimi fondamenti et veri segni di
paterno amore già alli mortali mostrati, nel haver col'adiuto della

* See notes, pp. 152–67.　　　　10. d'industriosa *Ed.*] l'industriosa
II^r:　7. COMPIEMENTO]　　　　B, E
　　　Compimento B　　　　　11. tempo B] temp E
　　　8. DI] de B　　　III^r:　7. col'adiuto] co'l'adiuto B

44

Serenissima Maria restituito, doppo questa scurita di nevole, la chiaressa del sole* à li suoi britanni, et il dolce riposo di pace doppo tal tempestuosa guerra all'altri provintie cristiani. Per la quale se 10 n'è renduto honore à Dio, felicita à gl'huomini, richezze alle citta, abondantia à le campagne, sicurità à gli stati, allegrezza à i cori, et in ogni secolo futuro al felice suo nome immortalità. La fama del quale gia sparsa p'el universo, isforza gl'animi delli principi d'ogni provintia cristiana, di venerare con fervidi cori l'alti pensieri di 15 sua Maiestà et inchinarsi àli piedi di quella. Et perchè la mansuetudine et clementia di lei, nel accrescimento d'imperio et di gloria // III^v somiglia alla magnanimita del leone (la cui natura è quanto più libero, tanto più mite et humile), il popolo anche lei chiama, lei adora, et al presente priega per la preservatione di sua eterna corona, non altrimente che facevano gia i romani per la vita del buon Augus- 5 to. Sendo, adunque, o Clementissimo Re, et soprano arbitro delle controversie mondane, che a la Vostra Maiesta, come ad un nume sublimi di cui secondario depende la salute del suo popolo, debbono d'ubligo i sudori, gli voti, et pensieri di tutti, non si turba s'io, servo di lei humilissimo, da questi bassi valli nelli quali con sudori continuoi 10 travaglio, porgo, al'altezza sua, questo picolo offerto accioche mediante cio ne potrei et fare fede insieme con tanti altri popoli della allegrezza et godio che tenga il core mio del bene publico che la Britannia et il mondo tutto ha ricevuta di Vostra Maiestà, et render anche l'eterna memoria alli meriti di Stephano Gardinero, 15 vescovo di Wincestria, grand Cancelliero di Britannia, autore del'opera presente, //la cui constantia nella fede catholica, eccellentia IV^r nelle scientie, prudentia nelle manegie publiche, modestia nelli honori, et fede singolare verso la Vostra Maiestà mi hanno dato l'ardire di tradure questo suo opera, et consecrarlo à l'eterno nome di quella. Et accioche nulla mancasse in questo picolo volume, che si 5 puole desiderare alla cognitione delle leggi, ordini, costumi, natura, et humori delli popoli di Britannia, ne ho composta et qui giunto un ritratto del realme, li quali insieme, inchinandomi a li piedi di Vostra Maiestà ne offero con devotissima affettione à la clementia di quella. Di Londra ali xvi di marzo MDLVI. Di Vostra Maiestà il 10 devotissimo servitore, Georgio Rainsfordo.

III^r: 8. nevole] *sic for* nuvole B, E   III^r: 16. àli] a li B
          12. abondantia] abondantie B;   III^v: 16. Wincestria] Wincestra B
               à i] ai B   IV^r: 4. questo suo] questa sua B

45

1^r

RAGIONAMENTO DELL'
ADVENIMENTO DELLI INGLESI ET
NORMANNI IN BRITANNIA

Stephano. Alphonso.

5 Discorrendo fra me stesso lungamente, honorato cavaliero, ne stio
(alquanto come tra Silla et Caribbe) sospeso et dubioso qual recca
1^v seco minore pericolo et manco biasimo, ò il concedere ò il negarvi
quello che tante volte me ne havete⫽richesto. Perche il negare una
cosa honesta et licita à uno gentilhuomo virtuoso et amico, egli pare
che il huomo non puole senza violare le sacre leggi di amicitia et
5 sospettione d'ingratitudine. D'altro canto, il promettere, et poi non
sapiando condurlo à quel desiderato et perfetto fine, che voi
paraventura ne spettiate, reccarebbe à me l'autore piu biasimo che
lode, at a voi l'oditore piu fastidio che piacere. Ma tutte le cose, tra
gli amici, soleanno esser in buona parte (qualecunque sono) accetate,
2^r pero ho deliberato meco, aprirevi in questo⫽caso piu presto il mio

Suggietto poco valore con benevolentia, che celare la, et d'essere giudicato da
della voi poco amorevole. Voi dunque mi richiedete, che io monstra il
materia parere mio circa gli mutationi piu memorabili accaduti nel reame
5 d'Ingliterra, et le cause d'essi, infin al tempo presente. Ma primo
ditemi, che cosa vi ha mossa à domandare quello, essendo voi
forestiero à cui i regimenti et governi di questo regno non toccano:
ne meno i mutationi ponno dare utile ò danno.
2^v *Alph:*⫽Illustrissimo signor, egli è bene vero, che li governi del
realme non pertengono à mi, ne io gli desidero per altro che per
sapere et contentare il mio avaro animo, bramoso di cognoscere
et sapere ogni cosa, et massimamente i regimenti et governi de
5 diversi provincie et realmi, acciò per gli diversi essempi d'essi
imparati, posso adiutarne (al mio ritorno) la mia patria, al qual tutti i
hommini sono nati. Questo desiderio, illustrissimo signor, mi mosse
3^r richidere il vostro appro-⫽vato giudicio nelle mutationi gia da voi
di sopra nominati.
Steph: La vostra lunga pelegrinatione (come me ne havete detto)
monstra veramente il grand desiderio che ne havete di sapere, il che
5 è tanto piu honorevole et lodevole quanto egli da pochi à tal fine

2^r: *marginal note lacking in B*   2^v: 8. richidere] richiedere B
   4. reame] realne B

cercato, perche in questi nostri giorni gli hommini bramano ogni
altra cosa piu che quello.

Alph: Anzi io credo che tutti i hommini naturalmente tengono
questo desiderio di sapere, ilche mi pare d'essere il sommo⫽bene
et solo contento di gli hommini, mentre che in questa valle
pelegrinanno.

Steph: Quali sono li ragioni che vi persuadino da creder quello?

Alph: Molti veramente, et primo per esser cio l'ultimo dono
ch'il omnipotente Iddio dette à i hommini. Perche havendo l'infinita
providentia de Dio data à tutte le altre creature i suoi numeri, i
suoi pesi, le sue misure, il modo, la spetie, l'ordine, l'essentia,
l'virtù, l'operatione; l'huomo (che per metter in lui la soprema mano
di tutte⫽l'opere Sue) non fece se non l'ultimo giorno. Accioche à
quella beatitudine et gloria che Egli possede per natura solevarsi
potesse, fra tante doti che varii sono, per gratia diede questa ingenita
proprietà naturale, che non contento d'esser come le pietre, non di
viver come le piante, non di moversi et sentire come le bestiae, ma
desiderasse d'intender et di saper ogni cosa come gli angeli. Percio mi
pare che la scientia è l'ultimo fine, et la somma felicitade di questa
vita non si⫽possede, non si trova, anzi non si cerca pure senza
scientia. La religione co'l dono supernaturale et infuso della sapientia,
lo possede. La theologia con la meditatione delle sante scritture, lo
trova. La philosophia co'l disputare et balbutire nelle cose naturale,
considerando le cause per li mirabili effetti, lo cerca. Le maneggie
publiche co'l continuo legere l'istorie et lunga esperienza, le acquistano. Non è huomo si vile, ne si idiota, si non e però piu statua di⫽
volto humano che huomo ch'à pena nato non habia un vehemente et
focoso desiderio di saper. Non desidera cosi l'aeria quando è piu
obscura la luce, ne la pietra quando è gittato di sopra il centro della
terra, come l'intelletto humano brama la perfettione della scientia,
per adornarsi, per illuminarsi, per quietarsi.

Gli uccelli nascono a volare, le fiere ad errare, i pesci a notare, i
cavalli a correre, gli houmini ogni loro gloria, ogni lor bene ripon-
gano nel sapere. Veggia-⫽mo che i grandi et picoli, maschi et
femine, quando si parla alzano la testa, aprono gli occhi, tendono
gli orecchi, sol per sapere. Per qual cosa habiamo tanto diletto quando sentiamo delle nuove, se non perche siamo bramosi di sapere

[marginal notes:]
3^v La scientia contenti l'animo
5 Discorso del saper'
4^r
5 Desiderio del huomo
4^v
5^r Le scientie adornano 5
Il fine dell' animali
La gloria del huomo
5^v

3^v: *margin.* contenti] contenta B   4^r: 8. vita non] vita. non B, E
4^r: *margin.* del huomo] *omitted in B*   4^v: 6. l'istorie] le istorie B
    1. giorno. Accioche]   5^r: 2. habia] habbia B
        giorno accioche B, E
    5. bestiae] bestie B

5 ogni cosa? Perche portiamo, quasi dalle fascie, una certa invidia à quelli che sanno piu che gli altri, se non perche pensiamo che chi sa piu che noi, tiene piu del' houmo che noi? Percio, i savii conchiudono

6ʳ Iddio niu-//na cosa haver potuto darci in dono piu utile, et piu

l sapere è cosa utile necessario all'vita humana che il sapere, veramente honorevole essercitio à i giovani, giocondissimo solazzo a gli vecchi, richezza incomparabili à gli poveri, et contentezza massima à gli ricchi. Il

L'amore di Platone verso le scientie desiderio di saper fece il divino Platone, la cui dottrina ribombava con si grand suono nell'academia d'Atene, che si dicea publicamente s'Iddio havesse da parlare con humana lingua, non potrebbe usare

6ᵛ piu//dotta, ne piu eloquente; et pure, va circondando* l'Egitto, la Calabria, la Puglia per trovare Archita tarentino, et vuole piu presto pelegrinare et esser suo discipulo, che stare nella patria et d'esser maestro di tante genti. Apolonio Tianeo andava tutta la

Travaglio di Tianeo vita sua errando per sequitare le scientie in ogni luogo, che se ne fugivanno dal mondo. Entrà primo tra i persi, passa il monte Caucaso, penetrà gli albani, i scithi, gli masageti, gli regni opulentissimi

7ʳ //dell'India. All'ultimo perveniva à i bragmani, et ode que' alti secreti* di nativita del gran Hiarca, che sedeva nel throno d'oro insegnando la divina philosophia, indi tornatosi in Alessandria, se ne và in Ethiopia per imperare da i gimnophisti, et vedere

5 quella famosissima mensa del sole, in quello arene dove se ensegnano alti misterii. Percio non maravigliate, signor illustre, s'io, spento di

7ᵛ questo desiderio di sapere le scientie, et cognoscere et vedere i// custumi, leggi, et ordini di varii genti et popoli, hò messo la vita in tanti pericoli, solcando l'impiacabile mare, pelegrinando gli aspri monti, si nell'a Europa come in parte dell'Affrica e Asia, et

5 al fino con grande contento d'animo qui giunto nel splendidissima corte de Philippo re d'Ingliterra, dove vedo per questa vostra authorità* (la qual mostra l'houmo) la singolare prudentia sua nelle maneg-

8ʳ gie publiche, la ferma constanza nell' //catholica fede, incorruttibile iustitia da voi à tutti ministrata, d'onde cognosco chiaramente che le sue qualitade non meritanno punto minore lodi (anzi molto magiore) che crida la publica fama d'esso (quantunque honoratissima) per

5 tutta Europa. Però confidandomi in questi suoi rare virtude, et pigliando ardire in questo suo cortesissima accoglienza, immenza liberalitade, et altri singolari beneficii verso di me usati, vengo

8ᵛ domandar il giudicio suo sopra// alcuni mutationi (sopra nominati)

5ᵛ: 7. houmo] huomo B   6ᵛ: 7. penetrà] *sic for* penetrò
6ᵛ: 5. sequitare] seguitare B   8ʳ: 6. immenza] immensa B
     6. Entrà] *sic for* entrò; passa]
     sic for passò

accaduti in diversi tempi in questo potentissimo realme d'Ingliterra.

Steph: Magnanimo cavaliero, vedo p'el vostro dotto et eloquente discorso il focoso et ardente desiderio che ne havete à sapere la mia opinione di questo suo dimando, il qual poi che io haveva meco 5 considerato, et gli circunstanti di quello, pesando il mio picolo valore con la grandezza de la materia, havrei senza dubio fugito // 9ʳ questa fatica per esser peso alli mei homeri molto inequale, s'el grand amore che porto à voi non mi persuadesse al contrario. Pero io monstrerò me stesso piu presto d'esser temerario, che ingrato à questo vostro lodevole desiderio. Ascultate dunque. 5

Alph: Asculterò attentivemente, senza interrompere punto il suo parlare.

Steph: Anzi no, domandate liberamente quello che voi piace, et ne renderò ragione à tutto che il mio saper se //estende: al resto 9ᵛ confesserò ingenuamente la mia ignorantia.

Verso il settentrionale, à la ponente giace l'isola gia Albion da gli albi scoglii detta, la qual per la bonta della terra, per il tempera- mento del cielo, per le commodità del paese, per la virtu de'i 5 popoli, non solamente ha da lungo tempo in qua i reali honori in se stessa havuta, ma è stata ad altre provincie vicine superiore et regina, et in tal modo allargò et stese l'ali //del suo realmi che di Francia, 10ʳ Normandia, Britagna, Gasconia, Scotia, et Hibernia luogi, citte, et provincie sottomise al imperio suo, et meritovelmente, conciosia che non solamente per gli armi et grand abondantia di tutte le cose al vivere humano necessario, à l'altre vicine superiore, ma anche nelle 5 littere et scientie liberali, come gli ingegni d'essa in ogni eta prodotti chiaramente all'posterità danno testimonianza. Ma poi (come sono tutte le cose huma-//ne soggetto al variare del cielo) travagliò 10ᵛ anche ella, di maniera che spesse sentiva la grand battiture di fortuna. Et in fine d'alcuni anni perse non solamente la libertà et il dominio degli altri, ma fu fatta serva, et sottoposta a l'innimici perdendo piu che una volta, insieme con la libertà anche il nome. 5

Primo Bruto,* figliolo di Silvio Ascanio troiano, con alcuni legioni suoi se impatronisse dell'isola senza grand fatica, per la rudezza del //tempo, essendo gli isolani alhora nella militia inesperti, 11ʳ et senza armi, et dal nome suo la chiamò Britania; i successori di cui godorono felicemente mille et quaranta anni al tempo di Julio Caesar dittatore, per la virtu di cui ella venne tributaria et dalli pretore romani governata. Al tempo di Valentiano imperatore, 5

Lodi della Britannia

Britannia di Bruto

9ʳ: 4 presto B] prestò E   11ʳ: *margin.* di] da B
10ᵛ: 1. soggetto] soggette B
     5. insieme] insiemme B

49

essendo alhora in Britannia pretore romano Aetio,* nell'absenza
di cui (essendo egli ito in Francia al socorso di suoi) i britanni
11ᵛ elessorono //per lor re Vortigerio, houmo britanico et lo primo
(con la corona d'oro) cororno, il qual in poco tempo di poi oppresso
quasi dalli scoti et pitti, chiamò in adiuto gli angli sassoni, popoli
della Germania ferocissimi et arditi, i quali havevano per duce et
Hengisto capitaneo Hengisto, della istessa natione, et nelle guerre esspertissimo,
capitan' qual vince non solamente i scoti et pitti, ma anche (per gli grand
delli
sassoni errori di Vortigerio re) lui stesso; et in breve mutò l'imperio da i
12ʳ bri-//tanni a gli angli et la chiamo Anglia.

Alph: O che perfidia di quelli genti, che voltaron l'armi contra
gli patroni, et quelli che gli chiamavano in adiuto!

Steph: Tal e l'effrenata cupidità di regnare, che gli hommini non
5 sparagono ne amici, ne parenti, ma attende varii successi. Poi
Cadavalladro gueregiavano insieme gli angli et britanni, fin ad Cadavaladro,*
ultimo delli
britanni ultimo re dell'sangue britanico, il qual dapoi molti bataglie vinto,
12ᵛ se retirò al esteriori parte dell' isola con // i rimanenti delli britanni,
iquali alhora furono chiamati dalli angli walli, che vole dire nel
lingua sassonica, hommini strangieri, perche chiamano gli italiani,
franciosi, et tutti altri forestieri, walli, et la patria Wallia.

5 *Alph:* Questo dunque è la vera origine del nome de' walli et
della patria loro?

Steph: Cosi egli e.

L'origine *Alph:* Ma que' popoli del continente che se chiamano britanni,
delli walli donde tragino l'oro origine?

13ʳ *Steph:* //dalle medesimi popoli sopra detti, perche sforsati dall'
sterilità et strettezza del luogo s'imbarcorno la magiore parte al
litto armorico, dove impetrorno sedia ad habitarne, et al fin di
hoggi la mantengono con l'antica lingua britanica.

5 Gli inglesi per questo mezo tenendo lo regno soli, lo divisorno in
setti regni, la qual dette animo a i daci, popoli crudelissimi d'invader
di nuova il regno, et occuparlo; i quali dopo trente anni che hebberò
13ᵛ l'imperio, furon cacciati dalli inglesi, i quali // erano dopo vinti due
anni sogiogati dal Normanno, i successori di cui regnoron felicemente fin a la morte d'Edouardo sesto, il che non lasciando del
corpo suo heredi, il regno venne à Maria sua sorella, laqual p'el
5 consentimente delli baroni, et per l'ordini del regno, hebbe per
marito et re, Philippo, di Carlo quinto imperator il figliolo, p'el bene

11ᵛ: 5. capitaneo] sic B, E   13ᵛ: 4. laqual] la qual B
12ʳ: 2. voltaron] voltarron B   6. imperator] imperatore B
13ʳ: 7. hebberò] hebbero B

commune del regno, et utilità (come poi se dirà) di tutta la cristianita.

Ho voluto contarvi succinttamente //li mutationi accioche meglio potrete intender cio che habiamo di dire sopra le particolari d'essi. Discorreremo adunque hora le cause et varii accidenti d'essi piu memorabili, lasciando indrio que' antichi di Bruto et di Caesare, et descendiamo à Vortigerio primo re delli britanni, poi che hebberò cacciati il giogo romano, et essaminaremo il regimento suo. Il testo* dice: 'Britanni principes cum viderent tantam tempestatem impendere à Scotis aeque ut a Pictis //hostibus crudelissimis statuerunt sibi regem aliquem optandum. Idque decus Vortigerio deferebant, quod esset vir inter viros authoritate, nobilitate, et virtute summus.' Per questa istoria se vede che la necessità fusse la cagione principale che nel principio mossi li huomini di eleggersi un re, chi in Britannia per conservare l'unione delli huomini insieme, per ministrare giustitia, per ridurre gli huomini ad un vivere civile, per rifrenare l'appetiti insatia-//bili, et finalmente per defendere lor popoli contra la violenza et forza delli inimici, come in tutti altri regni del mondo, et colui che fusse di magiore authorita et riputatione tra i popoli.

Alph: Ma ditemi Signor, quomodo erano governato que' popoli innanzi sendo senza re?

Steph: Io ne v'ho detto, che egli furon governati per i pretori romani, da iquali in quel tempo furono destituti, per esser ito Aetio (cosi //si chiamo il presidente romano) in Gallia al socorso delli romani, et però la necessità constrinse i britanni, circonventi dall'inimici, ellegersi Vortigerio per re, per esser egli di magiore reputatione.

Alph: Se io non pensava di molestarvi con questi presontuosi domandi, et tirarvi dal proposito, ne domanderei, pel mio contento, delle altre cose, ma temendo che non venessino al proposito, mi taceo.

Steph: Do-//mandate pure, perche il mio proposito è di rispondere et contentare in quanto posso, al vostro richesto.

Alph: Dite, adunque, per quali modi vengono li huomini reputati, perche dicesti che Vortigerio era di magiore riputatione.

(marginal notes)
14ʳ
Vortigerio primo re di britanni
Il testo
14ᵛ
5
Ufficio del re
15ʳ
5
5
15ᵛ
5
16ʳ

---

5   *Steph:* Gli vengono* riputati per la riputatione del padre, o delli predecesso, iquali erano stati huomini di grand authorità et

16ᵛ virtu. Se crede che i figliolo debbino esser simili a i padri in fin⫽à

Ondi li huomini sono riputati tanto, che per le sue opere non se vede il contrario, perche un popolo và driò quello che si dice di un huomo per la publica fama, o voce. Gli huomini acquistano riputatione appresso un moltitudine

5 per la compagna d'houmini savi et di buoni custumi, perche nessuno giudicio se puole havere magiore d'un huomo, che per la compagnia che egli tienne; et pero uno che uso la compagnia de

17ʳ savii acquista il nome di savio,⫽et che tiene la compagnia de virtuosi è tenuto buono. Perche non è possibile che non habia qualche similitudine con quello.

    Egli è un altra via per acquistarne riputatione, cioe per le proprie

5 virtude, et di monstrare essempi di sua virtu, et questo e il meglior di

Riputatione per propria virtu tutte l'altre, perche quella riputatione fondata solamente sopra li parenti è fallace: gli huomini vanno à relento, et à poco si consummi,

17ᵛ quando la virtu propria di colui, che ha desser giudicato, non⫽ l'accompagnia. L'altra che fa l'huomo d'esser cognoscuto per le sue practiche dura alquanto, ma ella è facillissima à cancellare. Ma questa ultima sorte che procede dalle proprie virtu, acquistà nel

5 principio tal home et fama che molte opere al contrario operate non l'annullano.

    Alph: Per quali di queste sorte era Vortigerio riputato?

    Steph: Per la prima, che nacque delli parenti solamente, perche

18ʳ l'opere sue propie non detteno mai⫽riputatione (perche non meritanno) anzi infamia a se stesso, et roina à sua patria, come se vedeva in poco tempo dapo che il hebbe lo governo del regno.

    Alph: Tale sgratie vengono piu volte à i huomini et à regni come

5 si furono destinati che non se puole rimediarle in conto alcuno, pero in simili casi gli principi sono senza colpa quando faranno lor dovere, perche contra il cieli chi puole operare?

18ᵛ   *Steph:* Le stelle non hanno tanta forza in⫽queste cose humane che

Le stelle inclinano et non sforzano la prudentia non puole mutarle; perche elle incitano l'huomo solamente et non sforzano. Pero non attribuisco tal colpa à le stelle, ne alli nascimento del huomo, ma à la poca prudentia. Dove* la

La fortuna vale poco dove è prudentia virtu è debole la fortuna è potente, et al contrario dove sia prudentia et buone discipline la fortune vale poco. Pero chi essaminarà il

16ᵛ: *margin.* ondi] onde B   17ᵛ: 4. nel] al B
       7. uso] usa B   18ʳ: 3. che il] ch'il B
17ᵛ: 2. l'accompagnia] l'accompagna   18ᵛ: 3. à le] alle B
       B; cognoscuto] cognosciuto B

governo di Vortigerio vedrà che altra non era la causa della perdita
et roina dell'imperio britanni-//co, che la sua poca prudentia qual   19ʳ
monstro nel principio del suo governo. Essendo alhora Britania
molestata con gli continuoi incorsioni delli scocesi et pitti, 'et iam',
come dice* la istoria, 'diffisus viribus suis, in mentem venit Anglos
Saxones rei militares illustres, ad resistendum inimicorum furorem   5
in insulam arcersere'. Eccò per questa deliberatione di Vortigerio   Il primo errore
se manifestà la poca prudentia sua, nel chiamare et totalmente   di Vortigerio
fidarsi sopra di forestieri //soldati mercinarii.   19ᵛ

Alph: Che altra cosa voresti che egli facesse essendo ridotto in
questa necessità?

Steph: Vorei quando uno e ridotto ad un tal pericolo, che il   Di duoi
habbia tanta prudentia di pigliare, di duoi mali, il minore, ma egli   male il
di molti partiti prese il pessimo, chiamando tali huomini per adiuto,   minore è
che furono poi piu crudeli et impii che non sarebbe mai i scocesi o i   meglio
pitti, quando egli havessino debellato nella campagna.

Alph: Se egli //havesse presaputo del fine havria fatto anche   20ʳ
altramente, ma in tale casi che ha tanta prudentia di presapere il fine?

Steph: Ogni uno che habbi esperientia; perche di mille principi à
pena se trova uno che habbia fatto profitto nel acquistare con li
soldati mercinarii. Ma l'errore di molti principi è che se attribuiscono   5
tanto à lor proprii ingegni che dispregino il consiglio di tutti altri.
Questi tali non sanno misurare lor forze con quella dell'inimico, i
pre-//sumano di saper ogni cosa, et credeno havere la forza sopra   20ᵛ
tutti altri, d'onde à la prova rimangono vinti et battuti della superbia,
et dellor sol sapere, come era Lotrecchio* innanzi la citta di Napoli.   La causa del
Tali principi lassino dar ad intender che egli sono quei, che non sono,   roina di
onde se mettino a pigliare imprese sopra lor forze. Stimandosi   Lotrecchio
d'aver la testa piena di sale, et le sono grilli. Se credino tal volta   5
d'esser sopra un cavallo grosso, et si trovino sopra un //gambero.   21ʳ
Pensando d'andare innanzi, se tornanno in drio come fece il re
Vortigerio che non si lascia governar' pe'l consiglio de houmini savi   Sol sapere
et esperti, iquali detteno consiglio piu presto d'accettare le conditioni
delli scosesi offerti, che servirsene delli inglesi sassoni, huomini   5
impii et crudeli, perche il picolo nomero delli soldati mercinarii   Consiglio
non bastavano contra il inimico, et il grand era pericolosissimo per   delli
torlo lo stato. Ma vedendo gli principi //suoi, che lor consiglio non   barroni
   21ᵛ

19ʳ: 4. dice la B] dicela E   19ᵛ: 2. che egli] che fa egli B
        4–6. *inverted commas beside*   21ʳ: 4. detteno] dettono B
        each line of text in E, lacking   *margin.* barroni] baroni B
        in B

piglio effetto, tentorno un altra via, con una piacevole favola, di farlo vedere il suo errore, il danno, et roina che sequitava il suo

consiglio, et gli disseno: Signor, egli era un cavallo,* il qual stava a pasturarsi alla campagna, et s'era fatto patrone di tutta la pastura, avenne che un cervo entrò in questa pastura tutto affamato, et mangiò senza discretione al mondo, talmente che il cavallo se

22^r corrusciò con esso, et li dette⫽la fuga parecchie volte. Ma il cervo alletto della dolcezza dal pastura, ne tornò incontinente, talché il cavallo vedendo che non puote mai soprafarlo, si per le sue duri corni, come per velocissimi suoi pedi, sene stava in tutto desperato.

5 Un di per caso vi capito un houmo, et il cavallo contandoli la sua sgratia gli chiese adiuto, per vendicarsi del cervo. L'houmo che era piu astuto che la bestia, gli rispose: Ser bestia, io solo non posso

22^v fare questa⫽impresa, ma si voi mi lasciarette montare sopra di ti, con una briglia in bocca, ne farò la tua vendetta d'houmo da bene. La bestia, per vendicarsi dell'altro bestione, si lassio cavalcare del houmo. Il cavallo adunque per questo modo vince il cervo, ma lui

5 resto prigioniero del houmo; perche mai piu non se cava la briglia foura della sua bocca. Cosi (dicevan i baroni) Illustrissimo Re, se

23^r Vostra Eccellencia chiamerà un moltitudine⫽di sassoni dentro il

regno potria esser che vindicarete l'ingiurie fatte dalli scocesi et pitti, ma voi et questa nostra patria stara sempre à la discretione di loro. Ma tutto questo non puote disuaderlo, egli volse haverli.

Pero se vede che tutte le parole che venne dette ad un houmo ostinato, sono gittate al vento.

Alph: Io non vedo che altro rimedio ne haveva in tal necessità.

23^v Se io mi trovai in simili pericoli credo havria fatto, ne piu, ne⫽ meno, che fece Vortigerio.

Steph: Cosi fanno tutti coloro, che non cosideranno il poco utile et grand pericolo che portino ad ogni principe (che gli adopera) tali

5 mercinarii, quando el nomero è si grande, che egli è sforzato da

mettere tutta la sua fidutia in essi; perche* i sono rapaci, ambitiosi, superbi, disobedienti. Alcuni ne sono instrutti (pel lungo uso) nella disciplina militare, ma pochi osservino l'ordini d'essa. Tengino

24^r poco timore verso Iddio, et meno⫽rispetto a li houmini, se la paura della pena non hebbe magiore forza in loro che la honestà. Et tutto* l'amore che portino à colui che servino, depende solamente di quel poco stipendio che egli donne, il qual non sarai mai tanto che

li basta di vivere, perche sono prodigi di suoi proprii, et avariosi di   5
quello di altrui: ne tanto che basta che moriranno per causa sua, ne
manco mettersi in pericolo si non sforzati di una grand necessità o
vergogna. Di tal⁄⁄fatti ne ho cognosciuto alcuni compagni, che   24ᵛ
militavano prima à la merce di Francesco* re di Francia, poi
s'accostorno ad Henrico de Ingliterra et al presente ne sono al servigio
d'Henrico di Francia tutti, eccetto quei, che per lor meriti son appi-
cati o per le privati questioni tra lor medesimi ammazzati.   5

Alph: Non credo che i mercinarii soldati sono obligati ad alcuno
oltra il tempo promesso, ma che li sia licito di servirene à cui gli⁄⁄   25ʳ
piacino, pure che se fanno ad intendere à colui che egli servino, di
loro partita, et quanto di non mettersi si temerariamente à li pericoli, meritanno (al parere mio) piu presto lode, che biassimo.

Steph: Dove sia licito di partirsi da colui che servino mentre che   5   Fanno
dura la guerra, non disputerò qui, ma dico, fanno ogni cosa licita,   ogni cosa
quando lor forza gli basta. Et dove (al vostro parere) meritanno lodi   licita
per non mettersi nelli pericoli, al mio, me-⁄⁄ritanno biassimo, perche   25ᵛ
egli usano d'imitare in alcune casi Fabio,* et in alcuni altri Varrone,
ma tutto al contrario. In questo imitanno Fabio che non vengono
voluntiere alimani co'l nimico se non sforzati, ma con ogni temerità
corrono adosso ai poveri contadini amici, robbando et spogliandoli   5   Natura de'
senza paura ò rispetto alcuno, tal che contra l'inimici (quando   mercinarii
conbattino per lor principe) sono rispettosi, et procedino come Fabii,   soldati
ma contra li amici⁄⁄per lor proprio utile diventino leoni ferocissimi.   26ʳ

Di questa ne fa fede un essempio fresco delli allemanni e spagnoli   Allemanni
alcuni, i quali venevano in Ingliterra come mercinarii* soldati nel
tempo di Edouardo sesto, quando i popoli di Cornowalli et Nordo-
vici ribellorno contra la nobilita. I mercinarii furono quei che primo   Danno riceputi
voltasseno le spale à i plebei. Laqual lor fuga era la cagione che i   per i
nobili restorno con dishonore grandissimo, sendo rotti,⁄⁄et presi   mercinarii
da i villani. Ma lasciando il campo poi, questi valenti houmini   26ᵛ
andavano senza ordine ò timore alcuno, robbando et spogliando le
case delli poveri houmini. Ma gli hebberò tal fine che meritanno
tali soldati, perche pochi d'essi godorno la preda male guadagnata,   5
essendo poi la piu parte amassati per mani di villani. Et per conchiu-
dervi, di pochi principi ne ho letto, che hanno hauti grand acquisti
per i soldati mercinarii, ma molti n'ho⁄⁄veduto che hanno hauti   27ʳ

24ʳ: 6. ne] *followed in E by* manco   26ʳ: *marginal notes lacking in B*
            deleted   6. spale] spalle B; Laqual] la
24ᵛ: 1. cognosciuto B] cognoscut E   qual B
25ʳ: 6. fanno] sanno B
25ᵛ: *marginal note lacking in B*

perditi grandissimi; et gli venitiani* tra i altri, i quali in un giorno perdevano tutto cio che in molti secoli ne havevanno acquistati. Infiniti altri sono gli essempi nell'istorie, che manifestino li grand

⁵ pericoli che portino l'armi forestieri à coloro che servino. I cartha-

ginesi dopoi la guerra con i romani era finita, furno per esser oppressi di lor mercinarii (quantunque hebberò per capitani lor proprii cittadini). Che altra cosa⁄ha ridotta la Grecia in servitu, se non gli mercinarii soldati, usciti di Turchia, quali l'imperatore di Constantinopoli vi messe dentro? I milanese soldorno Sforza contra i venetiani, il qual poi che hebbe superati l'inimici congiunse con loro per opprimere li suoi patroni, il che anche fece. Anzi come li mercinarii furon cagioni della roina di molti altre provincie, cosi li erano della distruttione del stato britannico, perche poi che Vortigerio hebbe⁄hauto una victoria delli scocesi et pitti p'el adiuto delli sassoni, per non monstrarsi* ingrato, detteli una provincia nel suo regno ad habitarne, et gli fece molti altri honori, che non doveva fare. Perche Hengisto (cosi era chiamato il capitano delli sassoni) che cognosceva hora la natura di Vortigerio, et che tutta la sua fidutia era posata sopra le virtu sua et di sue genti, imaginò seco, quomodo poteva impatronirsi del tutto, persuadendolo che l'e-⁄ra bisogna di piu genti di Sassonia per finire l'imprese comminciate, et vi condusse un nomero grandissimo insieme con la sua figliola di bellezza maravigliosa, nell'amore di cui Vortigerio il re era acciecato, et la prese per mogliere. La qual essendo fatto regina essaltò incontinente gli inglesi à i honori et officii del regno; il che alienò primo l'animo delli baroni del regno da Vortigerio lor re, et il nome suo da quel tempo indrio commin-⁄cio desser in odio appresso di tutti.

Alph: Il proverbio* dice quando Iddio vuole castigare un houmo, pigliarà primo il cervello, et quando li piace di casticare un popolo, li

⁵ manderà tal re, però chi considera come vanno le cose humane vedrà che alcune sono in tal modo ordinate dal cielo, che non si puole rimediarli; in tal maniera l'animi delli huomini sono accecati della fortuna, che non vagliono opporsi à la forze sue, come⁄⁄ pareva che fusse obfuscato l'intelletto di Vortigerio.

Steph: E bene vero che la fortuna (quando ella vuole condure cose grande ad effetto) elegerà uno che per prudentia cognoscera quelli

Margin notes (left column)

Pericoli delli cartaginesi

27^v
La roina della Grecia procedeva deli mercinarii

Milano perse la liberta per gli soldati mercinarii

Gli soldati
28^r
forestieri causorno l'estrema roina delli Britanni

Poca prudentia di Vortigerio

28^v
Astutia di Hengisto

Vortigerio inamorato

Alienatio delli barroni da Vortigerio

29^r

Proverbio

29^v

27^r: *margin.* cartaginesi]
    carthaginesi B
27^v: *margin.* gli B] gli i E
    2. mercinarii soldati] soldati
    mercinarii B

28^v: *margin.* barroni] baroni
29^r: 8. opporsi B] oppersi E
29^v: 2. fusse] fuesse B

occasioni che ella gli porge, cosi medesimamente quando ella 5
vuole condure grand ruine à una citta, ò ad un regno vi prepone un
houmo acciecato nelli suoi appetiti, che adiuterà tal ruina come fece
Vortigerio, il qual non conten-//to di commetter un errore nel
chiamare dentro que' crudeli popoli, ma concederli luogo ad habitarne, di farne con essi parentado, di participare con essi li honori et
secreti del regno, d'onde, sendoli in questa maniera accarezzati,
venorno in brieve tempo un nomero infinito. 5

Alph: Egli è da credere che questi sassoni non venivano in
Britannia tanto per le commodite d'essa, quanto per la discom-
moditade et sterilezza di lor propria patria, altre-//mente non hav-
riano lasciato un luogo certo per un altro incerto. Et percio sforzati
del mancamento del vivere, cercarno nuove sedie, et altre terre piu
fertile, che producevano piu abondantemente.

Steph: Della causa dell'advenimento di questi popoli in Britannia
ne sono varii opinioni. Alcuni* affirmano, che li detti sassoni
venisserò à caso, et non chiamati, perche l'era un costume anticho
tra quelli popoli di Germania che habita-//vano nelli luoghi freddi
et sterili (quando li houmini accressavano à tanta multitudine che la
paese non bastava à sostinerli) che i piu atti e disposti à la guerra si
partisserò per cercarsi nove sedie et habitationi, et per questo modo
dicono gli sassoni primo d'esser venuto in Britannia al stipendio di 5
Vortigerio. Ma quomodocunque fusse la cagione dell'advenimento
loro, questo è certissimo, che la paese d'onde venivano è molto
sterile, il che monstra l'etimologia del//luogo: Sassonia, quasi
piena d sassi. Et pero è di giudicare che li erano oppressi dalla
sterilità del paese, overo di qualche altra necessità grande. Laqual
cosa se puole facilmente indovinare d'esser vera, per la grand et
eccessiva virtu di quelli popoli, perche fra tutte laltre cose che 5
movino i huomini à pigliare l'armi, la necessità hà la magiore forza,
et quella guerra, tra tutte le altre, è massime pericolosa, la qual è
cagionata d'una necessità.

Alph://Mi pare che li houmini quando piglianno l'armi per il
commandamento del principe o sforsati della peste, o d'una guerra,
che tutto venne di necessità, perche è di necessità che il voler del
principe in questo caso sia obedito.

Steph: Nondimeno il commandamento del principe non ha 5

Fortuna accieco
l'animi delli
huomini

30^r

5

30^v

Varia opinioni
del'advenimento
delli inglesi in
Britannia

31^r

Costume
antico de
germani

31^v

Sterilita
di
Sassonia

5

La necessita
ha grand forza

32^r

29^v:	*margin.* accieco] accieca B	31^r:	2. la] lo B
30^r:	7. commodite] commodita B		7. la] lo B
30^v:	3. cercarno B] cercarne E;	31^v:	3. sterilità B] strerilità E
	nuove] nove B	32^r:	2. sforsati] sforzati B
	margin. Varia] Varie B		

57   3-2

tanto forza nelli cori d'una moltitudine quanto ha le altre detti necessitadi. Perche le cause de le guerre per le piu parti procedino

32ᵛ dalli principi, et l'honore o l'utile che dipen-//da della vittoria

L'honore della guerra è solo del principe, gli danni sono del popolo pertiene solamente a lui. Ma le discommodità che procedino d'una carestia, una peste, o di una guerra quando gli sono cacciati fuora de lor paese tocca generalmente à ciascaduna; per tanto potrete vedere che le guerre* tutte fatte tra li principi non procedono d'una

Guerra per ambitione necessità, ma alcune duna ambitione del principe, che è desideroso di propagare imperio suo et acquistarsi fama come Alessandro et

33ʳ Giulio Cesare. Altri ne sono commin-//ciate per vendicarsi del'

Guerra per ingiurie fatte ingiurie fatte, et per ricuperare citta, ò provincie ingiustamente tenute, come questa al presente tra Carlo imperatore et Henrico di Francia. Altri ne sono che piglianno l'armi mossi dalle commodi-

5 tati delle paese, alqual egli fanno la guerra, come i gothi* et vandale, i quali sentendo desser in Italia dolci vini, saporiti frutti, belle donne, poco freddo, temperati caldi, se miserò ad acquistarla, non

33ᵛ provocati da sdegno,//o desiderio di vendicarsi di lor inimici, ma d'una lussurioso desiderio di vivere una vita lasciva et delitiosa.

Guerra per avaricia Altre ne sono che procedono d'una avaricia. I romani et carthagi erano lungo tempo amici, ma sparsa la fama d'esser in Spagna

5 grand mine d'oro* egli venne voglia a i romani d'occuparla, d'onde nacque tra loro grand discordie, di modo che due amplissime

34ʳ republiche, per torre l'altrui destrussero i regni proprii.//Queste tal sorte* son pericolose, come tutte le sorti di guerra sono, ma non cacciano in tutto i habitatori d'una provintia, ma basta al vincitore sola l'obedientia, il tributo d'e popoli, et il piu delli volte li lasciano

5 vivere per lor leggi, et sempre con lor case et possessioni. Ma egli è

Guerra di necessità un altra sorta di guerra, quando un popolo se leva con tutti lor beni, d'un luogo necessitato dal fame, o dalla sterilità, o d'una guerra,

34ᵛ et va per cercare nuove//habitationi, non per commandarla et d'aver il tributo d'essa solamente, come quei di sopra, ma per possederla in tutto, et cacciarne gli habitatori antichi di quella.

Alph: Queste sorte di guerre sono spaventissime.

5 *Steph:* Del grand pericolo di tal guerra parla Paulo Diacono,

---

32ᵛ:	*margin.* sono del popolo] *illeg. in B*	5.	a i] ai B
	7. imperio] l'imperio B	34ʳ:	2. pericolose B] pericose E
	8. Giulio] Giutio E		3. provintia] provincia B
33ʳ:	5. delle] del B; alqual] al qual B;		6. sorta] sorte B
	vandale] vandali B		7. dal fame] dalla fame B
	6. desser] d'esser B	34ᵛ:	2. d'aver] d'haver B; d'essa]
33ᵛ:	*margin.* avaricia] avaritia B		dessa B
	3. I] Li B; carthagi]		
	carthaginesi B		

58

diceva che i romani combattorno con tutte l'altre genti solamente per dominare, ma con i franciosi et simili popolationi se combatte per la vita et salute di ciascaduno. //Ad un principe che assalta una provincia basta à spengere solo coloro che commandino: ma questi popolationi voglion spengere tutti accioche possino vivere di quello che gli altri vivanno.

Da questi popolationi Roma fu primo presa, cioe per i franciosi, che havevano tolti la Lombardia, et fattola lor sedie, et poi anchora presa, occupata, et l'imperio tutto distrutto da i gothi et vandali.

Alph: Quando un popolo occupanno cosi al primo advenimento una pro-//vincia, come faceano la Lombardia e di necessario ch'il nomero sia grandissimo.

Steph: Per la piu parte il nomero è grande, che in tal maniera partino per cercarne nuove habitationi, et oltra il nomero la virtu è sempre grandissima, quando ella è sforzata di tal necessita, che mancano le case per riposarsi, del pane per sostinere la natura, et delle altre necessarie, gli houmini diventino giganti, et non stimano in questo caso la vita, pero//se la forza che gli scontrerà non sia potentissima, restino sempre vincitori. Se vede parechie volte che gli houmini mossi da questa necessità hanno acquistato altre provintie cacciando d'inde li habitatori antichi fuora di quellae, che non potevanno diffendere lor proprie, come i maurisii* popoli di Soria, i quali sentendo venire i popoli ebraichi, et giudicando non poter resisterli pensorno esser meglio salvare lor medesimi, et lasciare la patria, che per salvare quella, perdere//anco loro; et levatisi con lor famiglie se andorno in Africa, dove cacciando via i habitatori che in quel luogo trovorono la chiamorono Marusia, secondo il nome loro. Moyse donque, capitano delli giudei, trovando i maurusii esser partiti, preso la provincia, et la chiamo Giudea, secondo il nome delli popoli che egli governava.

Per questi essempi se puole giudicare ch'il nomero di coloro che abandono lor patria per fame, per pestilentia, o per guerra, è sempre//grande (percioche la necessità tocca generalmente à tutti) et alhora al primo impeto (quando entranno in una provincia per forza) amazzano incontinente l'habitatori d'essa, possedono lor

Margin notes:
35ʳ Spaventose guerre
Roma sachegiata
35ᵛ
Necessita fa gli huomini senza paura
36ʳ
5
I maurisii
36ᵛ
Onde le provincie perdono lor nomi
37ʳ

34ᵛ: 6. diceva] diceve B
       7. et] i B
35ʳ: 3. popolationi] population i B
       6. anchora] anch ra B
       7. da i] dai B
36ʳ: 1. scontrerà] scontriraro B; non]
       omitted in B

4. quellae] quelle B
6. venire B] veniri E
7. poter] potere B
margin. I maurisii] Maurisii B
36ᵛ: 5. maurusii] maurisii B
       8. abbandono] abbandonon' B

Moyse chiamo Marusia Giudea

beni, fanno tutto nuovo, et mutano il nome della provincia, come fece Moyse et i franciosi, la Lombardia che se chiamo Gallia Cisalpina, l'Ungaria Pannonia, Gallia Transalpina hora Francia, da franchi. La Schiavonia se chiamava Illiria.

37ᵛ

Ma quando il nomero che si⫽parti d'una provintia non è grande che non ponno al primo impeto usar tanta violenza conviene loro con arte occupare qualche luogo, et mantenersi per via d'amicitia

Prudentia di Hengisto

et confederati come fece nostro Hengisto, capitano delli sassoni, perche primo egli fortificò il contado di Canterburia dal re Vortigerio li dato ad habitarne, poi fece una stretta amicitia con ello donan-

38ʳ

dogli per mogliere et regina la sua figliola, et in questo tempo non⫽ cessò mai da condure ogni giorno sassoni nell'isola, non in un tempo, ne gli teneva tutti in un luogo; gli fece arrivare in diversi porti, per non esser sospetti da' britanni, et in poco tempo il nomero

5

era si grande, che gli condusse dentro, che li pareva di non esser punto inferiore al re, et odendo gia li mormori delli principi contra

Hengisto inimico

di lui, facendo in uno tratto pace con i scoti et pitti alhora inimici delli britanni, gli monstrò se stesso apertamente anche inimico

38ᵛ

del⫽popolo britannico, i quali poi con molte bataglie gli ruppe in tal maniera che in nessuno luogo osorono piu comparere, non omettendo sorte alcuna di crudelità o tirannia che mai usava Nero ò

Crudelta de Hengisto

Domitiano, amazzando i miseri britanni senza misericordia conpassione o rispetto di età ò sesso, godendo et disponendo i beni, le case, et gli possessioni di quelli, secondo la volonta et il piacere suo et il regno in sette regni divise et lo nominava Ingliterra.

39ʳ
I Trogiani per amicitia occuporno Latio
I soldati mercinarii sono sempre pericolosi

Per⫽simili modi d'amicitia, i trogiani occuporno una parte di Latio, et anche i britanni gia cacciati mantenavano la provincia concedutoli apresso il litto armorico. Talche vedete sel numero è grand o picolo, il pericolo è sempre grande, come n'havete odito pel calamitoso fine delli britani. Quantunque il numero di quelli popoli che uscivano fuora di Sassonia primo non era grande, niente-

39ᵛ

dimeno il danno non era meno grandi à gli britanni, ch'il grand⫽ nomero de i franciosi erano à i lombardi, perche l'uno et l'altro hebbe il medesimo fine. La differentia è che la moltitudine occupan in un tratto la provincia, che invadino, et li altri, che sono in nomero

Il principe non si dee fidar delli mercinarii

inferiori, circano co'l tempo, et con l'arte da condure ad effetto cio, qual per aperta forza al primo impeto non bastono.

37ʳ: *margin.* Marusia] la Marusia B
37ᵛ: 1. parti] parte B; provintia] provincia B
38ʳ: 4. porti] parti B; da'] *above the line* E, de' B

38ᵛ: 6. volonta] voluta B
39ʳ: *margin.* Latio B] L'accio E
39ᵛ: *margin.* delli] deli B

Alph: Per questo mi par che volete conchiudere che un principe
non si dee fidarsi mai ne del uno, ne dell'altro, perche ne//cercanno 40ʳ
piu lor proprio utile, che il suo che li servino. Hor havendo hora
detto della prudentia di Hengisto che di privato se ne fece principe,
et lascio un tal regno à i suoi, contentate voi anche di monstrarne
la principal' cagione che fece Vortigerio da principe esser privato, 5
et della sua patria libera, da venire serva.

Steph: Delle cose sopra dette si puole giudicare la causa de l'uno
et laltro: nondimeno per satisfarvi in tutto quello//che posso, 40ᵛ
essaminarò il governo suo piu minutamente accioche gli errore de
lui commessi, ponno esser documenti à i suoi posteri, di non incorrere
nelli simili. Dico, pertanto, che Vortigerio ne fece, tra molti altri
errori, tre principalli, il minimo de i quali bastava di tore il stato da 5
ogni nuovo principe.

Alph: Questo è quello che io desidero di saperne volontieri.

Steph: Primo parlerò di quelli di Vortigerio fatti, nel suo governo,
poi//dirò generalmente di tutte le qualitade damnose ò giovevole 41ʳ
ad un principe per mantenere lo stato suo, o torlo. Il principale era Errore
di non haver indrizzato li suoi àla disciplina militare. Un altro per principal di
farsi una columna di foresteri, houmini maligni, inquinati d'ogni Vortigerio
sorte di vitio; poi nel dispregiare le leggi antiche del regno in admit- 5
tendoli detti sassoni al suo consiglio et primi honori del regno. Chi
considerarà bene questi errori//vedrà che ciascaduno d'essi lo fa 41ᵛ
dispregiato, et poi odiato delli piu parte di suoi subiti et tutti
quei attioni che producono simili effetti hanno sempre tal fine qual Colui e
hebbe l'errori suoi. Et quanto* al mancare armi proprii di suoi debole che se
soggetti, affermo che nessuno regno o principato è sicuro anzi fide de altri
tutto suggetto a le colpe di fortuna non havendo virtu in tempo di 5
necessità, che lo puole diffendere. L'era l'opinione de i savii, che non
è cosa si debole et infermo come il principato fondato sopra// 42ʳ
l'armi d'altrui. Percio* un principe debbe haver principal cura
d'instituire i suoi popoli piu atti et disposti nelli ordini della militia, La scientia
la qual è una scientia sola, che fa lo principe amato et honorato di militare e
suoi, et lo rende temuto dall'inimici. Questa scientia non solamente necessaria al
fa quelli che sono nati principi nelli stati lor sicuri, ma molte volte principe
gli houmini di basissima fortuna fa venire à tal grado come Agatocle* La peritia di
et Hengisto et infiniti altri.//Et il contrario se vede, quando i Hingisto 42ᵛ

40ᵛ: 2. errore] errori B; de B] li E   41ʳ: 1. qualitade] qualitadi B
    4. pertanto] per tanto B   *margin.* principal] principale B
    5. principalli] principali B   41ᵛ: 2. dispregiato] dispreggiato B
    7. volontieri] volentieri B   4. mancare] manchare B
        42ʳ: 5. temuto B] tenuto E

61

principi si danno buon tempo, et studiano piu al vivere delicato, che alli armi: diventino dispregiati dall'nimici et odiati di suoi proprii sogetti. Come Edouardo secondo, et Giovanne re d'Ingliterra, iquali tutti duoi, per lor ignavia venerò (come indegni di tal honore) di lor baronni privati del stato et poi delle vite anchora.

Alph: Io lodo grandemente quelli principi, che stimanno la milizia, perche nessuna cosa è piu necessario à chi governi, come quella. Pero il principe* non dee mai levare nel tempo della pace il pensiero di questo essercitio della guerra, il che egli puole fare facilmente legendo l'istorie, et considerare in queste l'attioni deli huomini illustri et eccellenti, essaminando le cagioni delle vittorie dell'uno, et la causa del perdita d'altro, per poter seguire quello, et evitare questo. Et nelle altre sue essercitii del corpo, d'usar spesse volte la caccia, laqual è viva imagine della guerra, perche mediante quella, cognoscerà la natura de gli monti et valli et siti dei fumi et palude; et per questo mezo l'userà il corpo à molti disagi, con questo piacevole essercitio, che quando venerà il tempo andar à la campagna, egli puole comportarlo senza disagio alcuno. Et quel principe, che con simili essercitii userà il suo corpo nelli tempi delli pace, quando si muta il tempo à la guerra, lo trovi sempre parechiato d'oviare et opponersi alli suoi dardi.

Ma per indrizzare un popolo intiero ne la militia et essercitarlo in quella, giudicò, che sarebbe cosa pericolosissima, perche la natura d'un popolo è licentioso, audace, desiderabile d'innovare, tumultuosa, morbida et massime (con licentia sia detto) i popoli inglesi, come se vede per l'istorie, perche chi legerà le vite delli re, comminciando dal Guilhelmo Normanno fin ad Edouardo sesto vedrà, come alcuni ne sono di lor regni cacciati altri morti di tumulti et conspirationi popolari, et pochissimi o nulli i quali hanno regnato intieramente senza tali tumulti. Per tanto, se questi popoli havessino l'arte della militia congiunta con lor alta natura, sdegnosa et morbida, diventerebbono in tal modo insolenti et disobedienti à lor principe, che sarebbono insopportabili ad ogni uno.

Steph: Non ho veduto mai, che la scienza fusse causa di male

Marginal notes:

Edouardo secondo et Giovanne

43ʳ

43ᵛ La caccia e viva imagine della guerra

44ʳ

44ᵛ

Scientia non e causa di mal, ma l'ignorantia

42ᵛ: 3. dall'nimici] dall'inimici B
6. baronni] baroni B
43ʳ: 4. deli] delli B
5. essamminando] esaminando B
6. del] della B; d'altro] de laltro B

43ʳ: 6. seguire quello. . . . evitare questo *Ed.*] fugire questo. . . . evitare quello E, seguire questo. . . . evitare quello B
7. nelle] nelli B; sue] suoi B
43ᵛ: 2. dei] de'i B
6. delli] della B
44ʳ: 2. essercitarlo B] essercitar fa E

62

alcuna, ma la ignorantia sempre. La poca pru-//dentia delli capitani   45ʳ
ha causato la roina di molti citta et provincie et la morte d'infiniti   Lignorantia
popoli, come ci insegna lo presente essempio di Vortigerio. Et   di Vortigerio
per il contrario se vede che grand prove hanno fatto i romani et
Alessandro, i quali hebberò lor popoli instrutti nella disciplina   5
militare.

Alph: Hora non siamo su quel medesimo caso, ragionando
d'Alessandro, delli romani, et di Vortigerio, perche à gli predetti,
che cercorno di sogiogare tutto il mondo//per larmi, era necessario   45ᵛ
di disciplinare loro popoli, accioche perdendo una giornata potevano rifarlo essercito di genti disciplinati incontinente. Ma à
Vortigerio et ali altri principi christiani, i quali debbono fare una   Cristiani
picola guerra per un continua pace, non per torre di altrui, non   debbono far
per sogiogare il mondo per l'armi, ma per diffender' i suoi, et gover-   guerra per
narli poi in pace, basta che una parte solamente siano disciplinati,   haver pace
et tanti soli, che risultarebbono//di fare un giusto essercito, che   46ʳ
puole comparere innanzi l'inimico à la campagna, et quando la
necessità mi stringesse d'aver piu genti, pigliarei piu presto mercinarii, i quali saranno piu utile (quando il nomero non sia grande) che   Mercinarii,
da disciplinare i proprii. Perche finita la guerra, i mercinarii vore-   finita la
bbono esser rimunerati (secondo lor meriti) et licentiati. Et alhora da   guerra,
quelli non resti piu pericolo, ma havendo una volte disciplinato i   vorebbono
suoi popoli nella militare//disciplina, et armatoli, egli starebbono   esser' licentiati
sempre su quella bravaria dell'armi, et la piu parte non tornerà   46ᵛ
mai piu ad coltivare la terra, ne al loro solito essercitio, qual innanzi   Bravaria di
usavano ma di robbare questo per la strada, et sacinare quell'altro   contadini
in le case, perche i contadini, i quali sono usati nel faticoso essercitio   5
della agricoltura, di state et di verno, nelli pioge, nevi, grandini,
venti, ardenti raggi del sole, hor co'l vomere, hor con la zappa//   47ʳ
spessando la dura terra, esporgando le spine, hor gittando i sassi,
et mille altri essercitii simili durissimi, lavorà continuamente,
nientedimeno non se faticà mai, ne gli pare travaglio alcuno, perche
credono che non sia altro cielo; non hanno provato altri piaceri: 5
ma havendoli una volta imparati molti di questi gentilezze che se   Gentilezzae
usano in la corrotta militia di nostri giorni, egli faranno piu presto   della guerra
ogni altra tristitia che tornarsi à lor//vechi mestieri, et per ogni   47ᵛ
capricio che li vendrà nella testa, i susciteranno nuove seditioni,
talche il principe sera sforzato di stare à la discretione loro (come
hanno fatto alcuni re di questo regno, et molti altri imperatori

---

46ʳ: 6. esser B] esse E   47ʳ: *margin.* Gentilezzae] Gentilezze B
        7. volte] volta B   47ᵛ: 2. capricio] capritio B

5 romani, à la discretione di lor soldati perche egli staranno à la
discretione di nessuno). Pero i principi temendo la natura di questo
popolo, hanno fatto molte buone leggi per rifrenarla, prohibendoli

48^r in tutto la cognitione della ⁄⁄militare disciplina, che non sia licito à

Lege persona di dar regole, ne stampare libri alcuni di quella materia,

d'Ingliterra l'uso del arcabuso ò balestra. Oltra che non partino fuora di caso
lor dopo otto hore à la notte; che non fanno ludi o giochi publici,

5 per non ragunare insieme il popolo, et che sera licito per ogni
uno d'accusarli à la ministri di giusticia ogni volta che se vedra il
nomero di dodeci houmini o piu ragunati insieme in casa alcuna

48^v sospetta ò in altre luogo, ⁄⁄il qual ministro di sua authorità puole
commandarli à la prigione tutti di tal iuditio accusati senza d'aver
cosa alcuna altra manifesta contra d'essi, et molte altre simile leggi
durissimi.

5 Tali savii principi, i quali sapevano quanto l'era pericoloso di
mettere la spada in mani di quelli, che non sapevano usarla, hanno
voluto in tempo opporsi con buone leggi àloro cattiva natura,
perche vedevano che tal disciplina sarebbe piu pericolosa et nocevole

49^r in tempo della ⁄⁄pace, che utile in la guerra.

Confutatione *Steph:* Mi pare che voi siate di natura di quelli, che non leggono

del opinione le rose per esser offeso delli spine: ma bisogna che gli houmini

predetta hanno tanta prudentia di pigliare la dolcezza del una, et scifare

Natura della l'asperità del altra. L'ape tira d'un fiore mele, et la ranea del mede-

ranea sima veleno. L'houmo che ha la febre non gusto altro che amarezza,
et l'houmo sano del medesimo cibo prende saporito notrimento.

49^v La colpa non è nel fiore che ⁄⁄rende al uno mele, et al' altro veneno,
ne nel cibo, che ad uno pare amaro, et al altro saporito, ma in la
diversa natura del ape et della ranea; et delli diversi humori del
houmo sano et del houmo amalado. Dico per tanto, che la disci-

5 plina et cognitione della scientia militare non recca seco mai male;

Se puole quantunque ella sia piu volte delli ignoranti et tristi male usata,

usare male non si dee pero imputare tal male à la scientia (qual per se è buona)

ogni cosa ma a i tristi che malamente la usano, perche non e cosa al mondo che

50^r non puole esser malae ⁄⁄usata. Pero le ragioni da voi preallegate
non provino, che la cognitione di questa arte non conviene à i
popoli generalmente, quantunque egli la usano qualche volte male.
La colpa di questo procede dalli principi et che debbono insignarli il

49^r: 6. gusto] gusta B
49^v: 4. et del] et del' B
5. recca B] rerca E
9. malae] male B

50^r: 4. il] *followed in B by* modo *deleted*

retto uso di quella. Di questo ne monstrerò un essempio frescho, 5
et di quelli medesimi popoli, che voi ne havete preso vostra authorita. Henrico ottavo quando venne a la corona trovo (per esser suo
padre trenta anni innanzi // senza guerra) lo regno senza soldati
disciplinati, et senza capitano che haveva militato: non dimeno egli
in breve tempo et in tal modo gli disciplinò che d'una banda
assalto* lo potentissimo regno di Francia, piena di soldati et capitani,
et del'altra affrontò (solamente con i suoi) tutto la forza di Scotia, 5
et hebbe in uno medesimo tempo gloriosa vittoria del'uno et de'
laltro, si per l'espugnatione di Turrino, Tornay, et per la ignominiosa
fuga de li // franciosi, come per la grand strage de scocesi et la
miserabile morte* di Jacomo lor re. Notate: Henrico in quel tempo
armava di suoi subditi ottanta cinque mila, et finita la guerra
tornorno à coltivare la terra, et far lor solite essercitii senza tomolti o
pensiero di tumultuare; ilquale nacque della prudenza del principe,
che seppe disciplinarli et servirsine d'essi ne la guerra, et con sua
authorita commandarli à lor mistieri ne la pace. Pero un principe //
non dee mai omettere un utile presente, sendo honesto et certo,
per la paura d'un danno che puole accadere dopoi. Voglio dire,
che non si dee temere da disciplinare i suoi subditi, et servirsi di
que' in la guerra per paura di ribbellare poi in la pace. Et si Vorti- 5
gerio havesse hauto tanta prudentia in questo caso come Henrico,
l'havria salvato in piede la sua patria, et fatto anche terrori a inimici.
Ma non havete male indovinato della natura delli // inglesi, perche
in vero nelli tempi passati sono stati inquieti, mutabili, desiderosi
d'innovare, et morbidi; et tutto procedeva delli fattioni et discordie
tra i nobili, d'onde egli presorno tal licenza che in molti anni poi
l'era difficile per tenerli in obedientia. Nondimeno si ne havete
bene considerato gli tumulti et conspirationi gia di voi mentionati,
vedrete che i popoli non sono stati cagioni sempre di quelli: ma il
piu delle volte i principe del // realme, accioche quei piu facilmente
incitando i popoli à tumultuare, potevano condurre ad effetto lor
desiderii, come fece gia Richardo, duca di Yorca, et vi voglio
contare il modo che egli usò, accioche potrete meglior sapere d'onde
nascono i spessi tomulti et congiure contra i re d'Ingliterra, et poi
giustamente imputare la colpa à chi la merita.

Il duca Richardo aspirandosi à la corona pensò con aperta forza

Margin notes:
- Prudentia di Henrico
- 50ᵛ
- 5
- 51ʳ Le gloriose vittorie di Henrico Morte di Jacomo. re di Scotia
- 51ᵛ Nota
- 5
- 52ʳ La licentiosita del popolo nacque delle fattione de i nobili.
- 52ᵛ
- Astutia del duca di Yorcha

50ʳ: *margin.* Henrico B] Hengisto E   52ʳ: *margin.* fattione] fattioni B
50ᵛ: 5. tutto] tutta B   52ᵛ: 5. tomulti] tomolti B; contra]
51ʳ: 4. solite] soliti B   *last three letters inserted above*
      margin. Scotia] Scot: E, Scocesi B   *the line in E*

53ʳ d'opporsi⫽a la potentia del re, ma temeva il popolo, perche non sapeva quanto la sua authorità valeva apresso desso, et trovo questo modo di provare l'animi del popolo senza d'esser sospetto di alcuno di cio, che egli haveva nel animo di fare. Nella citta* di Yorcka era
5 un hospitale per sostenire gli poveri, infermi, et altri pelegrini del regno, alqual (d'uno anticho costume) ciascaduno della provincia
53ᵛ dette ogni anno alcuni misure di fromento, et una certa⫽somma di denari (secondo la facolta loro) per mantenerlo; et furono preposti questori per colleggere il detto frumento, et gli denari. Il duca che cognosceva gia come era facile à persuadere il popolo da pigliare una
5 impresa qual reccava lor utile, fece sparger litere incognite et per incerti authori publicare, per tutta la provincia, che quel fromento,
54ʳ et quelli denari, quali erano dati à li poveri venne devorati⫽delli richi ministri di quel hospitale, et che i poveri non godevano la minima parte d'essi, disuadendoli per simili ragioni di non pagare piu nel fromento ne li denari.

Gli popoli adunque, communicando queste cose tra lor medesimi, et consigliandosi di quello, che havevano di fare, determinorno p'el commune accordo di negare constantamente tal pagamento (perche
54ᵛ pareva lor utile) quando che sarebbe dimandato. Il che anche⫽ facevano. Gli ministri del luogo se lamentorno al consiglio del re della disobedientia de' popoli contra gli antichi costume et leggi del regno. Il re Henrico sesto (nel regimento di cui questo tumulto
5 accadeva), il qual era osservatore delli costumi del realme, commandò, che quelli che negavano tal debito furono imprigionati et puniti come ribelli disobedienti. I popoli sentendo tal sententia data,
55ʳ si levorno in un tratto diece*⫽mila huomini marchiandosi contra, verso la citta di Yorcka, con animo di vendicarsi delli ministri, iquali hebbero procurati tal sententia contra di loro. Ma i cittadini sentendo venire il moto popolare, chiuserò le porte, et defendevano
5 le muraglie. In questo mezo il re vedendo quanto l'importava questa cosa commando il duca Richiardo, il qual era presidente della provincia da pacificare il popolo, con qualche bel modo, et la
55ᵛ piu presto che poteva. Egli per non d'esser sospetto⫽di favorigiare la parte del popoli prese lor capitano, et lo taglio la testa, commandando l'altri in publico che tornassero ciascaduno à casa sua. Ma

margin: E cosa facile a persuader' gli huomini le cose utile — Judicio temerario del popolo

53ʳ: 2. valeva B] voleva E
4. nel] in B
53ᵛ: 1. di] de B
2. facolta] faculta B
3. colleggere] collegere B
7. denari] dinari B

54ʳ: *margin.* temerario B] temerar E (end of word lost in cutting)
54ᵛ: 6. furono] fussono B
55ʳ: 7. da] de B; la] lo B
55ᵛ: 2. popoli] popolo B

in secreto per littere et romori incerti procacciavali d'andare à Londra di vendicarsi contra i ministri dell re; laqual cosa anche venne fatta. Il re, giudicando meglior per oviare alla furia dell popolo innanzi che venivano a Londra, ragunò dodeci mila huomini et si messe in viagio per affrontarli in // questo mezo. Il duca Richiardo era anchora in Yorcka, et cognoscendo che i popoli perseverorno nel lor furia, egli sequitò con un essercito, parendo à tutti ch'andasse in favore del re, contra i rebelli, ma giunto che egli era appresso il campo del re, misurando le sue forze con quella del re giudicò il tempo d'esser venuto di palesare quello che lungamente innanzi l'haveva celato nel'animo, et in uno subito giuntosi co'l essercito popolari, dette segno ad // investire l'essercito regale, et lo ruppe et presò tutta la nobilita dei quali decapito alcuni suoi inimici, et meno seco Henrico re a Londra prigioniero : et questo nondimeno è chiamato il tumolto delli popoli d'Yorcka.

Similmente concitorno i baroni contra Henrico ottavo cinquanta mila huomini quando commincio d'usurpare i beni spirituali, et quello era chiamato il tumolto* delli popoli di Linconia et commumente che considererà l'isto- // rie vedra che quasi tutti i tomolti fatti in Ingliterra eran comminciati delli barroni et principi del regno, o contra il re p'el suo mal governo, overo per vendicar i privati nimicitie, ingiurie, et odii iquali spessissimi nascono tra loro et nientedimanco il popolo vene incolpato come autori di tanti mali.

Alph: Et non senza causa, perche è sta veduto in questo realme molti tomolti causati del popolo solamente, non essendo altri capitani, che popolari // come quelli delli popoli di Canterburia essendo capo del uno Giovanni Caddo* et d'un altro Giovanni Strava, et novamente il tomolto de' popoli di Nordovico, i quali hebberò per capo uno che si chiamava Ketto, tre houmini vilissimi luogi nati, de'i quali duoi primi sacchegiorno la citta de Londra. Stravo taglio la testa d'alcuni consiglieri del re, et tenne il re stesso come prigioniero nella torre di Londra. Il tertio preso la piu parte della // nobilita della provincia, et la tienne incarcerata, facendoli rendere ragione à i piu infimi et fare restitutione à quelli che gli hebbero offesi. La cosa e si manifesta, che non se puole scusarla.

Steph: Non cerco d'escusarli di queste cose mal fatte, ne anche in nullo altro, anzi li vitupero, et condanno. Non dimeno quando

---

56ʳ

56ᵛ

Henrico re prigioniero

Barroni concitorno i popoli contra Henrico

57ʳ

Il popolo incolpato a torto

57ᵛ

Londra sachegiata

58ʳ

Tomolti contra nobili

56ᵛ: *margin.* i] *omitted in* B   57ʳ: 4. nimicitie] inimicitie B
57ʳ: 2. barroni] baroni B   6. causa] *above the line in* E; è sta]
                                                              esta B
                                                  57ᵛ: 4. houmini] huomini B

essaminaresti l'originale causa delli sopra detti tomolti, non darete la colpa solamente à i popoli, ma parte à nobili, et parte à i⫽re istessi come io vi faro vedere chiaramente.

Le fattione in Ingliterra
Nell'anno trenta del governo di Henrico sesto re d'Ingliterra, le fattioni di duoi amplissime famiglie, cioe di Lancastria et di Yorcka
5 comminciorno d'aver grandissime forze, sendo Henrico re capo di quella de Lancastria, et Richiardo duca di Yorcka capo della contraria. Il qual duca, non trovando altra via meglior per condure suo

59ʳ
desiderio ad effetto, suscitò in diversi provincie⫽del regno tomolti popolari, contra gli ministri del re, accioche sotto questo colore di castigare i cattivi ministri, gli puote piu facile privare Henrico del

Donde nacque la licentia del popolo
regno (come poi anche fece). Questi fattioni generò tanta licentia ne' popoli che per molti anni non si studiavano ad altro che ad innovare et mutare principe, hor prevaleva la famiglia di Lancastria, hor la famiglia di Yorcka, secondo che egli erano favoriti o dis-

59ᵛ
favoriti del popolo, come parse per la⫽grand calamitade del detto

La misera fortuna di Henrico sesto
Henrico, et per la sua varia fortuna, il qual primo venne in potestade del duca suo nimico. Poi p'el popolo era liberato, et volendo vendi-
5 carsi, suo essercito era rotto in la campagna, et lui necessitato di fugire in Scotia, dindi da poci giorni ritornò per ricoperare il suo regno, venne anchora preso, imprigionato, et privato della corona, et la seconda volta liberato et restituito al regno, et poi la tertia

60ʳ
volta preso, et amazzato⫽in prigione.

Le cause delle tumolti
In questo calamitoso tempo che le leggi erano calpestrate sotti li pedi, et che l'armi sonavano fin al cielo, et che era licito per cias-

Caddo scelerato
caduno tristo per metter' in effetto la sua tristezza, questo scelerato
5 houmo Caddo, da voi mentionnato, se ne fece capitano di tali, quali egli stesso era, et non lascio indrio sceleragine alcuno che un

Tomulti per colpa del re
houmo impio et tristo havria imaginato.
La causa del altro tumolto* qual Stravo era capitano nacque della

60ᵛ
straordinaria essattione di Richiardo secondo re, il qual commando⫽ di ciascaduno del regno, quantunque poverissimo, un pezzo d'argento volgarmente detto un stotere, et delli ricchi una somma magiore, secondo la facolta loro, la gravessa del qual generò tanto odio del
5 popolo contra il re, che dicevano publicamente, che si se soffrirorno il pastore tante volte all'anno tosare le pecore, che egli in breve tempo scortigarebbe anche, pero determinorno di non pagare tal straordinaria essattione, et fecero lor capitano questo Stravo.

58ᵛ: 6. Yorcka] Yorckca B   60ʳ: 8. tumolto] tomolto B
59ᵛ: 5. poci] pochi B   60ᵛ: 7. scortigarebbe] scorticarebbe B
         7. second la] above the line in E

in secreto per littere et romori incerti procacciavali d'andare à
Londra di vendicarsi contra i ministri dell re; laqual cosa anche 5
venne fatta. Il re, giudicando meglior per oviare alla furia dell
popolo innanzi che venivano a Londra, ragunò dodeci mila huomini
et si messe in viagio per affrontarli in //questo mezo. Il duca   56ʳ
Richiardo era anchora in Yorcka, et cognoscendo che i popoli
perseverorno nel lor furia, egli sequitò con un essercito, parendo à
tutti ch'andasse in favore del re, contra i rebelli, ma giunto che egli
era appresso il campo del re, misurando le sue forze con quella del 5
re giudicò il tempo d'esser venuto di palesare quello che lungamente
innanzi l'haveva celato nel'animo, et in uno subito giuntosi co'l
essercito popolari, dette segno ad //investire l'essercito regale, et lo   56ᵛ
ruppe et presò tutta la nobilita dei quali decapito alcuni suoi inimici,   Henrico re
et meno seco Henrico re a Londra prigioniero: et questo nondimeno   prigioniero
è chiamato il tumolto delli popoli d'Yorcka.

Similmente concitorno i baroni contra Henrico ottavo cinquanta   Barroni
mila huomini quando commincio d'usurpare i beni spirituali, et   concitorno i
quello era chiamato il tumolto* delli popoli di Linconia e commu-   popoli contra
mente che considererà l'isto-//rie vedra che quasi tutti i tomolti   Henrico
fatti in Ingliterra eran comminciati delli barroni et principi del   57ʳ
regno, o contra il re p'el suo mal governo, overo per vendicar i
privati nimicitie, ingiurie, et odii iquali spessissimi nascono tra loro
et nientedimanco il popolo vene incolpato come autori di tanti mali.   Il popolo
Alph: Et non senza causa, perche è sta veduto in questo realme   incolpato a
molti tomolti causati del popolo solamente, non essendo altri   torto
capitani, che popolari //come quelli delli popoli di Canterburia   57ᵛ
essendo capo del uno Giovanni Caddo* et d'un altro Giovanni Strava,
et novamente il tomolto de' popoli di Nordovico, i quali hebberò   Londra
per capo uno che si chiamava Ketto, tre houmini vilissimi luoghi nati,   sachegiata
de'i quali duoi primi sacchegiorno la citta de Londra. Stravo taglio 5
la testa d'alcuni consiglieri del re, et tenne il re stesso come prigioniero
nella torre di Londra. Il tertio preso la piu parte della //nobilita   58ʳ
della provincia, et la tienne incarcerata, facendoli rendere ragione à   Tomolti contra
i piu infimi et fare restitutione à quelli che gli hebbero offesi. La   nobili
cosa e si manifesta, che non se puole scusarla.

Steph: Non cerco d'escusarli di queste cose mal fatte, ne anche in 5
nullo altro, anzi li vitupero, et condanno. Non dimeno quando

56ᵛ: *margin.* i] *omitted in B*   57ʳ: 4. nimicitie] inimicitie B
57ʳ: 2. barroni] baroni B   6. causa] *above the line in E*; è sta]
                                                                esta B
57ᵛ: 4. houmini] huomini B

essaminaresti l'originale causa delli sopra detti tomolti, non darete
58ᵛ la colpa solamente à i popoli, ma parte à nobili, et parte à i⁄re
istessi come io vi faro vedere chiaramente.

Le fattione in   Nell'anno trenta del governo di Henrico sesto re d'Ingliterra, le
Ingliterra   fattioni di duoi amplissime famiglie, cioe di Lancastria et di Yorcka
5 comminciorno d'aver grandissime forze, sendo Henrico re capo di
quella de Lancastria, et Richiardo duca di Yorcka capo della contraria. Il qual duca, non trovando altra via meglior per condure suo
59ʳ desiderio ad effetto, suscitò in diversi provincie⁄del regno tomolti
popolari, contra gli ministri del re, accioche sotto questo colore di
castigare i cattivi ministri, gli puote piu facile privare Henrico del
Donde nacque regno (come poi anche fece). Questi fattioni generò tanta licentia
la licentia del
popolo   ne' popoli che per molti anni non si studiavano ad altro che ad
innovare et mutare principe, hor prevaleva la famiglia di Lancastria,
hor la famiglia di Yorcka, secondo che egli erano favoriti o dis-
59ᵛ favoriti del popolo, come parse per la⁄grand calamitade del detto
La misera Henrico, et per la sua varia fortuna, il qual primo venne in potestade
fortuna
di Henrico del duca suo nimico. Poi p'el popolo era liberato, et volendo vendi-
sesto carsi, suo essercito era rotto in la campagna, et lui necessitato di
5 fugire in Scotia, dindi da poci giorni ritornò per ricoperare il suo
regno, venne anchora preso, imprigionato, et privato della corona,
et la seconda volta liberato et restituito al regno, et poi la tertia
60ʳ volta preso, et amazzato⁄in prigione.

Le cause delle   In questo calamitoso tempo che le leggi erano calpestrate sotti li
tumolti   pedi, et che l'armi sonavano fin al cielo, et che era licito per cias-
Caddo scelerato caduno tristo per metter' in effetto la sua tristezza, questo scelerato
5 houmo Caddo, da voi mentionnato, se ne fece capitano di tali,
quali egli stesso era, et non lascio indrio sceleragine alcuno che un
Tomulti per houmo impio et tristo havria imaginato.
colpa del re   La causa del altro tumolto* qual Stravo era capitano nacque della
60ᵛ straordinaria essattione di Richiardo secondo re, il qual commando⁄
di ciascaduno del regno, quantunque poverissimo, un pezzo d'argento volgarmente detto un stotere, et delli ricchi una somma magiore,
secondo la facolta loro, la gravessa del qual generò tanto odio del
5 popolo contra il re, che dicevano publicamente, che si se soffrirorno
il pastore tante volte all'anno tosare le pecore, che egli in breve
tempo scortigarebbe anche, pero determinorno di non pagare tal
straordinaria essattione, et fecero lor capitano questo Stravo.

58ᵛ: 6. Yorcka] Yorckca B   60ʳ: 8. tumolto] tomolto B
59ᵛ: 5. poci] pochi B   60ᵛ: 7. scortigarebbe] scorticarebbe B
       7. second la] above the line in E

Quell'altro delli popoli di Nordovico⫽et di Cornovallia, na- 61ʳ
sceva per la insolentia d'alcuni nobili, i quali per la tenera eta ᴛᵘᵐᵒˡᵗⁱ causati
d'Edouardo re, manigiavano ogni cosa, non secondo le regole di ᵈᵉ ⁱ ⁿᵒᵇⁱˡⁱ
giustitia ma secondo lor appetiti et utile, pero per il secreto giudicio
di Dio lor insolentia, che gia commenciava d'esser insopportabili à ᴸᵉ ᶜᵃᵘˢᵉ ᶜʰᵉ
tutti buoni, venne castigata per mani di villani. ᵖᵒᵖᵒˡᵒ ᵈⁱ

Vedete hora, messer Alphonso, come ne havete incolpato à ᵖⁱᵍˡⁱᵃʳ ˡ'ᵃʳᵐⁱ
torto il popolo, et imputatoli l'errori et vitii d'altrui: perche i
nobili studiando⫽a li fattioni danno animo à i popoli (quali di 61ᵛ
natura sono desiderosi d'innovare) da fare il medesimo. Questa è
una causa mediante la qual un popolo se movi. Un altra è quando il
principe aggravò i subditi con straordinarie essattioni et tributi;
quando egli è notato immane, crudele, senza misericordia; quando ᴳˡⁱ ᵈᵉᶠᵉᵗᵗⁱ
non ascolterà le quaerele de' poveri, et farli giustitia. Simili enormi ⁿᵃˢᶜᵒⁿᵒ
vitii generanno mormori, i mormori dispregio, dispregio odio, ᵈᵉˡ ᵖʳⁱⁿᶜⁱᵖᵉ*
l'odio dal commune⫽accordo cerca vendetta; talche generalmente 62ʳ
i diffetti del popolo nascono della negligencia, poca prudentia,
overo per li cattivi essempi del principe che gli governa. Percio
commumente il venne detto, qual principe tal popolo. Per tanto è
facile à vedere che i popoli non movino si non causati. 5

Alph: Adunque vi pare licito, che il popolo si leva contra loro
principe, per causa alcuna che sia?

Steph: Quello non mi pare licito, anzi affermo ch'il sia damnevo-
⫽le, percioche egli e il ministro di Dio ordinato à tal ministerio per 62ᵛ
governar' gli popoli alla cura suo commessi: non fatto à caso come ᴺᵒⁿ ᵉ ˡⁱᶜⁱᵗᵒ
altri affirmano, ma per la providentia de Dio ordinato, et pero ᵃˡᶜᵘⁿᵃ ᵖⁱᵍˡⁱᵃʳ
nessuna cosa è piu chara a Dio, che i principe, et questo monstra la ˡ'ᵃʳᵐⁱ ᶜᵒⁿᵗʳᵃ ⁱ
straordinario dono datoli. Di chi ne havete mai letto che Iddio ᵖʳⁱⁿᶜⁱᵖⁱ
habia aggunto anni, ò giorni alla sua vita accetto a gli regi? L'essem- ᴱᶻᵉᶜʰⁱᵃˢ
pio di Ezechias,* il qual per le cause naturale doveva⫽morire Iddio 63ʳ
sopra l'ordinario corso gli prolungo la vita quindeci anni. Indi
sapete l'Omnipotente per dare caparra à loro di questa magioranza
in terra, gli assegna un archangelo, principe delli angeli, alla costodia
sua fin à la morte. Percio disse quel grand re Salomone* che il core ˢᵃˡᵒᵐᵒⁿᵉ
delli principe è nelle mani di Dio, volendo inferire che Iddio ha

61ʳ: 5. insopportabili] insopportabile 62ʳ: 2. negligencia] negligentia B
   B 5. si] *sic* B, E
61ᵛ: 4. aggravò] aggravà B 62ᵛ: 4. i] il B
   5. egli] *omitted in* B *margin.* principi B] princi E
   6. non] non egli B; quaerele] 7. naturale] naturali B
   querele B 63ʳ: 4. à la] alla B
   6. principe] principi B

69

una cura magiore di loro, che delli altri houmini privati, et pero
63^v tutti debbono honorarli, et obe-⫽dirli p'el sacro ministerio. Cio
David confermano anche le parole del re David,* quando li venne detto,
ch'il re Saul suo nimico dormiva, che egli puote senza pericolo
amazzarlo: Dio me ne guarda, rispose egli, di non violare le mani
5 sopra l'unto del Signiore.

Questi essempii manifestono, che Dio non vole, che sia fatto
violentia a li suoi ministri. Perche coloro, che gli resistono disobe-
64^r dianno anche l'ordinationi di Dio (come disse Paulo, et⫽in un
Paulo altro luogo* ad Ephesios: obedite i principi con timore, non come
desiderosi solamente di piacere gli houmini, ma come conviene
piacere à Dio, cognoscendo che ciascaduno riceverà mercede da
5 Dio per quel bene, che havria operato, dovunque sera libero, ò
servo). S'el principe fara l'ufficio suo verso i subditi, egli hanno
causa continuamente di ringratiare Dio del singolare suo dono,
che li è la piu eccellente gratia, che Dio puole concedere ad un
64^v popolo. Se egli fara altremen⫽te debbiamo cognoscere, che egli è
ordinato per i peccati del popolo perche se vede nelle sacre scritture
spesse volte che tal è lo castigo (et in vero non puote dar magiore)
che Iddio manda ad un popolo. Pero debbiamo con ogni humilitade
S. Augustino et patientia pigliarlo, e come dice S. Augustino, con riverentia
basciare il bastone, che ci batte, perche lo venne di sopra: che non
significa altro, che quantunque i principi si lascino se stessi esser
65^r menati di cattivo⫽consiglio, o di lor appetiti dal vero; nondimeno
Non e licito a i i popoli debbino sempre manere nella debita obedientia, et non
cristiani cercare da pigliare la spada fuora del mano di colui, alqual Dio ne
pigliare l'armi
per causa hà dato: ma lasciare la vendetta à lui (perche io* faro la vendetta,
alcuna contro dice il Signiore). Talche non sia licito in caso alcuno *quantunque*
loro principi *egli fusse tiranno, pigliar l'armi in contra.* Ma perche gli houmini
adunque sia
tyranni spesse volte cascono, per debolezza di nostra natura, e fanno molte
65^v cose⫽illicite et prohibite, instinti et mossi della occasione, egli è
buono anche che i principi, volendo assicurarsi di lor popoli,
hanno l'ochio e la mente al ufficio, per non darli occagione di
ribellare, ma monstrarne virtuosi essempi di se stesso, et come un
Il principe chiaro lume, che monstra nelle tenebre la retta via à tutti, perche
dee esser come
la squadra egli debbe esser come la squadra del arcittettore, il qual non sola-
66^r mente è retto e giusto, ma anche fa tutte le altre à le quale⫽sia

64^r: 3. houmini] huomini B   loro] i B; adunque sia
64^v: 7. lascino] lasciano B   tyranni *omitted in B*
65^r: 3. del] dela B   65^r: 5–6. quantunque.... in contra]
         margin. cristiani] christiani B;   *not underlined in B*
                                    65^v: 3. occagione] occasione B

70

applicato giusto. Il debbe havere singolare cura di tenere i suoi
baroni uniti, et ministrare giustitia egualmente senza d'esser notato
di percialita, perche quella generarà invidia a lui al qual tal favore è
monstrato, laqual invidia generarà inimicitie et odii. Ma hora siamo 5
alquanto digressi dal nostro proposito, per monstrarvi che l'originale
cause delli tomolti che sono stato in Ingliterra vengono dalli nobili,
et non dali plebei, pure⫽quando i sono in tutto popolari, non 66ᵛ
portino pericolo alcuno.

Torniamoci pero ad essaminare gli altri errori di Vortigerio fatti
nel fare amicitia et parentado con gli houmini malvagi et tristi,
dispregiando le buone leggi gia di lungo tempo osservate. Ogni   I cattivi
vicio in un principe quantunque picolo, pare grande, tamen non è   consiglieri sono
altro piu nocevole che la famigliarità e il consiglio delli houmini   pericolosi
corrotti nella conscientia ò nelli costumi, perche tra⫽il buono et   67ʳ
cattivo è tal differentia, qual è tra fogo et l'aqua. Si nelli consiglii,
studii, et tutti li altri attioni l'uno tende al bene commune, l'altro
al privato commodo solamente ha l'ochio, et quella è la meta alqual
egli tira. L'istorie affirmano, che chi ha per compagno nel suo   Proverbio
camino il zoppo, non puole andare drittamente. Colui, il qual è
amigo delli tristi, è di necessario ch'il sia nimico à gli buoni. Havendo hora gli buoni lor principe per nimico, staranno sempre su le sue
⫽apparechiati alla diffesa ogni volte che li accaderà bisogna (accioche 67ᵛ
non li intervienne come al pigro pesce) et non solamente per diffen-   Istoria
dre, ma per offendere anche colui, il qual in tal maniera favorigerà i
maligni et tristi, et dispregiare i virtuosi et honesti.

Di tal perversa natura era Edouardo* secondo re d'Ingliterra, che 5
in altri che in homini maligni et vitiosi non si diletto mai, la qual
cosa fece lo primo in odio delli suoi baroni, et poi cacciato del
regno, et in⫽fine privato della vita. Tra l'altri l'era à core uno 68ʳ
chiamato Petro Ganesto, houmo contaminatissimo, il consiglio del   Petro Ganesto
qual usava pre tutti gli altri, et à li commise il governo del regno, il   huomo tristo
qual governo ogni cosa non secondo giustitia et le leggi, ma secondo
l'appetito, et volontade sua. Gli baroni vedendo la giustitia corotta,   La giustitia
le leggi perverse, la nobilita in nullo honore, et molti altri disordini,   corotta
che nascevano ogni giorno nel regno, per il cattivo consiglio suo
non⫽imputando la cosa tanto al re, quanto a i tristi houmini p'el 68ᵛ
consiglio di cui era menato, speravano di rivocarlo al suo ufficio si

66ʳ:	7. in B] *omitted in* E	67ᵛ:	2. diffendre] *sic* B, E
66ᵛ:	4. houmini] huomini B		6. homini] huomini B
	5. lungo] longo B	68ʳ:	3. li] lui B
	6. vicio] vitio B	68ᵛ:	2. si] *sic* B, E

questi suoi malvagi consiglieri li fussino separati, et pero determinorno ad essequire quello, hora per la forza che altre volte in vano
5 tentavano con buone parole, et in un tratto assaltorno il detto
Ganesto, qual fugendo egli amassavano. Nondimeno l'absentia et
morte sua, non puote estirpare quelli cattivi pianti, che in vita
69ʳ haveva //piantato nel animo di Edouardo re perche egli incontinente
cercò di fornirsi di altri simili, trovo li duoi Spenserii, il padre et il
figliolo, adulatori perfetti, et corrottori di tutti buoni ingegni,
i quali accettò nella sua famiglia, et gli fece del suo consiglio, et
5 dopo pochi giorni li commise il governo di tutto, non altremente
che al suo charo Ganesto haveva fatto innanzi, et in questo mezo
egli si dette buon tempo con i suoi Spenserii vivendo una vita
69ᵛ lasciva, et lussu-//riosa senza cura ò pensieri del bon governo di
suoi subditi ò per difendere il realme contra l'inimici scocesi, con i
quali alhora hebbe guerra, con suo disavantagio. Talche per suo mal
governo tutto il regno haveva ogni giorno grand perdite e il nome
5 de li inglesi venne dispregiato apresso tutti i forestieri. D'onde i
principali del regno, quali hebbero chara l'honore et salute di lor
patria cognoscendo la causa (d'onde la procedeva) di tali grand
70ʳ perdite, et tanto //dishonore et infamia, non anchora desperato della
bontà del re (per esser egli giovane) se questi suoi consiglieri foron li
tolti, determinoro un'altra volta di purgare la corte di cattivi

I nobili
conspirorno
contra gli
cativi
consiglieri

consiglieri, et in lor luoghi mettere megliori. Di questa impresa
Thoma il conte di Lancastria et Humfredo conte di Herfordia erano
capi, i quali alla presentia del re dissero che era necessario per il
bene commune, et utile de la patria, che li gettasse fuora del suo
70ᵛ consiglio, et con-//sortio li duoi Spenserii, come authori (per lor
cattivo consiglio) di tal dishonore, et di tante perdite che era venuto
al regno, perche quello mentre che tali governavano, non puote
esser salva. Per tanto li prigorno pigliare in buona parte lor
5 domando, sendo che l'amore et salute di lor patria, et non malicia,

Parole delli
baroni

non invidia, ne altra privata ingiuria li havevo mossi à dire tanto.
Il re, vedendo i suoi baroni d'aver conspirato li incontra, et
71ʳ stare parechiati su le //armi, promise di fare tanto, quanto doman-
davan, et chiamato consiglio messe in eselio i duoi Spensieri, con
alcuni altri, et publico lor beni, ma in secreto il re gli commando
di non partir fuora del regno, ma scondersi in qualche luogo per

---

<table>
<tr><td>68ᵛ:</td><td>6. fugendo] fuggendo B</td><td>70ʳ:</td><td>3. volta B] omitted in E</td></tr>
<tr><td>69ᵛ:</td><td>2. l'inimici] omitted in B</td><td></td><td>margin. cativi] cattivi B</td></tr>
<tr><td></td><td></td><td></td><td>5. Herfordia Ed.] Hersordia B, E</td></tr>
<tr><td></td><td></td><td>70ᵛ:</td><td>4. salva] salvo B</td></tr>
</table>

alcuno tempo. In questo mezo egli rangunò un essercito facendo
visto d'andar contra i scocesi, ma subito li volto sopra il conte di
Lancastria, et del conte di Herfordia, et li prese con molti altri
conspirati, i quali tutti fece//morire, et richiamò li suoi Spensieri,
et li prepose ad magior honori che mai innanzi, la qual dispetto
mosse i nobili et gli popoli à tanto odio contra di se, che conspirandosi insieme determinorno di privarlo come disutile à la patria et
nimico à i buoni, et pertanto, indegno di tal dignità. Et rangunando
un essercito se venerò verso Londra, ma egli vedendo che non
poteva resistere la potentia di suoi baroni, si mise in fuga verso
Wallia dove nel castello di Brigenorto//scoso, era trovato et
imprigionato, et li suoi chari duoi Spensierii (per causa di queli
tutto questo intervenne) per coda di cavalli, nel suo conspetto,
stracinati per la città, poi per mani della moltitudine di villani in
mille pezzi tagliati. Egli renonciò la real dignità, et tutto l'interresse,
che haveva ò che mai pretendeva d'aver al regno, in speranza d'aver
la sua vita conceduto, ma tutto in vano, perche era poi in prigione
amazzato. Questo essempio puole esser do-//cumento à i principi
di non accomulare ingiure sopra un altra, et ogni di con nuove
offendere i suoi baroni, come fece Edouardo, il qual non solamente
non castigava i huomini malvagi, quali per la leggi erano alla
querela de i nobili condemnati, ma in dispregio di buoni li premiava,
et à queste ingiurie vi aggiunse parole vituperose rimprovando loro
viltà, la qual in tal modo incitò l'animi loro a vendicarsi, che non
stimavano beni, moglieri, ne fi-//glioli, anzi li dispregiorno, et la
propria vita desiderando piu presto di morire che lasciare tali
ingiurie inulte.

Alph: Senza dubio non e cosa piu accende il core alla vendetta,
come le parole obbrobriose quale oltra che le sono disconvenevole
per la bocca d'un principe ò altra magnanima persona, sono anchora
massime disutile: fanno* l'nimico piu cauto, et d'aver magior odio
contra di lui, et pensare con ogni industria ogni volta, che li venerà
//l'occasione d'offenderlo, talche tutte le parole che in tal maniera
venne detto al nimico diventino armi acutissimi contra se stesso.
Et di questo mi ricordo d'aver letto essempi infiniti, oltra questo
che ne havete monstrato di Edouardo, et tra li altri uno notabile
delli popoli d'Amyda, citta d'Asia, laqual era lungo tempo assediata

Marginal notes:
- 5
- Il re prese l'autori delli congiurati
- 71^v
- Nobili conspirorno seconda volta contra re
- 5
- 72^r
- Edouardo preso
- Fine delli cattivi consiglieri
- Morte d'Edouardo
- 72^v
- 5
- 73^r
- Le parole ingiuriose causino odio
- 73^v
- 5

71^r: 5. rangunò] ragunò B
          6. li] lo B
71^v: 2. magior] maggior B
          2. la] lo B

72^v: 2. ingiure] ingiurie B
          4. la] le B
73^r: 7. l'nimico] l'inimico B

Amyda, citta d'Asia
74ʳ

di Gabide* capitano de i persi, iquali gia stracchi dal tedio della lungo ossidione, et quasi desperati di non haver // la citta, levorno il campo per partirsi. I popoli della citta, vedendoli corserò tutti a le muraglie, insuperbiti, non pardorno ad ingiuria alcuna, che potevano fare con parole et segni, vituperando et accusandoli di vilta et

Le parole vituperose movino vendetta

poltronoria, d'onde Gabide tutto adirato muto consiglio, et ritornatosi al obsidione, tanto fu la indignatione della ingiuria che in pochi giorni la prese, et in vendetta l'amazzo tutti.

74ᵛ

Steph: Quanto pericolose sono simili opprobriose parole, // se monstra un essempio fresco nel tempo di Edouardo sesto, il qual quantunque di sua clementia pardonni à tutti (eccetto alli capi solamente) che havevano conspirati contra la nobiltà. Nondimeno i

5 delinquenti restavano non senza vituperio et infamia et che per ogni capricio che venne alla testa delli altri, li chiamorno traditori, ribelli, li quali rimproveri talmente entrorno nelli cori loro, che (quantunque plebei) elesserò piu presto di morire, che vivere con

75ʳ

tal infa- // mia, et raunati una moltitudine insieme, determinorno farne lor vendetta di quelli, che li hebbero tali obbropriose parole dette. Ma il re, sentendo la cosa, et considerando quanta dura cosa era di comportar simili parole, non solo non li puniva, ma fece*

Legge d'Edouardo sesto contra le obbrobriose parole

una legge che nessuno (sotto pena capitale) doverebbe piu imputarli tal colpa, ne chiamarli ribelli ò offenderli con tali parole obprobriose, perche in vero le sono insopportabile, massime quando hanno

75ᵛ

troppo // della verita. La prudentia di Edouardo sesto in questo caso riprese l'arrogantia di Edouardo secondo, il qual non cesso di

Edouardo secondo ingiurioso

comulare ingiuriose parole al suo cattivo governo, qual per se senza altro era ingiuria assai grande; et hebbe forza non picolo nelli cori

5 di suoi popoli, come monstrava chiaramente il fine che egli haveva. Questi medesimi errori alienò l'animi di suoi baroni à Vortigerio

76ʳ

anche, perche vedendo egli che il re haveva fatto parendo con i //

I boni sono offesi a vedere i tristi honorati

sassoni impii et scelerati houmini, et contra le leggi essaltandoli a li honori, se erano chiariti che non era piu luogo appreso di lui per i virtuosi et homini da bene, pero ciascaduno fece il miglior pro-

5 visioni per se stessi, che poteron (vedendo la roina di lor patria iminere) alcuni in Scotia, altri in Francia, et altri in Dacia lasciando Vortigerio solo consigliato delli sassoni suoi nimici (quantunque

76ᵛ

l'animo suo era acciecato che non vedeva tanto). //

75ᵛ: 4. picolo] picola B
     7. parendo] parentato B
76ʳ: *margin.* boni] buoni B
    4. homini] huomini B

76ʳ: 4. il] le B
    6. lasciando] *second* a *cancelling* e *in* E
    7. nimici] inimici B

Questa era la causa principale dela roina del imperio delli britanni, et il principio di quello delli inglese. Qual nacque di Vortigerio per haver nichilate le antiche legge, per admettere simili forestieri à li secreti del regno, perche tra le altre cose nessuna genera magiore odio al principe, ch'il dispregiare* le leggi antiche in alcuno regno osservate. Empedocles disse che una medesima cosa fusse la cagione che mosse nel principio gli huomini //di eleggere i principi, et fare le leggi, delli quali nessuna sarebbe necessaria, si li houmini fusserò giusti, et renderebberò à ciascaduno il suo, ma poi che gli diventino rapaci, disobedienti, crudeli, et ingiusti, le leggi per mancamento della iustitia era introdotti, accioche i boni non furono de i cattivi oppressi. Pero dice Solone* che i houmini debbono combattere, non meno per le leggi che per le muraglie, conciosia che i regni et principati senza muragli si //mantengono, ma senza leggi roinano immediate, perche sono instituti per la salute et vita si del principe come delli popoli. Le quale sendo è medio tolti, i subditi non solamente fanno mille oltragi impune, ma i principe anche et magistrati diveggono tiranni, et a questo fine, delli savi erano ordinati, desser la sicurta del uno et dell'altro. Pero* credo che non sia cosa di piu cattivo essempio in un regno, che fare una legge et non osservarla, et tanto piu //quando ella non sia osservata da chi l'ha fatto, et questo monstrò un essempio di Jacomo tertio re d'scocesi, il qual re, con suoi baronni et popoli ordinò per legge, che ne lui, ne altri re suo successore, mai determinarebbe cosa alcuna, di fare guerra o conchiuder' pace, ò vero di maridare i suoi figlioli, pigliare essattioni ò tributo senza il consentimento di suoi baroni. Nientedimanco, Jacomo, vedendo poi tal leggi per esser contra l'utile suo non //volse piu osservarla, anzi governava ogni cosa secondo il suo parere, dicendo d'esser re per dar leggi a tutti altri, et non per pigliare da nessuno. Il qual cattivo essempio del principe generò tanto odio nell'animi di suoi baroni, che subito colserò un essercito et hebbero per capitano il suo figliolo (quantunque contra la sua voglia) commincindo con furia di bacchare contra tutti quei, che seguirno la parte sua. Al fine, poi che vede il grand //pericolo, mandò à li suoi baroni, per

Margin notes:
Causa della roina de Britannia
Empedocles 77ʳ
Solone 77ᵛ
Le legge son la sicurta del popolo et del principe
Il despregiare la legge e odiosa al popolo 78ʳ
Lege scocesi 78ᵛ
79ʳ

76ᵛ: 2. dela] do' la E
3. inglese] inglesi B
4. legge] leggi B
7. Empedocles B] Empedoctes E
77ʳ: 3. houmini] huomini B
6. houmini] huomini B
8. conciosia B] consiosia E
77ᵛ: margin. despregiare] dispregiare B

78ʳ: 4. tolti] tolte B
3. baronni] baroni B
6. figlioli] figliuoli B
8. leggi] legge B
78ᵛ: 7. bacchare] andare B; seguirno B] seguorno B
8. vede] vide B

trattar della pace: ma egli non volserò ne conditione, ne patto sinon deponesse primo l'autorita regia. Ma Jacomo, giudicando quello d'esser il pegior che puote accadere deliberò primo di provare fortuna, et combattere con essi, et cosi l'era amazzato* nel mezo di suoi.

Jacomo re di Scotia amazzato

5

Giovanne re d'Ingliterra quantunque usurpò il regno, saria comportato se non havesse violate le leggi del realme, la qual incitò i nobili insieme con gli plebei, di cacci-//arlo del regno. Sapino* donque i principe, che à quel hora commincianno à perdere lor stato, quando essi comminciano à romper le leggi et mutare quelli modi et costumi, quali sono antiche, sotto le quale gli huomini lungo tempo hanno vivuti. Et poi privati che sono del stato diventassino mai tanto prudenti, di cognoscere con quanta facilità i regni si tengino da coloro che saviamente si consiglianno dorebbe molto piu loro tal perdita, et à magiore pena //se condamnerebbono se stessi che si d'altri fussino condemnati. Perche egli è molto piu facile d'esser amati delli boni, che delli cattivi; meglior obedire à le leggi, che commandarle: perche l'uno e pieno di pericolo, l'altro di sicurtà.

Giovanne cacchiato del regno
79ᵛ

5

80ʳ

E piu facile desser' amato dei buoni che delli cattivi

Esser rapace delli beni genera odio

Oltra il dispregiare le leggi, d'esser' rapaci deli beni del popolo generà anche odio commune. Questa ingordigia è madre di tutti li vicii, et colui che è sta preso con essa non puole stare lungamente in piede; per esser un regno, come un corpo naturale, nel //quale e capo il principe. Si come non dee si non il suo proportionato alimento pigliare, accioche le altre membri non divengino essangui, ne dar tanto ad un membro che l'altre non ponno nodrirsi (come interviene nel hydropico) cosi non debbe il principe tanto attribuire à se, ò dar tanto à suoi famigliari, che gli altri patiscono, percio si come con questo irregolato modo non puo lungamente vivere il corpo: cosi non potra lungamente esser in pie un regno. Gli// huomini si mettino à tutti pericoli per acquistar li beni, et quanto piu per conservarli acquisiti. L'huomo* dismentiga facile l'ingiurie fatte contra suo padre o contra suo fratello, perche non furono li sempre necessarii, ma la necessita delli beni venne ogni giorno, et pero ogni giorno si ricordi deli beni tolti, con odio mortale contra

Il re e come corpo naturale
80ᵛ

5

81ʳ

Gli huomini non dismentiganno mai i beni tolti

79ʳ: *margin. Scotia*] Scot: E, Scocesi B;   79ᵛ: 4. antiche] antichi B; quale]
     amazzato] amazato B; cacchiato]   quali B
     cacciato B   6. faciltà] facilità B
     8. la] lo B   7. si tengino *Ed.*] et si tengino
  79ᵛ: 2. principe] principi B; commin-   B, E
     cianno] comminciano B   80ʳ: 2. si] *above the line in* E
         81ʳ: 6. deli] delli B

colui, che li haveva tolto, et animo fermo di vendicarsi ogni volta
che li venerà occagione, et pero quel principe che e di natura avaro,
et rapace delli//beni di altrui non è mai sicuro in luogo alcuno,   81ᵛ
come parse per Rufo* re d'Ingliterra, ilqual essendo a la caccia in   Ruffo re per
mezzo di suoi nobili venne amazzato con una saetta d'un infimo   esser avaro
huomo tirato, il qual fugendo si salvo senza desser persequitato   amazzato
di persona alcuna: anzi sarebbe di loro premiati quando fusse   Essequie di
cognoscuto perche i popoli sentendo de la morte sua facevano   Rufo
grand fuogi, sonorno le campane per tutto il regno, et secondo lor
modo rallegrando, non altramente per la//morte sua, che sogliono   82ʳ
fare, per la coronatione d'un altro, ringratiando Iddio che per tal
mezo haveva il regno, et i popoli di tal tyranno liberato. Tali
principi, i quali per qualche modo havria l'odio del suo popolo
non è sicuro ne in la pace, ne in tempo della guerra, perche nella   5
pace se conspiranno incontra in secreto, et nella guerra, quando
lor forza propria non li basta diventino nimici aperti, herendosi al
tuo nimico.

   Giovanne re d'Ingliterra tra le altri suoi//vitii che haveva (haveva   82ᵛ
molti) era avaro et rapacissimo delli beni dell popolo, et li aggravò
ogni di con nove sorti d'essattioni, non sparagnando ne religioso, ne
altro talche venne in odio di tutti, et conspirandosi incontra alcuni   Congiurie
suoi baroni, et vedendo non poter soprafarlo corserò per adiuto ad   contra Giovanne
Philippo re di Francia, chiedendo Lodovico suo figliolo, promet-   re
tendo di farlo re, et cacciare Giovanne. Al advenimento di Lodovico
tutti si corserò//à lui, et Giovanne, fugendo nelle parte settentrionali   83ʳ
del regno per socorso, il venne tozzigato nel monasterio di Suinis-
hedo,* d'un monacho, il qual pensando fare cose grato à Dio, et al   L'impieta d'un
sua patria, beveva del vino anche lui, misto co'l veleno, accioche   monacho
non sospetasse cosa alcuna di male, et cosi amendue cascorno in   Giovanne re
terra morti.   tozzigato
   Questa avaricia et non altra cosa spogliò Richiardo secondo re del   Richardo
regno et della vita, perche dopo la morte del//duca Giovanne di   secondo privato
Lancastria, suo fratello, egli messò le mani nelli beni suoi, defrau-   della vita
dando Henrico suo figliolo senza causa alcuna. Il che cattivo essempio   83ᵛ
di avaritia causò i suoi d'aver male opinione di lui, temendo (se
non s'opponevanno in tempo à tal inconveniente con forza, poi   5
che le parole non giovorno) il simile di venire sopra lor figlioli,

81ᵛ: 2. parse B] parsi E   83ʳ: 3. cose] cosa B; grato] grata B;
        5. premiati] premiato B   al] alla B
        7. fuogi] fuoghi B   margin. Richardo] Richiardo B
82ᵛ: 3. nove B] illeg. in E   83ᵛ: 2. messò] messe B
        margin. Congiurie] Congiure B   4. d'aver] d'haver B

dopo lor morte. Pero (Henrico duca di Lancastria duce) si coniura-
84^r vano incontra // donde egli si retirò nel castello di Flinto abandonato di
tutti suoi, era preso solo, imprigionato, et poi che haveva rinonciato
la corona, fatto morire in prigione. Tanto è la forza di questo vitio
nel fare un principe d'un universale d'esser odiato. Queste dunque
5 sono le cose quali principalmente generanno odio commune al
principe, donde spesse volte li venne tolto li stati come era di
Vortigerio, con la roina et distruttione di tutto imperio britannico.

84^v *Alph:* Mi ri-//cordo haver letto nell'istorie che questo regno era
posseduta anchi delli daci.

Steph: Si. Egli è vero, perche cognoscendo egli che l'inglesi
hebbero divisi lo regno, et che egli furno tra lor medesimi anche
5 divisi, l'un facendo guerra contra l'altro, fecerò incorsioni continuoi,
come ladri, poi soldorno al stipendio d'il re di Nortumbria contra
gli altri principi inglesi, fin tanta che eran esperti nelli secreti del
85^r realme, cognoscendo la grand debolezza//di quello, causata delli
discordii civili, se assaltorno primo uno, poi l'altro, fin che hebbero
Dacii hebbero il tutto quale per trenta anni possedevano, fin al governo di Canuto
l'imperio in lor re, il quale poi tanto tempo (pensandosi d'esser sicuro), non
Ingliterra saspettando tal cosa, venne tozzicato in la villa di Lambeth* dell'altra
Canuto re parte di Tamesis per mezo di Westmonasterio. D'onde nacque un
tozzigato altra mutatione perche i inglesi ricordandosi d'esser in ogni tempo
85^v che governorno i daci senza gratia fa-//vore et authorità, anzi male
trattati et dispregiati, pensorno il tempo hora desser venuto di
vendicarsene del tutto di tal ingrati popoli, et cacciarli fuora del
regno, et in un tratto elegendosi re Aloredo, il figliolo di Etheldredo,
5 a la volta de'daci con furia grandi se voltavano, amazzandoli in
ogni luogo dovunque si trovorno per tutto il regno sparsi, senza
Crudelta deli rispetto d'eta o sesso. Magiore crudeltà in tempo alcuno non e
inglesi sta mai veduto. Perche //fin ale donne inglesi, quale eran maridate
86^r
L'animi delle con i daci, conspirorno contra lor mariti, et gli amassorno, ò nelli
done letti co'l ferro, o altrove co'l tozzico. Talche di tanti che n'erano,
non restò uno vivo, eccetto pochissimi che scamporno àla continente.

5 *Alph:* Io non mi maraviglio punto della crudeltà dell'inglesi

84^r:	1. Flinto] n *cancelling* a *in* E, Fliato B	85^r:	5. saspettando] *sic for* sospettando B, E
	7. imperio] l'imperio B		8. daci] *followed in* E *by* d'esser *deleted*
84^v:	2. anchi] anche B		
	4. divisi] diviso B	85^v:	4. Aloredo] *sic for* Alfredo B, E
	7. tanta] tanto B		5. grandi] grande B
85^r:	*margin.* Dacii] Daci B		7. e sta] *sic* B, E
	2. assaltorno] assaltorrò B	86^r:	1. ale] alle B
			4. àla] al B

quando si consideri la cause, che li mosse àquella. Perche gli e un cordoglio estremo a li houmini, di qual natione o provincia che //li 86ᵛ sono veder i altri forestieri, di posseder que' honori, officii, et dignitati che ne tempi passati lor padri o predecessori godorno, et gli stessi lor figlioli come indigni, senza causa esser privati.

Steph: E ben vero, ne sono anche delle ragione che stanno in 5 questo caso con essi. Sendo che lor predecessori, cioe parenti di lungo tempo passato, in ogni tempo alcuni hanno perse, chi la vita, che i beni per fare qualche bene, utile, o honore à lor patria, la ragione //non vuole, ne la natura del huomo puole con patientia 87ʳ sopportarli huomini incogniti, forestieri, godere il frutto della fatica d'altrui.

In questo caso Stephano* re d'Ingliterra uso una discretione grande, et considerò li pericoli, che spesse volte interveggono à que principi, quali si monstrino poco amorevole, et di non favorire lor subditi, perche questo è un grand iudicio ch'il principe non ami, et che non si fida di essi, poi che li distribuisse li //honori, et officii à li forestieri, 87ᵛ egli per tanto in tutti li negotii spettanti al governo di Ingliterra usò i consiglii delli inglesi, et li soli preposi a li ufficii et honori nel realme. Quantunque hebbe seco continuamente molti honorati persone, et franciosi, et normanni, per esser duca di Normannia, non 5 dimeno, non gli preferiva mai ad honori in Ingliterra, giudicando in questo caso il parere di Hannibal desser buono, il qual dopo una lunga //guerra, che hebbe con i romani disse che sarebbe per l'utile 88ʳ di tutti, che i romani governasse Roma, et i carthaginesi à Carthago. Cosi volse Stephano, che in Ingliterra gli inglesi et in Normania i normanni: è per questo modo l'era continuamente un amore fraterno tra li inglesi et normanni, et egli quantunque era francioso, 5 il nome del quale è in odio apresso l'inglesi, regnò fin ala sua morte natura-//le. 88ᵛ

Et quel principe che fara altramente troverà quelli pericoli quali Canuto predetto trovo, se non stara continuamente su larmi, come li spagnolo in Milano et Napoli. Et tal fine hebbero i daci in Ingliterra. Poi gli normanni, duce Guilhelmo, huomo di grand 5 animo et forza pigliando l'occasione conquisto il regno et cercò non altramente che il daco, anzi con un mano piu forte di spengere il nome //dell' inglesi. 89ʳ

Alph: Che occasione era quella che egli piglio?

Prudentia di Stefano

Detto de Hannibal

86ʳ:	6. la] le B	87ʳ: *margin.* Stefano] Stephano B
86ᵛ:	2. veder i] vedere B	87ᵛ: 3. preposi] prepose B; a li] alli B
	2. et dignitate] et di dignitate B	88ᵛ: 4. spagnolo] spagnoli B

79

Steph: La discordia, che alhora era tra Haraldo re, et Tosto* suo fratello. Perche quantunque egli fu di grand virtu et forza, se non havesse preso occasione non havria mai monstrato la sua virtu.

Alph: Quelli huomini sono veramente savi, che cognoscino questa occasioni.

Steph: Cosi ne sono, perche è cognoscuta à pochi: la piu sicura via è daffron-//tarsi innanzi, perche ella è femina mutabili, che ha la testa innanzi piena di capelli, per i quali l'houmo puole facilmente tenersi, ma per dietro calva. Guilhelmo normanno seppe in tempo pigliarla, perche trovando alhora i duoi fratelli divisi, et Heraldo non anchor firmato nel regno, èra facile opprimerlo, perche nulla è piu giovevole al nimico, che la discordia del adversario, ne cosa piu damnevole à lor, che //debbono esser amici come quella. Impero si da materia al nimico d'assaltarlo, et assaltando di poter con faciltà opprimerlo, aprendo la strada à la buona fortuna del nimico, et ala roina propria, con l'adiuto et favore della disunione; la quale egli sempre dè notrire, come fece Philippo* padre di Allessandro in Grecia, tra quelle republiche dove pose tante discordie, seditioni, et talmente le tenne in volte nell'armi et nel sangue intra di lor, soccorando sempre //mai le parte piu deboli, che finalmente sforzo l'uno come l'altra, li vittoriosi come quelli che eran vinti, sottomettersi a la dura servitu d'el suo imperio. Di che ne furon cagioni i thebani che lo ritornò in Grecia contra gli atenesi: perche l'odio occulto che era tra di lor, che non potendo un citadino tolerare la grandessa d'altro, volserò piu presto elegger Philippo forastiero per lor capitano, che nessuno cittadino, laqual cosa era la cagione dell' roina //di tutta Grecia appresso. Imperoche Philippo poi che hebbe vinto laltre citta si volto adosso à quelle delle quale era fatto capitano, et che c'ol favore di lor militia haveva hauta tante vittorie, et tutte l'occupo e sacchegio, non perdonando a i tempi, ne a quelle case dove era stato con tanto honore e cortesia ricevuto, ma dopo che hebbe predato cosi coloro, che li haveva condotto come quelli altri contra iquali era chiamato, et vendute le moglie et figlioli di tutti //se ne torno in Macedonia.

Alph: Senza dubio un principe non puo havere meglior occasione d'occupare una citta o un regno, che d'esser richiesto d'una parte di

Marginalia (left):
Egli è virtu grande de' pigliar l'occasione offerta
89ᵛ
Occasione
Guilhelmo normanno
90ʳ
Philippo
90ᵛ
Thebani
5
91ʳ
5
Ingratitudine di Philippo
91ᵛ

89ʳ: 3. Tosto] *second* t *cancelling* c *in B*; Tosco E
      8. cognoscuta] cognosciuta B
89ᵛ: 3. dietro] drieto B
90ʳ: 4. adiuto B] aduito E
      8. soccorando] soccorendo B
90ᵛ: 2. l'uno] l'una B
      4. ritornò] irritornò B; atenesi] atheniesi B
      5. grandessa] grandezza B
91ʳ: 3. hauta] hauto B

quella alla diffesa, overo mediante la discordia opporsi à tal impresa. Perche tanta è la forza della discordia tra l'inimici che cercando l'uno la roina d'el altro non pensano à la destruttione, che portino l'armi forestieri. Questa discordia fece grande Philippo, et distrusse //tutta la Grecia.

Ottavio Augusto, pigliando l'occasione della vita lasciva et deliciosa di Marco Antonio in Egitto con Cleopatra, hebbe la vittoria et lo fortunato imperio. La discordia del imperator* di Constantinopoli con alcuni principi del suo imperio favoriti deli dispoti de la Servia et di Bulgaria fu la grandezza della casa ottomanna, et l'accressimento del regno di turchi. Perche egli dimandando quinze mila cavalli//contra li suoi nimici, co'l adiuto de i quali gli vinse, ma diede occasione ad Amurato* lor imperator d'aspirare al imperio suo, è di quello della Grecia tutta, dove di la à poco tempo, sendo bene instruto del paese, con un grand essercito sotto pretesto di vendicare l'ingiurie fatte al imperador, passò contra i detti principi, con i quali venendo à la bataglia, non solamente li superò, ma simpatrono anchor d'una parte del stato d'esso// imperadore. Non passorno molti anni che à poco a poco i suoi successori se insegnorno poi del tutto, et hogi di l'ha talmente allargato suoi confini nelle parti d'Europa, che si la bontà di Dio, quanto piu presto non metti nelli cori de li principi christiani farlo incontra, non passerà molto, che egli sera fatta signior del resto, al dishonore, perpetua servitu de la christianità, per la discordia deli principi di quella.

La discordia et gelosia, che//nacque fra li confederati* contra i venitiani (quando tutta la Italia et altri principi si conspirorno contra) non solamente causò che egli ricoverrno lor dominio tutto perso, ma fu cagione che egli pigliando questo occasione si fecerò padroni di quello d'altri.

Et à questi vi aggiungero uno delli nostri. Henrico settimo sendo in Francia, et sapiando de la discordia tra Richiardo tertio re et suoi baroni per la crudeltà sua, //havendo per usurpare il regno fatto amazzare duoi suoi nipoti (a liquali per lor padre era fatto governatore) accusato la sua propria madre d'impudicitia, et cercando anchor di amazzare la mogliere con altre sue opere tirannica acquistato l'odio di tutti, Henrico per mezo d'alcunni suoi amici, venne nel

Marginal notes:
Discordia distrusse la Grecia

92ʳ

Vita lasciva di Antonio

La discordia tra l'imperator di Constantinopoli

92ᵛ

93ʳ

La discordia christiana ha augmentata l'imperio mahometana

93ᵛ

5

Henrico settimo

94ʳ

Crudelta di Richiardo

Il morte di Richardo

91ᵛ: 6. d'el] dell' B
92ʳ: *second marginal note sic* B, E
92ᵛ: 1. adiuto] adiutto B
      4. instruto] instrutto B
93ʳ: 6. signior] signor B

93ᵛ: 3. ricoverrno] ricovrorno B
      4. questo] questa B
      7. sapiando] sapendo B
94ʳ: 4. tirannica] tirannice B

94ᵛ realme, e affrontandosi co'l essercito di Richiardo re, dieci milia da Londra appresso la villa di Bernetto,* la ruppe et amazzò // portando il corpo morto sopra un vile roncinetto legato come un vitello, tutto sanguinato a Londra (spettacolo veramente miserabile) nondimeno non indegno della sua vita.

5 Se puole notare per questi diversi essempi quanto pericoloso sia la discordia dentro alcune regno o provincia, quando l'inimico e di fuora armato. Questo realme piu volte è stato in grand pericolo per 95ʳ i discordii delli barroni, et hora mancava poco che non era in // tutto distrutto et il nome de li inglesi messo in oblivione.

La causa della discordia tra Heraldo re et Tosto suo fratello
Alph: Donde nacque tal discordia tra Heraldo re et Tosto suo fratello?

Steph: De la emulatione del imperio, perche egli non ottenendo quelli gradi et honori che ricercava, se voltò incontinente con odio Haraldo re di Norvegia contra il re suo fratello, procacciandolo in ogni luogo dove pote nimici; et primo incitava i scocesi poi sene andò ad Haraldo* re di 95ᵛ Norvegia promettendoli cose grande, come medi- // ante lui egli facilmente potrebbe occupare tutto il regno d'Inghilterra. D'onde il re, credendo che Tosto ne haveva molti amici, et che tutto il resto che ne diceva era vero, venne da indi a pochi giorni con 5 cento cinquanta naviiri et arrivò nel porto hora Nuovo Castello detto. Et ivi ʼespettando alcuni giorni l'amici di Tosto, non venne mai persona: nondimeno se deliberò di provare la fortuna con suoi 96ʳ proprii (per esser il nomero grande) et affrontò col essercito // di Heraldo re d'Inghilterra apresso il fiume di Druenta, non lontano da Morte di Haraldo re di Norvegia Staffordia dove era rotto e vinto suo essercito, et gli stesso insieme con Tosto uccise. Per esser* alquanto temerario di pigliare l'imprese Non di dee credere de' parole de' sbanditi delle parole deli homini privi di lor patria, i quali piu volte dicono molte cose aliene de la verità, per tornar à lor patria, o vendicarsi di lor nimici, et pensano che tutte il mondo deventerà lor amici, et 96ᵛ se ingannono, talche tra quello, che credino, et quelle ragione che // sanno usar à proposito, riempino spesse volte gli principi ambitiosi di speranza pigliar imprese che poi li fanno consumere un thesauro in vano, ò vero che sara lor roina.

5 Di questo i libri vecchi sono pieni d'essempi, et non mancanno neanche delli moderni innanzi l'occhi. Che considererà le guerre al

---

94ʳ: 7. *second* la] lo B
94ᵛ: 6. alcune] alcuno B
95ʳ: 6. ricercava B] licercava E
95ᵛ: 5. Nuovo Castello *Ed.*] Nuovo Caresto E, Castello *preceded by* Nuovo *deleted* B

95ᵛ: 5. cinquanta] a *after* u *cancelling* e E; naviiri] naviri B
96ʳ: 4. uccise] ucciso B
7. tutte] tutto B

presente in Toscana, vedrà da non procedere d'altro, che dalli proccaciamenti delli fuora usciti di Fiorenza, Salerna, Napoli, et altre citta d'Ita-//lia, persuadino il christianissimo, che per mezo di loro et lor amici se impatronirà dela Toscana, et poi co'l tempo de la Italia tutta, et il principe valoroso et magnanimo li attruisse fede, perche gli huomini facilmente credino cio che desideranno d'esser, et l'ha anche speranza, per la divisioni de li principi d'essa, talche egli fa un spesa grandissima, et poi in fine sara come Dio vora.

Ma per la piu parte coloro, quali si fondano sopra li pro-// messe o amici di simili huomini s'ingangno, perche egli per man-tenere la guerra et intratenersi nel'estimatione dicano molte cose, che non ponno prestare, et l'amici lor, i quali sono a casa caldi, lascino i pensieri a i sbanditi, et non meteranno, ne la vita ne i beni in pericolo per far servigii o piaceri a essi, quali sarebbe incerti et dubiosi.

Alph: La ragione vole, che si facesse ogni cosa per li amici senza rispetto di beni, o della istessa vita, quando //la cosa che gli doman-dan è giusta, et honesta.

Steph: Si, ma la esperientia e contra la ragione in questo caso: tutti si corrino drio la fortuna, et pochi hanno rispetto a li amici sfortunati, et quando ella lascierà uno, tutti i suoi amici non lo cognossino piu. Pero è cosa legiere per un principe di fidare sopra di lor, ò lor amici, perche li restino parechie volte con le mani pieni di mosche con una vergogna, òvero roina grande come resto Heraldo re di Norvegia, //il qual per esser troppo credulo perse xxii mila huomini, insieme con la sua propria vita.

In questo mezo Guilhelmo duca di Normannia con cinquanta* navieri preso il porto d'Hastingo, dodeci milia da Dovero, verso il mezo giorno, e vi messe i suoi huomini in terra. Heraldo, che anchor era nelle parti settentrionali del regno, dove commise la bataglia co'l re di Norvegia, sentendo tal nuove se conturbò alquanto per //che una grand parte di suoi soldati eran morti nella bataglia norvegiense, altri feriti, il rimanenti fugiti con la preda del nimico gia vinto. Talche in tanto pericolo si trovo privo di soldati, nondimeno, con ogni celerita venne à Londra, et havendo raunnato un essercito venne a li mani con Guilhelmo duca di Normannia. Ma dopo un lunga bataglia era amazzato, insieme con xxv mila altri.

Margin notes (right column):

Causa delle guerre in Toscana

97ʳ

Henrico di Francia valoroso

Gli huomini credono facile cio che desideranno daver

97ᵛ

Gli huomini sequitano la fortuna

Proverbio

98ᵛ

Duca di Normannia entro in Ingliterra

99ʳ

Haraldo re amazzato

97ʳ: *margin.* cio B] cioe E; daver]   97ᵛ: 5. meteranno] metterano B
       d'haver B   98ᵛ: *margin.* Duca] Il duca B
       3. attruisse] attribuisse B   3. cinquanta] a *after* u *cancelling* e
97ᵛ: 2. s'ingangno] s'ingannano B   E; navieri] naviri B
      3. dicano] dicono B

83

99ᵛ Questa bataglia debilitò molto le forze de li in-//glesi, et li tolsi
tutt' il fiore de la gioventu, talche Guilhelmo senza esser impedito
(dapo tal vittoria) venne à Londra, et sendo coronato, con belle
parole li promesse molte cose che debbino sperare ogni bene di
lui, non altremente che d'un padre, ma li fatti eran tutto contrarii.

margin: Il duca di Normannia coronato in Londra

Perche, havendo fortificato se stesso dentro con suoi normanni
contra i paesani, et con un nomero di navieri, di fuora contra
100ʳ l'inimici, s'assicurò primo di tutti quelli de//la linea regale, et altri
che per titolo ò potere potevano aspirare a la corona, altri deprivo
delli officii et dignitati dandoli a i normanni, aggravando ogni
giorno i popoli con nuove tribute et essattioni non astenendosi ne
5 dale cose sacre ne prophane, non hebbe in stima la nobilita, talche
pareva a tutti che cercava la roina del regno. Molte se ne fugirno chi
in Scotia, altre in Fiandra, altri in Dacia procacciandolo nimici di
100ᵛ fuora et incitan-//do i popoli dentro a tumultuare. Guilhelmo*
vedendo per li spesse tomolti l'animi d'el'inglesi alienati in tutto da
lui, penso di non poter piu fidarsi d'essi, delibero per rifrenarli piu
stretto; edifico quatro fortrezze in diversi luoghi del regno. Li
5 tolse l'armi che hebbero tutti. Gli prohibeva d'andar fuora di lor
case dopo otto hore a la notte con molte altri sorti di servitu durissimi talche si monstro in tutti suoi procedimenti nimico et destrut-
101ʳ tore piu//che defensore o patre et senza dubio se la vita non lo
mancava havria in tutto spento il nome di lor.

margin: E stirpo la linea regale

margin: Crudelta

margin: Fortrezze

Alph: In vero* i principi nuovi et que' massime quali per forza
acquistano alcuna provincia non ponno non fare molte sorti di
5 crudelita perche innanzi che una provincia sia soggiogata e di forza
che gli amazza gli genti distrugge le campane, brusare le case con
mille altri ingiurie per le quale acquistera l'odio generale della
101ᵛ moltitudine//et havendo in questo modo ingiuriatoli bisogna che li
sta su le sue, et che non si fida piu d'essi. La clementia, la liberalità
non li gioverà anzi sarebbe la sua roina, quando la usava, perche*
non si cancellò mai un simili ingiuria vechia con la liberalita ò
clementia nuova, ma solamente si differri la vendetta fin a tanto che
il tempo li ministra buona occasione, pero quando il principe
102ʳ (quali innanzi haveva//giustamente incitato il suo popolo al odio,
et poi voleva con la clementia cancellarlo) fidasse di loro, veneria

margin: La clementia non vale quando l'ingiurie sono ancora in memoria

---

99ᵛ:	*margin.* Londra B] l'ondra E	100ᵛ:	7. in] uin B
	7. navieri] naviri B	101ʳ:	6. distrugge] distrugger B
100ʳ:	6. Molte] Molti B	101ᵛ:	1. havendo] havendoli B
	7. altre] altri B		3. usava] usasse B
	margin. E stirpo] *sic for* Estirpò		4. cancellò] cancella B; un simili]
	B, E		una simil B; vechia] vecchia B

ingannato nel sua opinione. Non è altra strada per mantener una provincia o regno con l'armi acquistato, se non con le medesime armi fin tanto che lingiurie da lui fatte sono dal tempo (qual mitigò ogni dolore) dismentigate. Pero mi pare, che in questo egli adopera la piu sicura et miglior strada//volendo mantenere l'acquisto.

Steph: Non in questo solo, ma in tutte le altre sue attioni monstrò grand prudentia, et piglio* sempre la via sicura senza cura d'esser tenuto ò avaro ò crudele, perche si messe le mani adosso di coloro, che per ragione ò titolo potorno aspirare a la corona, et li spense 5 tutti, insieme con li altri, i quali co'l favore del popolo, o per lor authorita giudicò, poter per adietro offenderlo.//

Alph: Questa è una usanza di tutti gli principi piu commune, che per la legge divina licita.

Steph: Il nostro proposito al presente, non e da monstrare la cosa licitae ò illicito d'un principe a fare, ma solo per monstrare per quale 5 via et mezi un principe puol mantenere o perdere suo stato. Per tanto dico, che colui che fara altramente troverà mille pericoli, et se stesso sempre in una continua paura, la quale è pegiore che la istessa morte, et sempre* in pericolo//di perder lo stato, et la vita mentre che coloro vivano, i quali sono stati spogliati o defraudati di quello, come monstrò l'infelicità d'Henrico sesto, il qual non volse per vana pieta assicorarsi del Edouardo quarto, il qual ne hebbe nelli suoi mani, ma lo lasciò fugire, dal qual dopo era privato del stato et dela vita. Quel principe nuovo (non parlo deli hereditarii) che lascierà vivo o in libertà colui alqual la provincia per qualche giure puole ve-//nire nodrisse la serpente in senno proprio, come* fece Luigi re di Francia il quale per l'ambitione* deli venitiani era fatto solo arbitrio d'Italia, et signor de la tertia parte di quella, vi misse un compagno nel regno di Napoli, il re di Spagna, accioche li malcontenti del suo governo havesserò dove ricorre à lamentarsi, et 5 mediante lui vendicarne lor odii, et questo caso è manifesto anche in Henrico settimo, il qual per compassione teneva vivo, inprigionato //Edouardo* figliolo del duca de Clarentia, alqual il regno pertineva, et non trovando i popoli et i baroni altro mezo di tumultuare fingevano d'aver seco questo detto Edouardo, sotto colore di cui raunorno un grand essercito, et non senza pericolo di Henrico era quietato. D'onde al fine era sforzato di sicurarsi del detto Edouardo, giovane innocente, per tor da li mani ogni occasione per adietro di

(marginal notes:)
Le cose acquistate per l'armi sono desser mantenuti per le armi 102ᵛ

103ʳ

103ᵛ

La vana pieta e dannosa

104ʳ
Proverbio
Errore di Luigi

104ᵛ
Pericolo di Henrico settimo
Morte di Edouardo figiolo del duca di Clarentia

102ʳ: 5. mitigò] mitiga B
103ʳ: 2. di] *above the line in E*
    5. licitae] licita B; illicito] illicita B   104ᵛ:
104ʳ: 3. arbitrio] arbitro B

5. recorre] recorrere B
7. inprigionato] imprigionato B
6. adietro] adrieto B

105ʳ tumultuare. Richiardo duca di Yorcka//et poi re tertio di quel nome, aspirando a la corona, imaginava molti modi, ma nulla riusciva mentre che i suoi nipoti (figlioli del suo fratello Edouardo quarto i quali erano commessi a la sua protettione) vivevano, però

Richiardo si assicuro tirranicamente di suoi nepoti

commandò tirannicamente d'amazzare gli innocenti, quali furno commisi à lui come ad un padre per diffendere, et havendo in questo modo spento la linea regale, la corona venne à lui senza contrasto.

105ᵛ Et come//gli predetti hanno regnato per sapere sicurarsi di coloro che poteron offenderli, cosi* sulthan Paiaxit imperador deli

Paiaxit perse la vita per vana compassione

turchi, perse suo imperio, et la vita per vana compassione del impio suo figliolo Selym, et accioche meglior intenderete vi conterò la istoria.

Questo Selym era di natura crudele, ambitiosa, et dissimulatore grandissimo alquale temendo ne uno delli altri suoi fratelli non

106ʳ occupasse imperio dopo la morte del suo padre, egli pen-//so di torlo per forza mentre che viveva, et uso questo modo. Sotto il pretesto d'andare in Ungaria per acquistarsi un stato* di vivere, raunò un grand essercito, et sendo gia in ordine di marchiare, se

5 volto verso Andrinopoli, dove era Paiaxit suo padre, pensando aver trovatolo dormendo, ma egli, sendo avertito del consiglio scelerato

La impieta di Selym

di suo figliolo, era proveduto, et l'affrontò con esso lui non lontano di Andrinopoli, dove apiccorno una bataglia crudelissima, nel

106ᵛ qual//Selym perse xxxv mila huomini, et egli non senza pericolo si

Il padre hebbe vittoria del figliolo

salvo fugiendo. Nondimeno di questo horrendo tradimento d'un figliolo, il padre non solo perdonava, ma li chiamo a Constantinopoli dandolo un salvocondotto promettendo di farlo generale del

5 suo essercito per mandarlo contra sulthan Ahamat suo altro figliolo, il qual alhora ribellò in Natatolia.

107ʳ Selym rispose al padre che egli farebbe tutto//cio che li piacesse. Ma che temeva ne Corcuth suo altro fratello sarebbe fatto imperador mentre che egli era in Natatolia. Il suo padre disse, che stesse di buona voglia, et che di cio non dubitava punto, perche dopo la

La parole sole non contentino

sua morte null'altro che lui sarebbe imperador. Ma le parole senza fatti non sodisforno a Selym. Non volse partire da Constantinopoli innanzi che l'era assicurato del imperio, pero vedendo Paiaxit la

107ᵛ grand importu-//nità che fece, et sendo anche consigliato d'alcuni bassi, *amici di Selym, renunciò a lui l'imperio e lo fece imperadore,

---

105ʳ:	6. diffendere] diffend *with contraction sign* E, diffenderli B	6. avertito] avvertito B	
105ᵛ:	6. ambitiosa] ambitioso B	8. crudelissima] a *cancelling* e E	
	8. imperio] l'imperio B	106ᵛ:	9. qual] quale B
106ʳ:	5. aver] haver B		3. perdonava *Ed.*] non perdonava B, E; li] lo B

et egli pensando di vivere vita privata, se parti da Constantinopoli per andare à Diametocca dove hebbe un palagio.

Selym fatto imperatore

Hor dopo' il partito de Paiaxit, Selym imperator fece un essercito per andare contra Ahamat suo fratello, et sendo parechiato di partire li venne un sospetto//grandissimo, che nella sua assentia suo padre non tornasse à Constantinopoli, et farsi di nuovo imperator, pero per esser senza paura, lo fece tozzicare innanzi che partiva. Talche in riconpenso della pietà et misericordia ch'il suo padre usò verso di lui nel pardonarlo, quando meritò non una, ma mille morte, egli senza causa alcuna, solo per un sospetto, li tolse (poi che di volontà hebbe donato imperio) anche la vita. Tanto che egli gia//insignato per l'infelicità del padre, che non volse quando poteva assicurarsi, determiniò di non fidarsi piu ne di fratello, nipote, o di altra persona del sangue reale, pero primo uccise suo fratello Ahamat, poi cinque suoi nipoti, et finalmente il suo fratello Corcuth, et per questo modo regnò con la felicità, et honore turchesco.

108ʳ

Selym fece tozzicare il suo padre

5

108ᵛ

La crudelta de Selym per regnare sicuramente

Alph: Ne havete in vero ne' luoghi proprii allegati insieme questi essempi del'//inglesi, perche in vero hanno piu del turchesco, che della christiana.

109ʳ

Steph: Io* non li lodo, anzi dico che sarebbe meglior per i christiani vivere privati, che con tanta crudeltà di regnare. Ma questo e un giogo di sicuro che puol farlo, et non vuole fidarsi di coloro iquali per adrio ponno offenderlo come s'assicuro Guilhemo, et poi con le fortrezze* quale edifico s'assicurò contra tutt' universale, ogni volta che comminciassino di tumultuare//quali anche li furno a proposito.

Proverbio

109ᵛ

Alph: E bene vero a proposito dessercitar crudelta, perche le fanno un principe piu audace, piu violento, meno rispettivo ad offender suoi subditi, et ministra magiore occasione ogni giorno d'incrudelirsi.

Le fortrezze fanno i principi meno rispettivi

Steph: Io non biasimo tal crudelta, quando un principe la fa quasi sforzatamente, da mantenere lo stato suo.

Alph: Ne io la posso lodare in caso alcuno, perche molto piu vale la clementia, che la crudeltà.

10

*Steph://*Habiate di saper, che dove la clementia ha luogo et forza, egli è piu che fiero, che usarò il contrario, ma dove la non vale, è necessario imitare il buono chirurgio, il qual non uso il ferro et il

110ʳ

108ʳ: 2. nuovo] novo B   110ʳ: 2. usarò] usara
108ᵛ: 2. determiniò] determino B   3. uso] usa B
109ᵛ: *margin.* fortrezze] fortezze B

Il ferro e
necessario dove
l'onguento non
vale

110^v

Nota

111^r

fuoco, si non dove l'uguento, o per la sua debilità, o vero pero per
la grandessa del ferito, non puol operare, et pero in questo luogo
non saria dal nostro proposito (havendo hora occasione del governo
di Guilhelmo) per monstrare quomodo, et in queli casi ella et la
cle//mentia giovino o nuocevo à quelli principi, che le usino. La
crudelta è un vitio che portori una certa infamia senza pericolo,
quando ella non vene fatto per le ingordigia de li beni, nondimeno
il principe dee esser pietoso et clemente, et non crudele, si non
sforzato per la malvagità delli huomini, et alhora anche monstrare
di farla contra la sua voglia sforzatemente, per causa di giusticia, o
per esser nuovo principe, il qual havra molte//occasioni desser piu
crudeli che li altri.

Il severo
governo
di Guilhelmo

111^v

La dannosa
clementia di
Henrico sesto

L'inconsiderata
clementia e
causa d'infiniti
male

112^r

L'essempio presente di Guilhelmo monstra le grand occasioni,
che hebbe per i continui tumolti et congiurationi et insidie che eran
stese per pigliarlo: nondimeno egli vince i suoi nimici, pacificò i
tumolti, transformò di nuovo il regno, lo dette leggi et insignia, et
lo lascio a suoi successsori in pace et fede con questa sua crudeltà,
la qual senza dubio era piu lodevole, che quella damnosa pietà et
clementia di Richiardo//secondo, Henrico sesto, i quali per lor
inconsiderata clementia perdorno molti luoghi et citta in Francia et
in Scotia, quali lor predicessori hebberò acquistati et dettero
occasioni a lor subditi spregiarli et congiurarne incontra. D'onde
ambedue perdovano lo stato et la vita. Per tanto* non si dee currare
un principe della infamia di crudele di tenere i subditi in ufficio et
uniti, perche con pochi essempi sara piu pietoso che//quelli, iquali
per non fare morire uno lascino sequire tumolti o altri disordini
onde nascino occisioni et rapine lequale offendono l'universale,
et l'essecutione del principe fatto offende solamente un particolare.

112^v

Alph: In questo caso di Guilhelmo la crudelta valse et giovava
piu che la clementia, per esser egli come ne havete detto principe
nuovo, il qual col'armi haveva acquistato il regno non haveva
altri mezi che gli istessi//armi di mantenerlo.

Cambise

Silla

Steph: La crudeltà* giovò a Cambise, il quale ottenuta la vittoria
non perdoni à persona. Silla medesimamente con crudelta mon-
strata a quelli che sono ossessi et poi espugnati è piu volte utile,
perche gli altri temendo la medesima crudeltà, si sottomettino
senza resistentia come tutte la provincie dove passò Attila et

110^r: 4. l'uguento] l'unguento B   111^r: 2. crudeli] crudele B
           5. grandessa] grandezza B   111^v: *margin.* male] mali B
           7. queli] quelli B   5. currare] curare B
110^v: 1. nuocevo] nocevo B   112^v: 6. la] le B
           2. portori] partori B

Tamerlanes fecerono, paurosi di lor crudeltà: ma tali non cercorno
d'esser amati, ma li bastava //solo esser temuti.

E buono* che un principe sia temuto et amato, ma perche e
difficile, che li stianno lungamente insieme, quando si habia di
mancare del'uno, è piu sicuro esser' temuto, che amato, perche
generalmente, gli huomini sono volubili, desiderosi d'innovare,
simulatori, cupidi di guadagno, et in tutto corrotti. Mentre che i
doni veggono sono servi et schiavi, offeriscono la vita et sangue
quando non havrete bisogna, ma venendo //il pericolo si discos-
tino. Pero colui che si fonda solamente sopra l'amore delli subditi,
nel tempo di pericolo venne qualche volta ingannato. Gli huomini
si mettino à gli pericoli, piu per lor officii et timore di lui che d'-
amore. L'amore è tenuto d'un legame d'obligo, quale per esser gli
huomini tristi, dogni occasione et di propria volonta, è rotto. Ma il
timore è tenuto d'una paura, che non abandoni mai la persona, et
in questo modo esser temuto non nuoce pure, che si astene del- //
la roba deli subditi, perche quando il principe h'a l'ochio à la roba,
et monstra crudeltade per ottenerla, l'acquistò timore con odio, il
qual è cosa pericolosissima. Pero vorei havendo giustificatione
conveniente, che egli procedesse contra il sangue, con ogni rigore,
che monstrare un minimo volere a la roba. Gli huomini dismentican-
no piu presto la morte del padre, che la perdita del patrimonio: il
padre era nato à morire, et il patrimonio per sostenere i figlioli.

Alph: Diciate //havendo egli causa puole procedere contra il
sangue, io credo che quella non è crudeltà alcuna ma giusticia.
Anzi il principe puole punire chi e sospetto colpevole, in alcuni
casi, quantunque non provato manifestamente, come i parenti ò
figlioli di ribelli come fece Henrico con Cortineo,* ilqual per la
colpa imputata al padre venne, innocente, prigionato. Questo il
principe puole giustamente fare, havendo locchio alla pace commune
deli subditi piu che al privato //commodo o particolar vendetta.

Steph: Et quanto* spetta a la militia non si curi il principe esser
tenuto crudele, perche colui che ha in governo una moltitudine
senza tal nome non tiendrà un essercito unito à li ordini militari.
Tra le egregii fatti d'Annibale si nomeri questo, che havendo un
essercito grossissimo, d'ogni generationi misto, condotto à militare
in paese d'altrui, non vi sursesse mai discensioni, ne tra lor, ne

Right margin notes:
Tamerlanes
113ʳ

E piu sicuro
desser temuto
solo che amato
solo

113ᵛ

114ʳ

E meno pericolo
procedere
contra la sangue
che contra la
roba

114ᵛ

Henrico
imprigiono
Cortineo per
colpa imputata
al padre

115ʳ

La severita e
necessaria in la
guerra

Hannibale

113ʳ: 2. *In E the paragraph begins with*   114ᵛ: 1. contra] *last three letters inserted*
           Steph: *which is superfluous*   *above the line in E*
113ᵛ: 6. volonta] voluta B   115ʳ: 3. una] sna B s *cancelling* u
114ʳ: 3. l'acquistò] l'acquista B   4. le] li B
           margin. la sangue] lo sangue B   5. nomeri] numeri B

115ᵛ disobedientia à lo capitano, cosi nell'ad-//versa, come prospera fortuna, il che non nacque d'altro si non di sua crudeltà, la qual insieme con li altri suoi virtude fece sempre nel conspetto di suoi soldati venerando et terribili et senza quella tutte l'altre sue virtu
5 (quantunque eran molti) non bastorno à far quel effeto.

La clementia di Scipione e dannosa

Del altra parte si vede che la troppa clementia di Scipione era la cagione che ribellorno* suoi esserciti in Spagna dandoli piu licentia,
116ʳ che non si convenia à la disciplina milita-//re et pero era rimprove-rato da Fabio massimo* nel senato, et nomato corrottor della militia romana et piu essendo i popoli locrensi, amici del popolo romano, offesi di un suo legato, non solo non furon di lui vendicato,
5 ne anche l'insolentia del legato gastigato, il che nacque di sua troppo facilità, d'onde venne chiamato dal senato in giuditio.

Alph: Questo essempio d'Annibale di voi allegato di crudeltà è
116ᵛ solo di tutti l'altri capitani, che fussero al mondo,//ma havendo l'occhio al fine vederete che piu valle la benignità di Scipione nell'-animi di soldati che la crudelta d'Annibale, laqual benche vaglia di tenere un essercito unito quando i sono discosto dal nimico, perche lor
5 disunione non havrebbe effetto, ma poi che si veggono in ordinanza, et gli nimici apresso piu giova la benignità del capitano il qual tal hora indarno supplica i soldati, che combattono valorosamente, si
117ʳ per innanzi e stato inhumano et crudele//et questo si vede in Annibale, ilqual benche sotto Carthagine haveva ordinato l'essercito con grand prudentia contra Scipione, nondimeno fu sconfitto, et non li valse esser feroce, per tenere i soldati in ordinanza, perche
5 senza dubio nelli pericoli piu vale la benignita che l'asperezza.

Steph: Hor sia detto della militia, ma torniamo al governo civile, et vedremo in alcuni luoghi, et tra alcuni popoli, che la crudeltà si
117ᵛ nella pace, come nella//guerra, è piu utile et necessario, che la clementia, et in altre provincie tutto contrario, pero volendo alcuno usare l'uno ò l'altro li bisogna considerare il luogo, tempo, et le

Senza crudelta l'imperio turchesco andarebbe in roina

persone. Sensa la crudelta, l'imperio turchesca anderebbe in pre-cipitio, et questo avenne, che tutta la authorita è in tal manera rinchiusa nella persona del signore che ogni altro principe del suo regno espetta aver la testa tagliata, per ogni capricio che venerà
118ʳ nella sua testa;//perche i sono tutti suoi schiavi, egli lo muta di ufficii et dignitate, come pare a lui senza altro rispetto.

115ᵛ: 3. li altri suoi virtude] le altre sue virtudi B
117ʳ: 4. tenere] tener B
117ᵛ: 3. ò] a B

117ᵛ: 4. sensa] senza B; turchesca] turchesco B
5. avenne] avvene B
7. aver] haver B

Ma si un principe di Francia o d'Ingliterra procedesse in tal maniera, si roinarebbe incontinente. Ma colui che ha in governo un nomero di schiavi o servi per tenerli in spavento, che non ardiscono levarsi, in contra piu vale la crudelta, che la clementia, come hebbe Dario, Allessandro, et il Turcho al presente. I romani* et altri principi christiani⫽hanno in governo subditi, et non servi. La plebe romana haveva equale quasi imperio co'l senato, et i baroni in Ingliterra et Francia participanno del stato co'l re, et i hanno privilegii et authorita grandissima co'l popolo talche non si puole intieramente usare tal severità, ne con la crudeltà manegiarli.

I baroni d'Ingliterra participano del stato co'l re

Alph: Che authorita hanno i baronni in Ingliterra co'l popolo?

Gli popoli sono sogetti alli baroni

Steph: I popoli per le legi antiche sono in alcuno modo soggietto ali baroni,*⫽perche egli lascino lor possessioni et case senza denari al popolo, chiedendo certi servitii, tante volte al'anno, et che non ponno andare con nullo altro a la guerra, se non con essi o per il commandamento d'essi et molti simili servigii, quale e una certa servita, laqual il popolo e obligato osservare per giuramento, di modo che s'el principe usasse tal crudeltà, i baroni menarebbono il popolo incontra. Pero si vede in quel regno, che i regi⫽hereditarii, o l'altri, quali per mezzo d'amicitia hanno hauto l'imperio, facevano meglior frutto, co'l amore et benignità, che li altri hanno fatto con ferocità et crudelta.

119ʳ

5

119ᵛ

Alph: Questo non e stato peculiare a li regi d'Ingliterra, ma a molti altri imperatori, come di Alessandro, Cyro, Cesare, il qual vivendo hebbe un tempio in Roma commune con la dea Clementia, perche non lasciò mai da parte opera alcuna che sia ricercato ad un principe man-⫽sueto et clemente, et quanta riputatione acquisto Camillo con humanita, che non vede* che ha letto Livio.

5

Julio Cesare clemente

120ʳ

Essendo egli co'l essercito romano intorno la citta di falisci, venne un maestro di schola sotto colore d'essercitio con alcuni fanciulli nobili della citta, pensando di gratificare Camillo et il popolo romano, gli condusse tutti nel campo devanti lui et presentandogli disse come mediante quelli figlioli la citta si darebbe nelli sue mani. Il quale presente non⫽solamente egli non ricevo, ma fatto spogliare il maestro et legato le mani, dà a ciascaduno di quelli fanciulli un verge in mano, lo fece da quelli con molte bastiture accompagnare à la citta. La qual cosa intesa da i cittadini, piacque

L'humanita di Camillo

5

120ᵛ

118ᵛ: *margin.* baroni d'Ingliterra] baroni
    in d'Ingliterra B
    6. baronni] baroni B
    7. soggietto] soggietti B
    8. ali] alli B

119ʳ: 5. servita] servitu B
120ᵛ: 3. bastiture] batiture B
    4. accompagnare] acompagnare B

5 tanto lor l'humanità et integrita di Camillo, che senza voler piu diffender se determinorno darli la citta, donde se vede qualche volte che l'essempio humano, et pietoso ha magiore forza nelli

121^r cori delli huomini, che un atto feroce⫽et crudele, et come quelle provincie et regni, che ne l'armi, instrumenti bellici, ne ogni altro humano forza ha potuto aprire, che un essempio di humanità, di pieta, di castità, o de liberalita ha aperte, et di tali essempi l'istorie

5 sono pieni.

La liberalita di Fabritio   Tutta la forza romana non bastò a cacciare Pirrho fuora d'Italia, et la liberalità di Fabritio ne lo caccio, quando gli manifestò l'offerto

121^V che haveva fatto un suo famigliare d'avelenarlo. Tutte⫽le vittorie

Castita di Scipione   di Scipione non lo dette tanta reputatione, quanto un essempio di castità d'aver renduta la moglie giovene, bella, et intatta al suo marito. La fama di quella attione fece amica tutta la

5 Spagna.

Steph: Questi essempi da voi legate sono rare, et fuora d'uso in questi nostri giorni, anzi sarebbe stimato d'aver poco practica, che facesse, come fece Camillo o Fabritio, pero dico al proposito dela

122^r clementia et crudelta, che giove ad⫽un principe talhora monstrarsi crudele, pure che non habi l'animo pregno di crudelta, accioche facendo poi mistero di monstrarsi benigno, lo possa fare agevol-

La clementia dee vincer' la crudelta   mente. Perche ad ogni modo la clementia debbe vincere la crudeltà, altremente il principe non rassimigliarà à Dio, di cui è il vivo imagine. La scrittura sancta chiamo Iddio misericordioso* et giusto mettendo innanzi la misericordia.

122^V *Alph:* Talche voi conchiuderete, che il principe⫽dee esser piu tosto clemente, che feroce.

Steph: Si, che habi l'animo semper pietoso et benigno, ma non tanto benigno, che non puole quando havra occasione monstrarsi

5 anche crudele. Egli e un bel nome clemente principe, pure che non sequitase magiore inconveniente che del contrario. Si che ne havete l'opinione mia circa la clementia che un principe dee usare, et

123^r similmenti il modo che Guilhelmo duca di Normannia tenne, nel⫽ sogiogare, spengere i seditiosi, pacificare i tumolti, et lasciare il regno in fede et pace a li suoi successori.

·   *Alph:* Al parere mio sarebbe piu sicuro per un principe di pro-

5 cedere p'el contrario à quello di Guilhelmo, cioe per clementia,

---

120^V: 7. volte] volta B	121^V: 6. legate] legati B; rare] rari B
121^r: 3. altro] altra B; humano]	7. practica] prattica B
humana B	122^V: 8. similmenti] similmente B

humanità, liberalita, eccetera, et volere piu presto regnare nelli cori dell'huomini, che nelli fortrezze di sassi.

Steph: Ne havete di sapere che colui che acquistò un realme o una provincia per forza d'armi⫽ha una via da tenere, et egli che per 123^v favore d'amici, per iure hereditario o per matrimonio, ha un altra strada di proceder di manternerlo stato. Il fondamento di questo voleva esser clementia, affabilità, et liberalita, la quale tra le altre penetrà i cori d'huomini (quantunque durissimi). Queste qualità al   La liberalita principio li danno riputatione et fama, fanno anche la strada aperta   rompe le esser amato et obedito. Et le sono necessarie à colui che vuole   porte di ferro acquistare amore d'un popolo forestiero. Alessandro,⫽Caesar, 124^r Alphonso re di Napoli, Stephano re d'Ingliterra per queste qualità   Principi acquistorno regni, et li mantenevano. Perche in vero* le difficulte   liberali non sono grande di mantenere un regno per un principe nuove,   Le qualita quale per via d'amicitia è intrato, quando egli è sicuro di quelli del   mediante le sangue reale. Questo e il magiore pericolo che puole accadere in   quali principi alcuno regno, à chi governo, perche vive sempre in paura, et mai⫽   mentengono sicuro. I huomini naturalmente desideranno mutationi. Ma havendo   lor' stati assicuratosi di questi l'ha tolto ogni occasione dali nobili di procu-   124^v rare tal innovatione, et anche dali popoli di seguirli, perche li huomini non si movino mai senza una spetie almanco de la verità.   5

Poi gli è un grand adiuto, quando il principe andasse ad habitarne. La presenza sua è di grand efficacia, la qual sola refrena l'appetiti⫽ 125^r deli seditiosi, et li impaurisse di fare quello, che lor appetiti desi-   La presentia deranno. Et sendovi,* si vede i disordini nascere, et presto vi si   del principe ha puo rimediare. Ma sendo assente, s'intendino quando i sono grandi,   grand forza et alhora non è piu rimedio.   5

La presenza del principe refrena l'avaricia delli ministri, iquali sogliono scortigare i poveri huomini, ma havendo egli propinquo concorso da lamentarsi a lui, si satisfanno, et havranno magiore occa-⫽sione d'amarlo volendo esser buoni: et volendo esser altri- 125^v mente di timerlo. Si per caso l'inimici di fuora pensassino di assaltar il stato, havrebbono piu rispetto, tantoche habitando vi, puole con grand facilà mantenerlo. Pure che non alterasse lor leggi, ne li aggravasse con nuovi essationi o datii, egli in breve tempo venerà 5 antico nel principato, che habi singulare cura a tenere i suoi baroni uniti; ad oviare⫽a li principi deli disordini, innanzi che nascono 126^r

123^v: 5. durissimi B] *final two letters*   124^r: 7. governo] governa B
         cancelled in E   *margin.* mentengono] mantengono
124^r: 3. difficulte] difficultà B   B
       4. nuove] nuovo B   125^r: 4. s'intendino] l'intendino B

Uffitio
del principe

forti; ministrare giustitia egualmente à tutti, senza esser partigiano
ad alcuno, perche quella generara invidia; di premiare i virtuosi, et
castigare i tristi; monstrarsi facile humano et affabile à tutti; ascoltare
5 volontieri le quereli deli poveri, d'onde in poco tempo l'acquisterà
riputatione, et serà piu sicuro che un hereditario.

126^v

Stephano, re d'Ingliterra usando questi mezi, mantenavasi
sicuro quantunque era francioso, i quali //inglesi odino, et che
usurpò anche il regno. Ma tra tutte le qualità non e altra di magiore

La afabilita
acquista grand
riputatione

forza, per adquistare fama et riputatione d'un popolo, che d'ascoltare le querele et supplichi, et vendicare l'ingiurii de li poveri.
Questo confirmano l'infiniti essempi deli istorie, deli quali ne
adducerò alcuni.

Absalon

Absalon* figliolo del re David (dice la scrittura) che la matina era
salitota à porse nell'intrata del palagio reale del padre, et quantunque

127^r

che vedeva venire per audienza del re, egli //benignamente à se lo
chiamò, et con grand clementia l'ascoltava, il qual benche con animo
sincero non operasse, nondimeno venne in tanta gracia, et hebbe
tanta riputatione del popolo, che tutto Israel ribellava del suo padre,
5 ascoltandosi à lui. Il medesimo si vede di Salomone, et di Ottavio

Ottavio

Augusto, i quali in persona spesse volte sedeano in tribunal per
videre le cause di lor popolo, per laqual et grand humanita, conse-

127^v

quirno amore, fede, et sicurta di lor popolo. //Henrico ottavo, si

L'affabilita
di Henrico
ottavo

come non era inferiore à nullo principe nelli suoi giorni, per virtu
del corpo, et del ingenio (quando havesse usatole bene) cosi in questa
virtu d'affabilità superò tutti l'altri. Egli in vero ministrava grand
5 occasione nel tempo quando comminciò da rapire li beni spirituali,
et evertere li monasterii, al suo popolo di conspirarli incontra, et
massime quelli dela contadi di Linconia, et di Yorcka per esser

128^r

eglino piu contrarii //à la sua opinione, che tutti l'altri del regno,
d'onde egli adirandoli fortamente con essi, per li tumulti et conspirationi, quali spesse volte fecerò contra, usò grand crudeltà nel
privarli chi dela vita, et chi de la roba per ogni delitto quantunque
5 picolo. Del'altra parte i gentilhuomini, quali sequitavano le parti
del re (cognoscendo lui esser adirato con gli popoli), li gettavano

128^v

fuora della possessioni, tollevan ingiustamente i beni senza //
rispetto delli leggi, o compassione alcuna, talche i poveri contadini
venerò desperati, sendo ogni giorno con nuove ingiurie oppressi.

126^r:	*margin.* Uffitio] Ufficio B	127^r: 7. consequirno] q *cancelling* g *in* B,
126^v:	*margin.* afabilita B] fabilita E	cosegnorno E
	8. salitota] salito B; intrata]	127^v: 7. dela] dele B
	intrate B	

Accade che un di questi poveri* huomini vechio si mise in viagio
con suo mogliere et figlioli verso la corte di lamentarsi de li ingiurie 5
fattoli d'un cavaliero suo vicino, Henrico che per caso, venendo
dalla caccia, et ochiando qual povero su'l ginochi, lontano posto
tutto straciatto, et pieno de fango,//frenò suo cavallo in mezo   129^r
della corona di molti nobili, ascoltò con grand humanità tutto
cio che voleva dire et poi con fronte allegro et benigne parole li
disse che stesse consolato et di buona voglia, perche io (disse il re)
defenderò li mei simplici pecore dalla ingordigia deli lupi et vendi- 5
carò le ingiurii d'essi, et cosi con gratiosi parole commandò ch'il
povero huomo hebbe danari datosi per ritornari ala sua patria, lo
licentiò et essaminando//poi la causa delli poveri contadini de la   129^v
provincia, et trovando li detti gentilhuomini in colpa li fece primo
far restitutioni a li detti poveri, et poi li fece apicare per la gola à
lor proprii porti. La fama del quale gia sparsa per la provincia,
come egli haveva con tante benignità ascultato alla querela del 5
povero huomo, facendolo giusticia, et vendicando lor ingiurii
acquistò tanto amore et fede del popolo, i quali innanzi (per che
hebbe//usurpato li beni delli religiosi lo hebbero in odio) levorono   130^r
li mani al cielo, ringratiando Iddio che li hebbe dato un tal re, il
qual ascoltò le quereli delli poverli, et li facesse ragione. Talche dopo
restorno sempre obedientissimi et fideli.

Similmente nel principio del suo regnare monstro un altro essem- 5
pio raro, d'onde l'acquistava l'animi et cori di suoi popoli, i quali
eran gia molto offesi per la leggi,* che Henrico settimo suo padre//   130^v
fece la quale era che chiunque persona che era trovato d'aver
violato le leggi del realme anticamente fatte (quantunque nel
tempo passato) pagasserò tamen la pena, qual nelle leggi era
commandata di quella violationi et ordinò duoi giudici et molti 5
delatori in ogni provincia, che accusassero tali delinquenti, intanto
che in breve tempo hebbe raccolto una somma di dinari grandissima,
perche gli huomini dogni conditioni vene ogni di accusati://si   131^r
l'innocenti, come altri per questi delatori (troppo intento à lor
utile), d'onde i popoli mormorassero contra la crudelta di tal lege, et
infrotto corserò ad Henrico ottavo (dopo la morte del suo padre)
re, per rivocare* quella iniqua legge, et d'aver lor beni restituiti, i 5
quali eran innanzi per li avari ministri iniuste tolti. Ma egli,

128^v: 7. qual] quel B   129^v: 6. facendolo] facendoli B;
129^r: 4. disse B] lisse E   giusticia] giustitia B;
          7. ritornare] ritornari B   ingiurii] ingiurie B
                                      130^r: 2. *first* li] le B
                                      130^v: 5. violationi] violatione B

95

giudicando che non facesse per lui di restituire a ciascaduno li
beni tolti per la detta lege, trovò un modo di pacificare la furia del
131ᵛ popolo⁄⁄et gratificarle anche. Perche cognoscendo l'odio che il
popolo hebbe contra li giudici et delatori, quali nelli giudicii et
sententie erano troppo severi, commandò che li sopradetti giudici
Il modo che et delatori fussero chiamati in judicio, et dopo à la morte condam-
Henrico uso nati, et gli delatori in varii modi puniti, chi il naso tagliato, chi
di contentar'
il popolo orrecchio, chi la lingua, et altri brusati nel fronte. Per questo modo i
popoli restorno satisfatti et contentissimi di lui, che haveva fatto lor
132ʳ ven-⁄⁄detto delli cattivi ministri, et si egli godeva lor dinari senz'-
altri mormori o dispiacere d'alcuno.

Alph: Egli non e cosa, che acquista ad un principe i cori delli
popoli, che di parere di favorire quello che li amano, et odiare
5 quello che li odono.

Steph: Oltra le cosa sopradette, un principe acquista riputatione
Grandezza nel monstrare in tutti li suoi attioni una grandezza, fortezza, et
d'animo gravità d'animo, et circa li manegie de li subditi privati, che la sua
132ᵛ opinio-⁄⁄ne et sententia sia irrevocable. Et quel principe che si
mantiene in tal opinione nullo ardirà d'ingannar, ne di aggirarlo, et e
riputato assai. Et contra, chi e riputato, con difficulta si congiura,
la qual è causa doncque d'una grand sicurtà. Et in l'altre attioni*
5 suoi, di parere pietoso, humano, affabile, clemente, liberale, et
osservatore della fede.

Alph: Queste qualitade sono massime lodevole, ma alquanto
duro per un principe d'osservare.

133ʳ *Steph:* È ben vero⁄⁄neanche la conditioni delli principi non
consenti intieramente d'osservarle, et pure quando l'osservasse
sempre, sarebbe à lui piu damnose che utile, pero egli è assai s'el
principe è tanto prudente ch'il sapia schifare la infamia delle con-
5 trarie, quando è sforzato d'usarle, et fugire quelli vitii, i quali
torrebbono il stato, come d'esser rapace de li beni deli subditi, di
violare li antichi leggi, dispregiare i nobili, et li huomini virtuosi, et
133ᵛ quanto*⁄⁄d'esser tenuto clemente, liberale, et osservatore de la
fede, io li commendo sommanente, pure che l'osservarle non porti
piu danno che utile. Li contrarii di questi qualche volte giovino
grandemente à chi le usa, massime quando sono bene, et con arti-
5 ficio testuti.

131ᵛ:	*margin.* di] de B	132ᵛ:	4. doncque] dunque B; qual]
	4. judicio] juditio B		*inserted above the line in* E
	8. vendetto] vendetta B	133ʳ:	7. li] le B
132ʳ:	8. li manegie] le manegie B	133ᵛ:	2. sommanente] *sic* B, E

96

Alessandro* papa sesto era nel suo tempo il grand maestro di   Alessandro papa
questa arte, dico da coverire una ambitiosa impresa con una vela
di pieta et cetera. Et senza dubio tal vele giovino piu volte∥piu   134ʳ
che la simplice verita. Perche colui che procederà realmente con i
volpi et huomini tristi se roinerà come Henrico sesto. Neanche un
principe nuovo non puole (quando volesse) osservare tutte le cose,
per le quale i huomini sono tenute buoni, essendo piu volte neces-   5
sitato per mantener lo stato, d'operare contra la clementia, contra la
religione, et contra la fede, per tanto bisogna che habia un animo
disposto à volgersi∥come il vento, secondo la varieta di fortuna   134ᵛ
nelle sue fatte, ma nele sue parole di parere pieno di fede, di clemen-   Consiglio
tia, et di charità, perche questi parere l'acquistono apresso la molti-   d'huomo politico
tudine grand riputatione et un popolo nota piu l'effetti delli occhi
et dela lingua, che quelli delle mani, et si per adventura li fatti del   5
principe non rispondono per tutto alle sue parole, et le suoi pareri,
tal sera imputato alli errori delli ministri, et non∥al re, come si   135ʳ
vede nel essempio di Henrico ottavo sopra mentionato.

    Questo ne ho detto fuora del proposito per rispondere ali vostri
domandi. Hora non mi resta altro da dire di questa materia havendo
monstrato quale era il modo di Guilhelmo nel soggiogare il realme   5
d'Ingliterra, et lasciarlo in fede a li suoi successori, fin all'adveni-   Philippo re
mento del potente et clementissimo Philippo figliolo del Carlo
quinto imperatore. Questo io non chiamo∥mutatione, ne altera-   135ᵛ
tione del regno ma successione legitima, confirmata per tutti gli
ordini, alla restitutione della religione, honore del regno, et utile
delli popoli. Il che il nobilissimo sangue di quel invitto seme dela   Lodi della
potentissima Germania, di quel felicissima casa del glorioso Carlo   sangue de la nobilissima
imperatore augurio, et la somma bontà et propria virtu in lui   casa de Austria
creata manifestamente promette et confirmà lo medesimo. Chi non
sappia la grandessa coniuntta∥con virtude di Federico* tertio   136ʳ
imperatore, duca di Austria, per non comminciare piu alto, che
come un Fabio con la sua pacientia con prudentia inconparabile   La grandezza di Federico tertio
coniuntta, restituò quasi tutta la christiana religione dinanzi à lui
gravamente caduta. Il grand Maximiliano suo figlio, chi non sa   Lodi di
quanta pietà, bontade, et virtu era in esso, et quanto honorevole   Maximiliano
impressi egli fece in Brabantia, Fiandra, et in Italia, et quanto zelo∥   136ᵛ
grande hebbe sempre verso la religione, et a tutti gli huomini

---

133ᵛ: 6. il] *above the line in E*   135ᵛ: 4. quel] quella B
134ʳ: 3. come B] come come E   8. grandessa] grandezza B;
134ᵛ: 2. nelle sue fatte] nelli suoi fatti B   coniuntta] coniunta B
       6. le] li B   136ʳ: 4. coniuntta] coniunta B
135ʳ: 6. a li] alli B   7. impressi] impresi B

virtuosi? Io non parlo di Philippo suo figliolo per esser arretto
della crudele morte, dinanzi che hebbe tempo monstrar grand opere
5 degni di questa nobilissima sangue. Ma habbiamo Carolo quinto suo

Lodi di Carlo padre,* chi di dieciotto anni soli, ne fu fatto imperadore et monarcha
del mondo, il nome di cui fa impalladire i turchi et gli mori, e tutti
137ʳ l'inimici del nome christiano//temono la buona fortuna, la quale

Il detto del Dio lo dette. Pero Ottomanno, grand signiore et imperatore dili
imperatore turchi soleva dire che non temeva Carlo, ma la sua fortuna, la cui
turchesco
grandessa ha piu ornato l'imperio che non e stato ornato del imperio,
5 àguisa del sole con i raggi grandi delle sue valorissime imprese ha
illustrato il vechio, et il nuovo mondo, et tanto piu chiaramente
ch'il sole, quanto il splendore suo cede a la notte, il suo non cederà
137ᵛ mai ad alcuno//tempo. Et che cosa possiamo dunque sperare del
magnanimo, di Philippo suo figliolo, coniunto con tanta religione,

Simili pietà et clementia? I leoni non generanno conili, ne gli aquili
producono colombi. Ma i leoni procudono leoni, et gli aquili coano aquili.
simili
L'ha piacuto per tanto all' immenso Iddio, che el sia preposto a le
signorie di tanti provintie et regni, non a caso o per sceleratessa come
138ʳ molti altri principi sono preposti, ma per giustitia et per la somma //
providentia divina, produtto in questo tempo accioche la christia-
nita dopo tanta scurita di nevole habia la chiara luce del sole, et i
popoli christiani dopo si lungi et crudeli guerre goderebberò lo

La pace e precioso et inestimabile gioio della pace, tanto desiderata et bra-
figliola de Dio mata d'ogni persona: chiamata la figliola de Dio, norice di natura,
conservatrice della humana spetie, seminatrice de la virtu, et madre
138ᵛ d'abondantia. Non si ode voce piu grata ali orrechi de li//huomini,
che lo nome della pace, ne si trova cosa, che si desidera con magiore
voglia, o che si gode con piu diletto. Perche vi non e contento, ne
allegrezza di core alcuno dove non è la pace.
5 Chi adonque levara la pace delli huomini leva il sole dal mondo,
et la vita dalle creature. Ma Philippo e quello che è ordinato per
restituirli l'uno et l'altro, et la spada di tanti amplissimi regni nel
139ʳ suo mano destro, da sopremo motore a quel//fine, posta, accioche
con la potentia di quella egli puole come leone fortissimo debellare i
superbi tigri, giungere gli vitiosi volpi, et castigare li disturbatori de
la concordia christiana. Et come padre clementissimo premiare i
5 virtuosi, deffendere gli innocenti, et mantenerli subditi in pace.
Questo solo è quello che il core di lui magnanimo cerca, desidera,

136ᵛ:	6. soli Ed.] soll B, E	137ᵛ:	5. piacuto] piaciuto B
137ʳ:	2. signiore] signor B	138ᵛ:	7. nel suo] ne la sua B
	4. grandessa] grandezza B		8. destro] destra B

et brama. Et io che lo sapia vi dico. Questo amore et zelo grande Innata bonta
all'comune bene //et utile christiana li mosse cercare p'el honorevole di Philippo
139ᵛ
mezo del santo matrimonio di signorigiare (come padre piissimo)
lo potente realme d'Ingliterra, per loquale* sendo la sua potentia et
regni (in questi parti) insieme gia uniti, egli sensa controversia è
fatto arbitro della pace et guerra di tutta la christianità, nome Arbitro delle
veramente dignissimo della sangue d'Austria, et conveniente a la controversie
mondane
sincerità de religione, di pieta, et di //clementia del sublimo animo 140ʳ
di Philippo.

Alph: L'immortale Dio concede ch'il usa la sua auctorita et potentia al'honore di Dio, et (come ne havete detto) à la pace et tranquillità
di tutta la christianità. 5

Steph: Quello anche noi con le mani al cielo levate continuamente
supplicamo, et che il sommo donatore di tutte le cose buone, li dia
insieme co'l imperio felice, lessecutione di tutte suoi desiderii
santi. Ma ascoltate, signior Alphonso: // l'ora è sesta. Il duca di 140ᵛ
Norforchia* se espetta. Andiamoci à cenare.

Il Fine

139ᵛ: 1. *E repeats the last word of 138ᵛ:*
               bene; christiana] christiano B;
               li] lo B
          4. sensa] senza B

A Discourse on the Coming of the English and Normans
to Britain, Showing How Princes Have Succeeded or
Failed Depending Upon Whether They Ruled According
to Reason or Appetite

by

The Most Reverend Bishop Stephen Gardiner, K.G.,
Lord Chancellor and Royal Councillor. Translated from
English into Italian by George Rainsford, with a
Description of England by the Translator

II^r   To the most powerful and merciful Prince Philip, by the grace of God King of Castile, Leone, Aragon, England, France, the two Sicilies, Jerusalem, Ireland, Archduke of Austria,* Defender of the Catholic Faith: felicitations and fulfillment of your holy wishes.

Eternal God, purest fountain of ineffable bounty and sacred majesty of industrious nature, has brought forth in diverse ages for the benefit of mortals great-spirited men, wondrous in every kind of virtue, who have made the same journey (although by diverse

II^v   paths // according to the diversity of celestial influence), reaching, by determined aspiration, the highest peak of fame, the eternal palm of glory, and those spacious fields of blessed life. Thus Hercules was exalted above human felicity by the ancients for the incredible strength of his body, while Alexander was called the Great for qualities of spirit. Caesar was called Clement because in all his conquests and triumphs he showed unparalleled mercy to the conquered. Antoninus,* the most devout of the emperors, was called Pious. Titus, who believed that the height of human happiness consisted in helping the needy, was called Liberal. And Octavius, who governed the empire in peace, was the first to be honored as Augustus.

If the pagans gave these men, who were foremost in one virtue only, immortal titles appropriate to their virtues, with what surnames can we Christians now honor the happy name of the most powerful Philip, defender of the faith, merciful king and father of so many peoples, who seeks the perfection of all the virtues, just

III^r   as the burning flame // seeks to surpass the other elements? For he has been raised by divine providence to the rule of such large and powerful kingdoms for the benefit of the true faith, for the harmony of the Christian flock, and for the ancient glory of Britain. Clear testimony of this has been given to the world by his excellent beginnings and the true signs of paternal love he had already shown to mortals in having restored (with the help of the Most Serene Mary) the light of the sun* to Britain after such stormy darkness and the sweet repose of peace to the other Christian domains after such tempestuous war. By this he has given honor to God, good

---

* See notes, pp. 152–67.

fortune to men, abundance to the countryside, security to states, delight to hearts, and immortality through all future ages to his happy name, whose fame, already spread throughout the world, makes the spirits of the princes of every Christian land venerate the lofty thoughts of his Majesty with fervid heart and bow themselves at his feet. And because his kindness and mercy in the growth of his power and glory //resemble the magnanimity of the lion, whose III^v nature is as kind as it is mild and humble, the people also call upon him, adore him, and now pray for the preservation of his eternal crown just as the Romans did for the life of the good Augustus. Since the sweat, the praises and the thoughts of all are your due, O most merciful King and highest arbiter of the controversies of the world, as the heavenly agent of God's will on whom depends, as upon a secondary cause, the well-being of his people, do not take it amiss if I, your most lowly slave, offer you, from these low valleys where I work and sweat ceaselessly, this little gift, so that through it I may show the delight and joy that I share with so many others in the public benefit that Britain and all the world have received from Your Majesty, and also so that I may give eternal remembrance to the merits of Stephen Gardiner, Bishop of Winchester, Lord Chancellor of Britain, author of the present work, //whose constancy in IV^r the Catholic faith, pre-eminence in learning, prudence in public affairs, modesty in the midst of honors, and singular loyalty to Your Majesty have moved me to translate this his work, and to consecrate it to his eternal name. And so that nothing might be lacking in this little book that might contribute to an understanding of the laws, procedures, customs, nature and humor of the people of Britain, I have composed and here appended a portrait of the realm, and, bowing at your Majesty's feet, I offer them both, with devout affection, to your kindness.

At London, 16 March 1556.
Your Majesty's most devoted servant,
George Rainsford.

A DISCOURSE ON THE COMING OF THE ENGLISH AND NORMANS TO BRITAIN

Stephen. Alphonso

Steph: Honored sir, I have considered it at length, and remain uncertain and undecided (almost as if between Scylla and Charybdis) which would entail less danger and less blame: to yield or to deny 1^v you that which you have ⫽asked me so many times. For it would seem that one cannot deny a virtuous and amicable gentleman something proper and lawful without breaking the sacred rules of friendship, and without being suspected of ingratitude. On the other hand to promise and then not be able to achieve the perfect results which you perhaps expect would bring me the author more blame than praise and you the hearer more annoyance than satisfaction. But among friends all things, whatever they are, should be taken in good part, and therefore I have decided to disclose my small skill 2^r in this matter ⫽with good will, rather than to hide it and be thought wanting in friendship.

Subject of the work
You ask me, then, for my opinion on the subject of the more memorable alterations that have occurred in the realm of England and their causes, up to the present time. But first tell me, what made you ask this? You are a foreigner: the rule and governance of this kingdom have nothing to do with you, and still less can the changes in its governance affect you for better or for worse.

2^v *Alph:* ⫽Most famous sir, it is true that the governance of the realm does not pertain to me: I ask only in order to know: my spirit is greedy for every kind of knowledge and understanding, and particularly for knowledge of the rule and governance of different countries and realms, so that taught by diverse examples I can help my country when I return, as all men were born to do. This desire, 3^r most famous sir, prompted me to ask for your considered ⫽opinion on the alterations you have just mentioned.

Steph: The long pilgrimage you have told me of truly shows the great desire you have for knowledge, which is the more honorable and praiseworthy in that so few seek such a goal: today men are greedy for everything else, but not for knowledge.

Alph: Yet I think that all men naturally have this desire for 3^v knowledge which seems to me the highest ⫽good and only happiness of men while they sojourn in this valley.

Steph: What are your reasons for believing this?

Alph: There are many, in fact, and the first is that the desire for
knowledge is the greatest gift the Almighty God gave to men, for
the infinite providence of God (having given to all the other creatures their number, weight, measure, mode, species, order, essence,
virtue, and operation) made man only on the last day, as the final
touch to all ⫽His works; and so that he could lift himself to that
blessedness and glory which were His by nature, He gave him, of
His grace, among so many various gifts, this inborn and natural
characteristic: that he is not content to exist like the stones, to live
like the plants, to move and feel like the beasts, but wants to understand and know everything like the angels. Therefore it seems to me
that knowledge is the final goal; and the highest felicity of this life
is not ⫽possessed, is not found, indeed cannot even be sought
without knowledge. Religion with its supernatural gift and infusion
of sapience has it. Theology finds it with meditation upon Scripture.
Philosophy seeks it by disputation and babbling upon natural things,
discovering causes by their marvelous effects. The management of
public affairs acquires it through long experience and frequent
reading of history. There is no man so vile nor so idiotic, unless he
is more a statue with a ⫽ human face than a man, that he has not,
from birth, a vehement and ardent desire for knowledge. The air
does not so desire the light when it is dark, the stone does not so
desire the center of the earth when thrown above it, as does the
human intellect long for the perfection of knowledge to adorn
itself, to illuminate itself, to quiet itself.

The birds are born to fly, the beasts to wander, the fish to swim,
horses to run, but men reckon their value and their glory in terms
of knowledge. We see ⫽that the great and small, men and women,
when they are spoken to lift their heads, open their eyes, strain to
hear – all only for knowledge. Why have we such delight when we
hear of new things, if not because we are eager to know everything?
Why have we almost from our swaddling clothes such envy for
those who know more than others, if not because we think that he
who knows more than we do is more fully human than we are?
Therefore the wise conclude that God could have given us no ⫽gift
more useful and more necessary for human life than knowledge,
a truly honorable activity for the young, a most pleasant solace to
the old, an incomparable fortune for the poor, and for the rich a very
great satisfaction. The desire for knowledge even made the divine
Plato (whose teaching resounded with such great stir in the
Academy of Athens that it was said openly that if God had to speak

Marginal notes:
Knowledge contents the soul
Discourse on knowledge
4^r
Human desire
4^v
5^r
Knowledge adorns
The aim of the animals
The glory of man
5^v
6^r
Knowledge is useful
Plato's love for knowledge

6ᵛ with a human tongue He could not employ one //more learned or more eloquent) travel* to Egypt, Calabria, and Apulia to find Archytas of Tarentum: he preferred to journey and be this man's disciple than to stay in his own country and be the master of so many others.

Labors of Apollonius of Tyana went wandering all his life, seeking knowledge
Tyaneus wherever it fled from the world. He went first among the Persians, passed the Caucasian Mountains, penetrated the territory of the
7ʳ Albani, the Scythians, the Masagetae, and the most rich kingdoms // of India; then finally he reached the Brahmans, and heard the deep secrets* of the birth of the great Iarchas who sat on a golden throne teaching divine philosophy. From there he returned to Alexandria and thence to Ethiopia to learn from the gymnosophists and to see that most famous altar of the sun in the arena where they taught the deep mysteries. Therefore do not be amazed, illustrious sir, if I, con-
7ᵛ sumed by this desire to learn the sciences and to understand and see // the customs, laws, and procedures of various people have placed my life in such dangers. Furrowing the implacable sea, crossing harsh mountains in Europe as well as in regions of Africa and Asia I have at last arrived with great contentment of mind at the most splendid court of Philip, King of England, where I find that your authority (which shows the man), your singular prudence in public affairs,
8ʳ your firm constancy in the // Catholic faith, and the incorruptible justice you minister to all, show me clearly that all your qualities merit no less praise (rather much more) than their public repute throughout Europe, however honorable. Therefore trusting in these your rare virtues and taking fire from your most courtly welcome, your immense liberality and your other singular kindnesses towards
8ᵛ me, I come to ask your judgment on certain above- // mentioned alterations which occurred at various times in this most powerful realm of England.

Steph: Magnanimous knight, I see by your learned and eloquent discourse the burning and ardent desire you have to know my opinions on this your question, and having considered it and its circumstances, weighing my small power with the greatness of the subject,
9ʳ I would without doubt have fled //this labor, for its weight is too great for my shoulders, had not the great love I have for you persuaded me to the contrary. Therefore I shall show myself to be rather rash than ungrateful with respect to this your praiseworthy desire. Listen then.

Alph: I shall listen attentively, without interrupting your talk.

Steph: But no, ask freely what you wish and I shall reply as far

as my knowledge permits. //For the rest I shall candidly confess my 9ᵛ
ignorance.

Northwards in the west lies an island formerly called Albion for Praise of Britain
its white cliffs, which for the bounty of the soil, the temper of the
skies, the commodity of the land and the virtue of the people has
not only enjoyed royal honors in itself this long time, but has also
been leader and queen to other neighboring regions, and has so
grown and spread the wings//of its kingdom that it has brought 10ʳ
cities, districts and provinces of France, Normandy, Britanny,
Gascony, Scotland, and Ireland under its empire, and deservingly,
since it is not only superior to its neighbors in arms and everything
necessary to human life, but also has made its mark for posterity in
the practice, by its men of wit in all ages, of letters and the liberal
arts. But then, as all human things//are subject to the variations of 10ᵛ
the skies it has had trouble also, so that it has often felt the great
buffetings of fortune. And finally, in certain periods it has lost not
only the freedom and domination of other lands, but has been
enslaved and subjected to enemies, losing more than once not only
its liberty but also its name.

First Brutus,* son of Silvius Ascanius the Trojan, with certain 'Britain' from
of his legions made himself master of the island without much 'Brutus'
trouble because of the rudeness of the//time, the islanders being 11ʳ
then inexperienced in warfare and unarmed, and he called it Britannia after his own name. His successors ruled securely 1040 years
until the time of the dictatorship of Julius Caesar, through whose
power the island came to be tributary of Rome and governed by
Roman praetors. In the time of Valentian the praetor was Aetius,*
in whose absence (he was in France aiding his own) the Britons
elected//for their king Vortigerius, a Briton himself and the first 11ᵛ
to be crowned with the crown of gold. Shortly afterwards, when he
was almost beaten down by the Scots and Picts, he called the Anglo-
Saxons to help, a most fierce and aggressive German people whose
leader and chief was Hengest, a man of the same nation who had Hengest, the
great skill in warfare, and who conquered not only the Scots and Saxon chief
Picts but also (through his own great mistakes) King Vortigerius
himself and in short transferred the sovereignty from the Britons// 12ʳ
to the Angles and called the country Anglia.

Alph: What perfidy of those people, who turned their arms against
their patrons and those who had called for their aid!

Steph: Such is the unbridled greed for rule that men spare neither
friends nor kinsmen, but follow the changing course of success.

Cadwallader, last king of the Britons

The English and Britons then struggled against each other until Cadwallader* the last king of British blood who, after losing many

12ᵛ battles, retired to the outlying parts of the island with ⫽the British remnant which then was called by the Angles Welsh, which meant in Saxon foreigners (they call the Italians, French and other foreigners Welsh and their country Wales).

The origin of the Welsh

Alph: This, then, is the origin of the name of the Welsh, and of their country?

Steph: Yes, it is.

Alph: But what then is the origin of the continental people called Britons?

13ʳ *Steph:* ⫽They come from the same people I have just spoken of who were forced to emigrate to Armorica because of the sterility and harshness of their land. There they begged for a place to settle, and to this day they have held it and continue to speak the ancient British language.

Thus the English held the kingdom alone and divided it into seven kingdoms, which gave the Danes, a most cruel people, courage to invade the kingdom anew and to occupy it. After 30 years of rule

13ᵛ they were driven out by the English, who ⫽were subjugated after 22 years by the Norman, whose successors ruled securely until the death of Edward VI. Since he had no bodily heir the kingdom passed to his sister Mary, who with the consent of the lords and in accordance with the procedures of the kingdom took for husband and king Philip, son of the Emperor Charles V, for the common good of the kingdom and for the good (as will afterwards be said) of all Christendom.

14ʳ I wished to list these alterations in brief ⫽so that you would be better able to understand what I have to say concerning specific details. And now accordingly let us set forth the causes and the more

Vortigerius, first king of the Britons

memorable events of those alterations. Leaving aside the ancient cases of Brutus and Caesar, we come to Vortigerius, first king of the Britons after he had thrown off the Roman yoke. Let us examine

The text

his rule. The text* says: 'When the British lords saw what a great storm was threatening from the Scots as well as from the Picts

14ᵛ (most cruel enemies) ⫽, they decided to choose a king and they decided it was fitting to confer the title upon Vortigerius because he was greatest among them in nobility, authority and virtue.' By this account, one can see that necessity was the principal reason that

The duties of the king

moved men in the beginning to choose a king, a man who would be of great authority and reputation among the people and who would in England as in all the other kingdoms of the world conserve unity, administer justice, reduce men to a civil life, bridle insatiable // appetites, and finally defend the people against the violence and force of enemies.

Alph: But tell me, sir, how were these people governed previously, when they had no king?

Steph: I have told you that they were governed by Roman praetors, by whom they were abandoned at that time, Aetius (for so // the Roman governor was called) having gone to Gaul to help the Romans. And therefore necessity constrained the Britons, surrounded by their enemies, to choose Vortigerius as king, on account of his great reputation.

Alph: If I thought my presumptuous questions would not bother you and draw you from the purpose, I would ask about other matters for my own satisfaction: but fearing that we should not be advancing our purpose, I shall keep silent.

Steph: Please do ask //, then, because my purpose is to answer your questions satisfactorily, if I can.

Alph: Tell me, then, how men gain repute, for you have said that Vortigerius was of great reputation.

Steph: They can gain repute* through the reputation of a father or of ancestors who were men of great authority and virtue: it is thought that sons should be similar to their fathers // as long as their actions do not show them to be otherwise, for people follow the common opinion and public repute of a man. Men can acquire reputation with the multitude by the company of wise men who have good habits, for there can be no better measure of a man than the company he keeps; and therefore one who keeps the company of the wise acquires a name for wisdom, // and one who keeps company with the virtuous is thought good, since it is impossible that he should not bear some resemblance to his companions.

There is another way to acquire reputation, which is by one's own virtue, and by giving evidence of it; and this way is best, for a reputation based solely upon ancestors is false: men slacken, and when the man in question has no virtues of his own, his reputation will gradually diminish. // The other kind, in which a man is known by his dealings with others, lasts for a while, but it is easy to erase. But this last kind, which comes from a man's own virtue, acquires at the outset such name and fame that many deeds to the contrary do not destroy it.

Alph: Which kind of reputation had Vortigerius?

95

15ʳ

15ᵛ

16ʳ

How men gain reputation

16ᵛ

17ʳ

Reputation by one's own virtue

17ᵛ

Steph: The first kind, which springs from ancestry only, for his
18ʳ own actions never brought him⫽reputation (because they did not
merit it) but instead brought infamy to himself and ruin to his
country, as was seen a short time after he began to govern the
kingdom.

Alph: Such disgraces come very often to men and kingdoms,
as they were destined, and they cannot be corrected by any reckon-
ing, and therefore in such cases princes who do their duty are blame-
less, for who can do anything contrary to the heavens?

18ᵛ   *Steph:* The stars have not such power over⫽our human affairs
The stars that prudence is not able to affect them: the stars only prompt
influence but men; they do not force them. So do not lay the blame upon the
do not force stars nor upon a man's geniture, but attribute it rather to lack of
prudence. Where* virtue is weak, fortune is powerful, and on the
Fortune is contrary, where there is prudence and good discipline, fortune
weak in the face counts for little. Thus whoever examines the government of
of prudence Vortigerius will see that there was no other cause of the loss and
19ʳ ruin of the British hegemony⫽than the lack of prudence he showed
in the beginning of his reign. Britain was being molested at the time
by the continuous incursions of the Scots and Picts, 'and now (as
the history says)* distrustful of his own forces, it came to his mind
to call for the Anglo-Saxons, illustrious in war, to come to the
Vortigerius' island to resist the fury of the enemy'. Note how this decision of
first mistake Vortigerius shows his lack of prudence: he summoned foreign⫽
19ᵛ mercenary troops and placed utter trust in them.

Alph: What else would you have had him do, being reduced to
this necessity?

Steph: I would want someone in like difficulty to have enough
Take the lesser prudence to take the lesser of two evils; but he took the worst of
of two evils several courses, calling upon such men for aid who were, when they
had conquered the countryside, more cruel and impious than the
Scots and Picts had ever been.

20ʳ   *Alph:* If he⫽had foreknown the outcome, he would also have
done otherwise, but in such cases who has enough prudence to
foretell the end?

Steph: Everyone who has experience, for it is difficult to find one
prince in a thousand who has profited in a bargain with mercenary
soldiers. The mistake of many princes is that they attribute so much
to their own wits that they ignore the counsel of all others. Such
princes do not know how to measure their own forces against
20ᵛ those of the enemy; they⫽presume to know everything and they

believe they are stronger than others, and thus when it comes to a
test they are beaten and conquered by pride and narrow-mindedness,
as was Lautrec* before the city of Naples. Such princes allow themselves to believe that they are what they in fact are not, and so they
start to engage in enterprises beyond their strength. They think
their wits are sharp, and in fact they are as foolish as crickets. Often
they become persuaded they have a great horse to ride, and it turns
out to be a //crayfish. They think they are making progress when
they are going backwards as did this King Vortigerius who was not
content to govern with the advice of wise and experienced men who
counselled rather to accept the conditions offered by the Scots than
to employ the cruel and impious Anglo-Saxons, since such a small
number of mercenaries could not beat the enemy, and a large
number could effect a coup d'état.

But his lords, //seeing that their counsel did not take effect,
tried a pleasant story to make him see his error and the harm and
ruin that would follow his plan and they said to him: 'Sir, there
was a horse* who used to graze in the countryside, and he had
become the boss of the whole pasture. It happened that a stag came
into that pasture completely famished and began to stuff himself
indiscreetly. The horse became angry with him and //chased him
away several times, but the stag, enticed by the sweetness of the
pasture, returned to it at once, and the horse, seeing that he could
never overcome him because of his hard horns and his great speed,
was quite desperate about it. One day a human being chanced
upon the scene, and the horse told him of his disgrace and asked
his help in taking revenge upon the stag. The man, who was cleverer
than the horse, answered him: "Sir beast, I cannot do this job alone,
//but if you would let me mount you and put a bridle in your
mouth I would accomplish your revenge like a good fellow."
The beast, to take revenge upon his fellow brute, let the man ride
him. The horse overcame the stag this way, but he remained
prisoner to the man, for he never again got the bridle out of
his mouth. So (said the barons), most illustrious king, if Your
Excellency will call a multitude //of Saxons into the kingdom, it is
possible that you would revenge the injuries done by the Scots and
Picts, but you and this our country would always be at their mercy.'
But all this could not dissuade him – he wished to have them.
Whereby it is seen that words spoken to an obstinate man are
thrown to the winds.

Alph: I do not see that he had any other remedy in such a

The cause of
the failure of
Lautrec

Narrow-
mindedness
21ʳ

Counsel of
the barons

21ᵛ

The fable of
the horse

22ʳ

22ᵛ

Application of
the fable
23ʳ

Words spoken
to the obstinate
are wasted

necessity. If I found myself in similar difficulties I think that I should
23ᵛ have done neither more nor //less than Vortigerius did.

Steph: So do all those who do not consider the little good and the
great danger that these mercenaries bring to every prince who uses
them, when the number is so great that he is forced to place all
his trust in them, for they are rapacious, ambitious, proud, and
disobedient.* Some are instructed (by long use) in military discipline,
24ʳ but few observe its rules. They have little fear of God and less //
respect for men unless the fear of punishment motivates them when
honesty cannot; and any affection* they have for him whom they
serve depends solely upon that little stipend he gives them, which is
never enough for them to live on, for they are prodigal of their
own means and greedy for the goods of others: nor is it enough for
them to be willing to die for it, or even put themselves in danger
24ᵛ unless compelled by great necessity or shame. //I have known certain
fellows of this kind who fought first in the pay of Francis* of France,
then went over to Henry of England, and at present are in the service
of Henry of France; all except those who were hung for their
merits or killed in private quarrels amongst themselves.

Alph: I do not think mercenary soldiers are obligated to anyone
25ʳ beyond the promised time: they can serve whomever they //wish,
provided that they inform their employer of their departure; and
as for not putting themselves in danger so rashly, that seems to me
to merit more praise than blame.

Steph: I shall not dispute here whether it is permissible for them to
leave their employer while a war lasts, but I will say that they can
make anything permissible when their force suffices: and whereas
in your opinion they merit praise for not putting themselves in
25ᵛ danger, in my opinion they merit //blame, for they are imitating
in some cases Fabius,* and in others Varro, but in reverse. They
imitate Fabius in that they do not willingly come to blows with
their enemies unless compelled, but heedlessly attack the poor
country people on their own side, robbing and despoiling without
fear or respect. Thus when they fight for the prince against his
enemies they are respectful and proceed like Fabius, but against
26ʳ their friends //and for their own profit they become fierce as lions.

A recent example affords evidence of this: in the time of Edward
VI, when the people of Cornwall and Norwich rebelled against the
nobility, certain Germans and Spaniards came to England as
mercenaries.* They were the first to turn their backs to the plebeians,
and their flight was the reason that the nobles were dishonored,

Marginal notes: Habits of mercenaries. They make everything permissible. Nature of mercenaries. Germans. The harm caused by mercenaries.

beaten⫽and taken prisoner by the peasants. Then, leaving the field, 26ᵛ
these valiant men without fear and without order went robbing
and despoiling the homes of the poor. However they had the kind
of end such soldiers deserve: few of them enjoyed their ill-gotten
booty, for afterwards most of them were killed by the peasants;
and to conclude, I have read of few princes who have made good
bargains with mercenaries, but I have seen many of them⫽who 27ʳ
have had very great losses, as, among others, the Venetians,* who
lost in one day all that they had gained in many centuries. There
are countless other examples in the histories which demonstrate
the great dangers which foreign arms bring to those they serve.
When the war with Rome had ended, the Carthaginians were Perils of the
overwhelmed by their mercenaries even though those troops had Carthaginians
been under the command of their own citizens. What⫽reduced 27ᵛ
Greece to servitude but the mercenaries brought from Turkey by The fall of
the Emperor of Constantinople? The Milanese hired Sforza against Greece due to
mercenaries
the Venetians and when he had overcome the enemy he joined with Milan lost her
them to overwhelm his patrons, which he succeeded in doing. liberty because
of mercenaries
As mercenaries were the cause of the ruin of many other states, Foreign soldiers
so they were of the overthrow of the British state, since after were disastrous
for the Britons
Vortigerius⫽gained victory over the Scots and Picts with Saxon 28ʳ
assistance, in order not to seem ungrateful* he gave them a province Lack of
in his kingdom to live in, and gave them many other honors, prudence of
Vortigerius
which he ought not to have done. By this time, Hengest, the Saxon
chief, had come to understand Vortigerius' character and knew that
the king relied completely upon his power and that of his Saxons,
and he devised a plan for taking possession of the whole country. Hengest's
cleverness
He persuaded Vortigerius that more Saxons were needed⫽to 28ᵛ
finish the job, and he brought in a great number including his
daughter who was extremely beautiful. The king fell blindly in Vortigerius
love with her and married her, and as soon as she became queen in love
she preferred the English to the honors and offices of the kingdom. Alienation of
the barons
This alienated the barons of the kingdom from Vortigerius, and from Vortigerius
his name from that time forward⫽began to be hated by all. 29ʳ
Alph: The proverb* says when God wishes to punish a man he Proverb
first makes him lose his mind and when he wants to punish a
people, he sends them such a king; for he who considers how human
affairs go will see that some things are ordered by the heavens in
such a way that they cannot be remedied: Fortune blinds men so
that they are not equal to the task of withstanding its force, and⫽ 29ᵛ
Vortigerius would seem to have been thus blinded in this case.

Steph: It is quite true that when Fortune wants to bring great things to pass she picks a man prudent enough to recognize the opportunities she offers him, and conversely, when she wishes to bring ruin to a city or to a kingdom she gives it a ruler blinded by his appetites who will assist calamity as Vortigerius did. Not⫽ content with the mistake he made in calling in these cruel people, he also gave them a place to live, married one of them and allowed them to share in the honors and the secrets of the kingdom. And since they were treated so well, a multitude came over to Britain in a short time.

Alph: One would think that these Saxons came to Britain not so much on account of its convenience as on account of the inconvenience and barrenness of their own country (otherwise⫽they would not have left a certain place for an uncertain) and that they sought new homes and more fertile soil yielding more abundant crops because they were conpelled by the need to make a living.

Steph: There are various opinions as to why these people came to Britain. Some* affirm that the Saxons came by chance, and were not summoned, for there was an ancient custom among those peoples of Germany who lived⫽in cold and sterile places that when a population increased to such an extent that the land could not sustain them the most active and warlike would leave to look for new homes and habitations, and they say that in this way the Saxons first came to Britain in the pay of Vortigerius. But whatever the reason for their coming this is certain: that the country they left is very sterile, as the etymology of the⫽place shows: Saxony means full of rocks, and therefore we may conclude that they were oppressed by the sterility of the land or by some other great necessity. The great, even excessive valor of these people confirms this conjecture, for of all the things that move men to take up arms, necessity has the greatest power, and that war is most dangerous of all which is caused by necessity.

Alph: ⫽It seems to me that whether men take up arms because of a prince's command, or because compelled by famine or war, they do so in all cases because of necessity: it is a necessity that the prince's will be obeyed in such cases.

Steph: Nonetheless a prince's command has less effect on the hearts of a multitude than the other necessities you mention because most wars are caused by princes and the honor and the profit⫽of the victory are theirs alone, but the suffering which comes from famine, plague or from a war in which people are driven from their land touches everyone, and thus you can see that wars* made among Wars of
ambition princes do not come of necessity, but rather from the ambition of the prince who wishes to increase his empire or gain fame for himself like Alexander and Julius Caesar. Other wars are begun // to revenge injuries or to regain cities or territories unjustly held, like the one at present between the Emperor Charles and Henry of France. There are others who are moved to take arms by the richness of the land upon which they wage war, like the Goths* and Vandals, who heard that Italy had sweet wines, savory fruits, beautiful women, little cold weather, temperate warm weather, and undertook to conquer it, not provoked by insult // or desire of revenge upon their enemies, but because they wanted to live a pleasant and luxurious life. Other wars are caused by avarice. The Romans and Carthaginians were friendly for a long time, but when the rumor spread that there were great gold mines* in Spain, the Romans wanted to take possession of it, and thereby great discord arose, and these two great republics each brought destruction upon itself by trying to conquer the other.

Wars of ambition

Wars to revenge injuries

33ʳ

33ᵛ

Wars for avarice

//This kind of war* is dangerous, as all wars are, but not in all are the inhabitants driven out, but rather the victor is satisfied with the obedience and tribute of the people, and most of the time lets them live by their laws, and always leaves them their houses and property. But there is another kind of war, in which a whole people leaves a place with all its goods, constrained by famine or the sterility of the land or war, and goes in search of a new // place to live, not for dominion and tribute merely, as in those wars mentioned above, but to take full possession and to drive the former inhabitants out.

34ʳ

34ᵛ

Wars of necessity

Alph: This kind of war is terrifying.

Steph: Paul the Deacon speaks of the dangers of such a war when he says that the Romans fought all others for domination alone, but they fought the Gauls and peoples like them for their very lives, and for the safety of all. // When a prince assaults a province, it suffices for him to eliminate the rulers, but whole peoples have to eliminate everyone, so that they can live on what the others used to live on.

35ʳ

Terrifying wars

Rome was first taken by such people – the Gauls, who had taken Lombardy and established themselves there. And later Rome was taken, occupied, and its empire destroyed by the Goths and Vandals.

Rome sacked

Alph: When a people occupy a territory at the first impetus, // as the Gauls did in Lombardy, they must come in very great numbers.

35ᵛ

115

Steph: In most cases in which people set out in search of new homes the number is great, and aside from the number their valor is always

Necessity makes men fearless

great. When people face necessity, when they have no houses to lie down in, no bread to keep them alive, when they lack the other

36ʳ

necessities, they become giants and think little of their lives,⫽ and thus they always win unless opposed by an exceptionally powerful force.

It often happens that men who act from such necessity have gained other territories and have driven out the former inhabitants, even though they could not defend their own. Such were the

The Moors

Moors,* a Syrian people. When they heard that the Hebrews were advancing upon them, they decided they could not resist them, thinking it better to save themselves and lose their country than to

36ᵛ

try to save it and lose their lives as well,⫽and they left with their families and went to Africa where they drove the inhabitants out and called the region Maurusia, after their own name. Then Moses,

How countries lose their names

leader of the Jews, finding the Moors gone, took the territory and called it Judea after the name of the people he governed. From these examples one can conclude that the number of those who abandon

37ʳ

their land because of famine or pestilence or war is always⫽great because the necessity touches everyone generally, and in that case when they invade a territory they kill its inhabitants at the first rush, take their goods, make everything over, and change the name

Moses called Maurusia Judea

of the territory as Moses did, and as the Franks did in Lombardy which was called Cisalpine Gaul. Hungary was called Pannonia, Transalpine Gaul is today called France from the Franks, and Slavonia was formerly called Illyria.

37ᵛ

But when the number that⫽leaves a territory is not great enough to employ such violence on the first thrust, they must use cunning to occupy some site and maintain themselves by means of friendship

The prudence of Hengest

and confederation as did our Hengest, leader of the Saxons, for he first fortified the district of Canterbury, given him to settle in by King Vortigerius. Then he made a close alliance with the king, giving him his daughter for wife and queen and during this time

38ʳ

he never⫽ceased bringing Saxons daily into the island. So as not to arouse the suspicion of the Britons he had them arrive at various ports rather than all at the same time and place, and soon their numbers compared favorably with those of the king's forces.

Hengest as enemy

Then, once he heard the murmurs of the lords against Vortigerius, he suddenly made peace with the Scots and Picts, at that time enemies of the Britons, and revealed openly that he too was an enemy.⫽

38ᵛ

He then beat the British in so many battles that they dared no longer show themselves. Nor did he omit any kind of cruelty or tyranny that was ever used by Nero or Domitian, killing the wretched Britons without pity, compassion or respect of age or sex, enjoying and disposing of their goods, houses and possessions according to his will and pleasure; and he divided the kingdom into seven kingdoms, and called it England.

By // similar means of friendship, the Trojans occupied one part of Latium, and also the Britons, when they were driven out, maintained the territory conceded to them on the Armorican shore; so you see that whether the number is small or great, the danger is always great as you have heard in this account of the calamitous end of the Britons: however small at first the number of these people who came out of Saxony, nonetheless the danger was no less great to the Britons than the great // number of Franks were to the Lombards, because in both cases the outcome was the same. The difference is that a multitude occupies the territory which they invade at once, and those others who are inferior in numbers seek by cunning and passage of time to bring to pass that which cannot be done by open force at the first rush.

Alph: In that case it seems to me that you would conclude that a prince ought to trust neither the one nor the other, because // they seek their own interests rather than those of him they serve. Having now spoken of the prudence of Hengest who from a private man made himself a prince and left such a kingdom to his own, would you now also explain the principal cause of the fall of Vortigerius from prince to private person and that of the enslavement of his once free country?

Steph: You can judge the causes of both of these events for yourself: nonetheless to satisfy you in all // that I can, I shall examine his rule in greater detail, so that, learning by his errors, his posterity can avoid the like. I say then that Vortigerius made, among many others, three principal errors the least of which is sufficient to lose any new prince his state.

Alph: This is what I eagerly wish to know.

Steph: First I shall speak of those errors Vortigerius committed in his rule, and then // I shall speak generally of all the qualities harmful or helpful to a prince in the keeping or losing of his state. The principal error was not to have trained his people in military discipline. Another was making himself a column of foreigners, malignant men, polluted with every sort of vice, then defying the

117

ancient laws of the kingdom in admitting the Saxons to his counsel
and to the highest honors of the kingdom.

41ᵛ Whoever considers these errors well⫽will see that every one of
them made him despised and then hated by most of his subjects,

He who relies on others is weak and that every course of action that produces that kind of effect
will have the same result as his errors. And as for his subjects lacking
their own arms,* I affirm that no kingdom or principality that
has no strength to defend it in time of necessity is secure, but utterly
subject to the blows of fortune. The opinion of wise men has been
that there is nothing so weak and infirm as a principality founded

42ʳ on⫽the arms of another. Therefore* a prince must have particular

Military science is necessary for a prince care to train the more apt and inclined of his subjects in military
discipline, which is a peerless science for making a prince loved
and honored by his own people and feared by his enemies. This

Hengest's ability science not only makes those who are born princes secure in their
rule, but often elevates men of lowest fortune to such a station as

42ᵛ Agathocles* and Hengest and many others.⫽And the reverse is
seen when princes have a good time and concern themselves with
luxurious living rather than with military matters: they become
despised by their enemies and hated by their own subjects, like

Edward II and John Edward II and John of England, who were both deprived of their
state (as unworthy of such honor) and later of their lives because
of their laziness.

43ʳ *Alph:* I praise greatly those princes who value military matters,⫽
for nothing is more necessary to a ruler than that. Therefore, the
prince* should not leave off thinking of the practice of war in peacetime, which he can easily do by reading histories and taking note in
them of the deeds of famous and excellent men, examining the
reasons for the victories of some and the defeats of others, in order

Hunting is an image of war to be able to follow the one and avoid the other, and he ought to
include frequent hunting among his physical exercises. Hunting

43ᵛ is the⫽living image of war, since through it a prince will become
acquainted with the nature of the mountains and valleys and the
location of the rivers and swamps, and he will accustom his body to
many discomforts through this pleasant exercise, so that when it
comes time to go on campaign, he will be able to endure without
any discomfort: the prince who accustoms himself to such exercise
in peacetime will find himself well prepared to avoid and with-

44ʳ stand⫽the barbs of war when the times change.

But as for training a whole people in the practice of warfare, I
judge it to be a most dangerous thing, for the nature of a people is

licentious, bold, desirous of change, rebellious, soft, and particularly so, begging your pardon, are the English people as history shows, for whoever reads the lives of the kings beginning with William the Norman down to Edward VI will see that some //were deposed and others killed in popular revolts and conspiracies, and that there are very few or none who have reigned entirely without such revolts. Consequently, if these people had combined the art of war with their arrogant, contemptuous and weak-willed nature, they would have become so insolent and disobedient to their prince that they would have been intolerable to everyone.

44^v

Steph: I have never seen that knowledge was the cause of any evil, but always ignorance: the lack of //prudence of leaders has caused the ruin of many cities and countries, and the death of countless people, as the present example of Vortigerius teaches us, and conversely it appears that the Romans and Alexander the Great, who had their people instructed in the discipline of war, accomplished great things.

Ignorance, not knowledge, is the cause of evil

45^r

The ignorance of Vortigerius

Alph: Now we are not dealing with the same case when we discuss Alexander and the Romans along with Vortigerius, because for the former, who sought to conquer the whole world //by arms, it was necessary to discipline their people so that if they lost one battle they would have troops disciplined to regroup immediately; but for Vortigerius and for other Christian princes, who ought to wage limited wars to secure lasting peace and should not seek to overturn other states or conquer the world but rather to defend their own people and govern them in peace, it suffices that only part be disciplined, and only so many as will yield //a suitable army which can stand up to the enemy in the field; and when necessity demands more, in my opinion it is more advantageous to engage mercenaries (in moderate numbers) than to train one's own. For when the war is finished, the mercenaries want to be paid according to their deserts and set at liberty, and then there is no longer any danger from them; but once your people are armed and trained, //they will always retain the bluster of a soldier, and most of them will never return to cultivating the land nor to their former customary occupations. Some will become highway robbers, others will pillage homes. For peasants are used to the tiring work of agriculture in winter, summer, rain, snow, hail, wind and sun, breaking the earth //with plow or hoe, turning up thorns, casting rocks and thousands of other arduous tasks. They work continually and never get tired, nor does it seem like work to them because

45^v

Christians should make war to have peace

46^r

When a war is over, mercenaries want to be set at liberty

46^v

47^r

they think there is no other world, they have not experienced other

Refinements of the camp pleasures: but once they find out about some of those refinements customary in today's corrupt armies, they will accept any hardship

47^v rather than return to their//old trades, and because of all the fancies that their heads have been filled with they will stir up fresh sedition, so that the prince will be forced to take orders from them, as several kings of this kingdom and many Roman emperors had to take orders from their soldiers, who would take orders from no one.

Therefore princes, fearing the nature of this people, have made

48^r many good laws to restrain them, totally forbidding them// acquaintance with military discipline, not allowing anyone to give

Laws of England instruction or print books on the subject of the use of the harquebus or crossbow, setting an eight o'clock curfew, prohibiting public games or sports in order to limit public assembly, and permitting informers to report to the magistrates any assembly of twelve or

48^v more persons in a suspected house or other location,//authorizing the magistrates to imprison those so accused without additional evidence, and many other similarly harsh laws. Such wise princes who knew how dangerous it was to put a sword in the hands of those

Refutation of the preceding opinion who did not know how to use it wished to counter bad character in good time with good laws, for they saw that such discipline would

49^r be more dangerous and harmful in//peacetime than useful in war.

Steph: You seem to be like those who will not pick roses for the thorns; but men must have enough prudence to take the sweetness

The nature of the frog of the rose and shun the sharpness of the thorns. The bee takes honey from a flower and the frog poison. The feverish man tastes nothing but bitterness, and the healthy man takes savory nourishment from

49^v the same food. The fault is not in the flower that//yields honey to the one and poison to the other, nor in the food that seems bitter to one and tasty to another, but in the different natures of the bee and the frog and of the different humors of the healthy man and the sick. I say, therefore, that the discipline and knowledge of military science never of itself entails evil. Though it be often used ill by

Everything can be misused ignorant and wicked men the evil ought not to be therefore imputed to the science (which in itself is good) but to the wicked

50^r who misuse it, for there is nothing in the world that cannot be// misused. Therefore the arguments you adduce do not prove that acquaintance with this art is unsuitable for the general populace even though they may sometimes use it wrongly. The blame for this belongs to the princes, who ought to teach the people the right use of the science.

I shall offer a recent example of this, from among those same people from whom you have taken your authority. When Henry VIII came to the throne he found the kingdom without trained soldiers and without an experienced commander (because his father had gone thirty years // without a war). Nonetheless he trained them so well and quickly that with one force he attacked* the most powerful kingdom of France, full of soldiers and officers, and with the other force, composed entirely of his own men, he confronted the whole force of Scotland and achieved glorious victory in both engagements, as much by the conquest of Thérouanne and Tournai and the ignominious flight of the French as by the rout of the Scots // and the miserable death* of James their king. And mark well, Henry at that time armed eighty-five thousand of his own subjects and when the war was over they returned to cultivating the land and to their usual activities without tumult or the thought of it, which came of the prudence of the prince, who knew how to train them and make use of them in war and how to use his authority to order them back to their trades in peacetime. Therefore a prince // ought not to reject a present benefit, honorable and safe, for fear of harm that might happen later. I mean that he should not fear to train his subjects and make use of them in war for fear that they will rebel afterwards in peace; and if Vortigerius had had as much prudence in this matter as Henry, he would have kept his country on its feet and also terrified his enemies.

But you have not guessed badly as to the nature of the // English, for truly in past times they were restless, mutable, desirous of change and soft, and all of this resulted from the factions and discord amongst the nobility, whence they took such license that for many years afterward it was difficult to hold them in obedience. Nevertheless if you carefully considered the tumults and conspiracies you have already mentioned, you would see that the people have not always been the cause: rather most of the time it has been the princes of the // realm who have incited popular revolt the more easily to achieve their aims, as Richard Duke of York did formerly, and I wish to relate to you how he went about it, so that you can understand more fully the origin of these insurrections and conspiracies against the kings of England and justly lay the blame where it belongs.

Duke Richard, aspiring to the crown, thought to challenge the power of the king by open force, // but feared the people because he did not know how much they respected his authority, and he

The prudence of Henry

50^v

Henry's glorious victories

51^r

The death of James, King of Scots

51^v

52^r

The license of the people comes from the factions of the nobles

52^v

The cleverness of the Duke of York

53^r

found this means of testing their spirit, without anyone suspecting what he intended to do: In the city* of York was a hospital for the maintenance of the sick, the poor, and the travellers of the kingdom, for the support of which, by ancient custom, everyone in the region

53ᵛ gave yearly a certain measure of grain and a certain ⁄⁄ sum of money, according to their ability; and constables were in charge of collect-

It is easy to persuade people of their own interests

ing the grain and the money. The duke, who knew how easy it was to persuade people to take up an enterprise to their own advantage, caused anonymous information to be spread and published through-out the region that the grain and the money given for the poor

54ʳ were devoured ⁄⁄ by the rich administrators of that hospital, and that the poor did not enjoy the least part of them, dissuading the people by such arguments from paying the grain and money any

The rash judgment of the people

longer.

The people then discussing these things amongst themselves and deciding what they should do determined by common agreement stoutly to deny such payment when it was demanded, because it

54ᵛ seemed in their interest to do so. And they ⁄⁄ did deny it. The administrators complained to the king's council of the people's disobedience to the ancient customs and laws of the kingdom. Henry VI (in whose reign this revolt occurred) was observant of the customs of the realm and ordered that those who would not pay the debt be imprisoned and punished as disobedient rebels. When the

55ʳ people heard of this decision they rose at once, ten* ⁄⁄ thousand strong, and marched against York to take revenge on those adminis-trators who had obtained such a judgment against them. But the townspeople, hearing the approach of the popular movement, closed the gates and defended the walls. The king understood by this the seriousness of the situation and ordered Duke Richard, who was the lord of the region, to pacify the people in any effective way

55ᵛ and as quickly as he could. He, so as not to be suspected ⁄⁄ of favoring the people's party, took their leader and cut off his head, and commanded the others publicly to return to their homes. But secretly by letters and rumors he got them to go to London to revenge themselves upon the ministers of the king – and they went. The king, judging it better to prevent the fury of the people before they got to London, assembled twelve thousand men and set out to

56ʳ confront them ⁄⁄ that way. Duke Richard was still in York, and knowing that the people persevered in their fury, he followed with an army, apparently in order to help the king against the rebels. But when he arrived near the king's camp, he measured his force against that of the king, judged that the time was come to reveal that which he had long concealed, suddenly joined with the popular army, gave the sign⫽to attack the royal army, smashed it and captured all the nobility of whom he decapitated several who were his enemies, and even took Henry with him to London as a prisoner. And this is nonetheless called the revolt of the people of York.

56ᵛ

King Henry a prisoner

Similarly the barons stirred up fifty thousand men against Henry VIII when he began to usurp church property, and that was called the revolt* of the people of Lincoln; and likewise whoever considers history⫽will see that almost all the revolts in England were begun by barons and princes of the realm, either against the king for his bad government, or to revenge the private enmities, injuries and animosities which often arise among them and nonetheless the people get the blame as authors of such evils.

The barons stirred up the people against Henry

57ʳ

The people blamed wrongly

Alph: And not without cause, for many revolts have occurred in this realm caused only by the people, and under solely popular leadership,⫽like those of the people of Canterbury, Jack Cade* being leader of one and Jack Straw of another; and like the recent revolt of the people of Norwich which was led by one called Kett. Of these three men (who were of the lowest class), the first two sacked the city of London; Straw cut off the heads of some of the king's counselors, and held the king himself prisoner in the Tower of London; and the third captured the greater part of the⫽nobility of the region and held them in prison, making them account for themselves to the basest people and to make restitution to those whom they had offended. The case is so clear that it cannot be excused.

57ᵛ

London sacked

58ʳ

Revolts against the nobility

Steph: I do not seek to excuse them for these evil deeds nor for anything else. In fact, I revile and condemn them. However when you examine the original cause of the aforementioned revolts you will not assign the guilt solely to the people, but part to the nobles and part to the⫽king himself, as I will clearly show you. In the thirtieth year of the reign of Henry VI, King of England, the factions of the two greatest families, those of Lancaster and York, began to build large forces with King Henry as head of the Lancastrians, and Richard Duke of York of their opponents. The duke, finding no better way to achieve his aims, stirred up popular revolts in various regions⫽against the ministers of the king, so that under color of castigating the evil ministers he could more easily deprive Henry of the kingdom, which he later accomplished. These factions produced such license in the people that for many years their only

58ᵛ

The factions of England

59ʳ

How the license of the people began

concern was novelty and change of princes. Now the House of Lancaster prevailed, now that of York, according to who was 59ᵛ favored or disfavored by the people, as is seen by the // great calamity of the said Henry and by his changing fortunes. First he came under the power of the duke his enemy, then he was set free by the people and when he sought revenge his army was smashed in the field and The wretched he had to fly to Scotland; he returned thence in a few days to regain fortune of his kingdom and was again taken, imprisoned and deprived of the crown, then a second time set free and restored to rule, and then the 60ʳ third time he was taken and killed // in prison.

The cause of In this calamitous time when laws were trampled underfoot, revolts when arms rang out to heaven, and when every wicked man was Cade the permitted to effect his wickedness, this criminal Cade you men- criminal tioned made himself the leader of such as he was himself and left Revolts caused undone no villainy human impiety or wickedness could devise. by the king The cause of the other revolt* of which Straw was leader had its 60ᵛ origin in the extraordinary taxes of Richard II, who demanded // of everyone in the realm, even to the poorest, a piece of silver known as a stater, and from the rich a greater sum according to their means. The hardship of this created such hatred among the people against the king that they said openly that if they allowed the shepherd to shear the sheep so many times a year he would shortly skin them too; and therefore they decided not to pay such an extra- ordinary tax and made this Straw their leader.

61ʳ The other revolt of the people of Norwich // and Cornwall arose because of the insolence of certain nobles, who because of the tender age of King Edward managed everything not according to Revolts caused the rules of justice but according to their appetite and advantage. by the Therefore, by the secret judgment of God, their insolence, which had insolence of the nobles already begun to be insupportable to all good men, came to be What makes a punished by the hands of villains. people take up arms You see now, Signor Alphonso, how you have blamed the people wrongly, and have imputed to them the errors and vices of others, 61ᵛ for the nobles' involvement // in faction gives the people, who are The defects of by nature desirous of change, courage to do the same. This is one the people come from the cause of popular uprisings which also arise when a prince oppresses princes* the subjects with extraordinary taxes and tributes, when he is known to be monstrous, cruel, without pity, and when he does not listen to the complaints of the poor and give them justice. Such enormous vices generate grumbling, grumbling scorn, scorn hatred, and hatred, 62ʳ as is well known, // seeks revenge; so that generally the faults of the people are caused by the negligence, lack of prudence, or by the bad example of the prince who governs them, wherefore it is commonly said: as the prince so the people. Thus it is easy to see that the people do not revolt without cause.

Alph: Then you consider it permissible for the people to rise against their prince for any cause at all?

Steph: I do not think it is permissible, rather I affirm it to be damnable, //for he is the minister of God ordained to such office 63ʳ to govern the people committed to his charge not by chance, as others affirm, but by the providence of God; and therefore nothing is dearer to God than the prince, and this is shown by the extraordinary gifts given them. Have you ever read that God has added years or days to anyone's life except a king's? Take the example of Hezekiah:* he ought to have died of natural causes, //but God 63ʳ prolonged his life fifteen years beyond its natural span. Thus you may see that the Omnipotent, in token of their preeminence on earth, assigns kings an archangel, a prince of the angels, to guard them until death. Therefore the great King Solomon* said that the hearts of princes are in the hands of God, implying that God has a greater concern for them than for other, private men, and thus all ought to honor and obey them //for their sacred ministry, which is 63ᵛ also confirmed by the words of King David* when it was told him that his enemy King Saul was sleeping and he could kill him without danger. 'God forbid', he replied, 'that I should lay violent hands upon the Lord's annointed.'

These examples show that God does not want violence done to his ministers, for as Paul said those who resist them disobey also the commandment of God. (And //in another passage* in Ephesians he 64ʳ said: 'Obey princes in fear, not as you would please men merely but as you should please God, knowing that each will receive mercy for the good he has done whether he is a slave or free.')

If the prince performs his duty to his subjects they have continual cause to thank God for his singular gift, which is the most excellent favor God can give a people. If he does otherwise //we have to 64ᵛ realize that he is ordained for the sins of the people, for many passages of Holy Scripture show that such is the punishment God sends a people (and truly He cannot send one greater). Therefore we ought to endure it all with humility and patience, and as Saint Augustine says, reverently kiss the rod that beats us because it comes from above, which means nothing else but that however princes stray from a true course, led either by evil //advice or by their 65ʳ

Margin notes:
It is not permissible to take arms against princes for any reason

Hezekiah

Solomon

David

Paul

St. Augustine

125

It is not permissible for Christians to take arms against their prince, even if he is a tyrant
65ᵛ

The prince ought to be like a square
66ʳ

66ᵛ

Evil counselors are dangerous
67ʳ

Proverb

History
67ᵛ

appetites, nonetheless the people are always obliged to obey them and not seek to take the sword from the hand of him to whom God has given it, but to leave vengeance to Him (for ' "vengeance is mine",* says the Lord'). Thus it is never permissible in any circumstances to take arms against a prince, even if he is a tyrant. But because men often stumble, through the weakness of our nature, and do many ⫽ illicit and prohibited things on the impulse of the occasion, it is good also that princes who wish to take precautions against their people attend carefully to their office, so as not to give them occasion to rebel, but rather set a virtuous example themselves like a bright light showing a path through the darkness to all. For the prince ought to be like the square of the architect which is not only right and just itself but also makes everything ⫽ it is applied to right as well. He ought to take particular care to keep his barons united and to administer justice equally without being noted for favoritism because that generates envy of the favored and envy generates enmity and hatred. But now we have somewhat digressed from our intention, to show that the original cause of the revolts that have taken place in England came from the nobles and not from the plebs and that ⫽ when revolts are fully popular they pose little threat.

Let us turn therefore to examine the other errors made by Vortigerius in making friends and relations of evil and wicked men and defying good laws long observed. Every vice, however small, seems great in a king. Nevertheless there is none more harmful than the company and counsel of men corrupt in conscience or behavior, for between ⫽ the good man and the bad there is such difference as between fire and water. If in counsel, studies, and all other activities the one tends to the common good, the other looks only to his private interest and that is the goal he aims for. Histories confirm that he who has a cripple for a companion cannot go straight. He who is a friend to the wicked is necessarily an enemy to the good. Now when good men have their prince for an enemy they will prepare ⫽ to defend themselves and keep at the ready, simply in order not to be taken like lazy fish. And not only will they defend themselves, but they will also take the offensive against a prince who favors the malignant and wicked and scorns the virtuous and honest.

Of such perverse nature was Edward* II of England that he preferred the company of the malignant and vicious to that of all others, for which he was first hated by his barons and then deposed

and //finally killed. Among others there was in his affection one
called Peter Gaveston, a most defiled man whose counsel he heeded
above all others and who, when the king had given him the governance of the kingdom, ruled everything not according to justice and
laws but according to his appetite and will. The barons seeing justice
corrupted, laws twisted, the nobility dishonored and the many other
disorders in the kingdom which came to pass daily because of his
bad counsel, did not //blame it so much on the king as on the wicked
men by whose counsel he was led, and hoped that he could be
recalled to his duty once the evil counselors were dismissed; and
therefore they decided to accomplish now by force that which at
other times they had attempted in vain by kind words and on the
sudden they attacked Gaveston, whom they killed as he fled.

Notwithstanding his absence and death it was not possible to
uproot those evil growths Gaveston had seeded //in Edward's
mind while he lived, for the king immediately sought to furnish
himself with others like him, and found the two Spensers, father and
son, perfect flatterers and corruptors of all good wits. He accepted
them into his family, made them counselors, and after a few days
gave them control over everything just as he had given it to his
dear Gaveston before. And in this way he enjoyed himself with his
Spensers, living a lascivious and luxurious //life without a care or
thought of the good governance of his subjects or of defending the
realm against the Scots with whom he was then at war to his
disadvantage, so that by his ill government the whole kingdom
suffered great losses daily, and the name of the English came to be
scorned among all foreigners; whence the great lords of the realm,
who held the honor and safety of their country dear, recognizing
the source of such great ruin and such //dishonor and infamy, but
not yet despairing of the goodness of the king (for he was young)
once his counselors were removed, decided again to purge the court
of bad counselors and to put better in their place. Of this endeavor
Thomas Earl of Lancaster and Humphrey Earl of Hereford were the
leaders, who said in the presence of the king that it was necessary
for the common good and advantage of the fatherland to get rid
of the counsel and //company of the two Spensers whose counsel
had brought such dishonor and ruin to the kingdom, for it could not
be safe while such men governed it. Thus they prayed him to take
their request in good part since it was love for their country and
concern for its safety rather than malice, envy or private injury that
moved them to speak.

The king, seeing his barons had conspired against him and that
they were ready to take//arms, promised to do what they had
requested; and, having summoned his council, sent the two Spensers
into exile with several others and attainted their property. But he
secretly ordered them not to leave the kingdom, but to hide some-
where for a time. By this means he assembled an army pretending
to go against the Scots, but suddenly turned it against the Earls of
Lancaster and Hereford and took them, along with many other
conspirators, had them all//killed, recalled his Spensers, and
advanced them to greater honors than ever before. This contemptuous behavior made the nobles and the people hate him so that
conspiring together they decided to depose him as useless to the
country and an enemy to good men and therefore unworthy of
such dignity, and assembling an army they marched on London.
But the king, seeing he could not resist the power of his barons,
took flight to Wales where he was routed from Bridgnorth Castle//
and imprisoned, and his two dear Spensers (because of all that had
happened) were drawn through the city at the tail of horses in his
presence and were then torn in a thousand pieces by the peasants.
Edward renounced the royal dignity and all the interest he had or
pretended to have in the kingdom in the hope that his life would be
spared, but all in vain, for he was then killed in prison.

This example should be a lesson//to princes not to pile injustices
one on top of the other and not to offend their barons with daily
innovation as Edward did, who not only did not punish evil men
who were condemned by law at the complaint of the nobles, but in
scorn of the good rewarded them and to these injuries added
vituperation, reproving the barons for baseness, which so moved
their spirits to revenge that they did not think of their property,
wives or//children, but held them and life itself in little regard,
wishing rather to die than to leave such injuries unavenged.

Alph: Doubtless there is nothing that kindles the heart to revenge
more than opprobrium, which apart from being indecorous from
the mouth of a prince or other great person, is extremely harmful:
it makes his enemies more cautious,* and makes them study carefully every opportunity for attack that arises;//so that insults to
an enemy become weapons sharpened against oneself. I can recall
having read infinite examples of this in addition to the one of
Edward you have cited, and among the rest the notable one of the
people of Amyda, a city of Asia, which was for a long time besieged
by Cobades,* leader of the Persians. He had become weary of the

71^r

The king took
the leaders of
the conspiracy

71^v

The nobles
conspired
against the
king a second
time

72^r

Edward taken

The end of
evil counselors

Death of
Edward

72^v

73^r

Insults cause
hate

73^v

Amyda, city
of Asia

long siege, all but despaired of taking⫽the city, and broke camp 74ʳ
to leave. The people of the city, seeing this, all ran to the walls and
arrogantly heaped every kind of insult by word or sign upon him,
vituperating him and accusing him of baseness and cowardliness,
which so utterly enraged Cobades that he changed his plans and
returned to the siege. So great was his indignation at insult that in a
few days he took the city and in revenge killed them all.

Vituperation stirs revenge

Steph: How dangerous such opprobrium is⫽is shown by a 74ᵛ
recent example from the time of Edward VI. Although the king
had pardoned all those who had conspired against the nobility,
except for the leaders, the offenders were nevertheless beset by
vituperation and infamy, and on every whim that came into other
men's minds were called traitors and rebels. These reproofs so
entered their hearts that (despite their plebeian status) they chose
rather to die than to live in such⫽infamy, assembled a multitude 75ʳ
together, and decided to take revenge on those who had so insulted
them. But the king, hearing of the case and considering what a hard
thing it was to suffer such insults, not only did not punish them, but
made a law* that no one (on pain of death) could any longer accuse
them of such crimes, nor call them rebels, nor offend them with such
opprobrium: for it was truly insupportable, especially as it con-
tained so much⫽truth. The prudence of Edward VI in this case 75ᵛ
recalls the arrogance of Edward II who never ceased to add verbal
insult to the insult of bad government (great enough itself without
addition); and this had no small effect on the hearts of his people,
as his end clearly showed.

The law of Edward VI against opprobrium

The insults of Edward II

The same errors alienated the barons from Vortigerius also, for,
seeing that the king had married with the⫽Saxons, impious and 76ʳ
criminal people, and against the laws had exalted them to honors,
it became clear to them that there was no longer a place near him
for men of virtue and good will; so each made the best provisions
for himself that he could, expecting the imminent ruin of their
country, some in Scotland, others in France, and others in Denmark,
leaving Vortigerius alone, counseled by the Saxons who were his
enemies, though his mind was so blinded that he could not see it.⫽ 76ᵛ

The good are offended to see the wicked honored

This was the principal cause of the fall of the British dynasty and
the beginning of the English, and it happened because Vortigerius
had nullified the ancient laws in making such foreigners privy to the
secrets of the realm, for of all other things nothing generates greater
hate for the prince than defying* the ancient laws observed in any
kingdom. Empedocles said that it was a like reason that first moved

Cause of the fall of Britain

Empedocles

129

77ʳ men to∥elect princes and make laws: none would be necessary if men were just and would render to each his own: but since they become rapacious, rebellious, cruel and unjust, laws were instituted to fill the deficiency in justice, so that the good would not be

Solon oppressed by the bad. For this reason Solon* said that men should fight no less for their laws than for their walls, since kingdoms and

77ᵛ principalities can∥survive without walls, but without laws they fall into ruin immediately; for laws were instituted for the health and life both of the prince and the people and when they are taken away

The laws mean not only do the subjects perform many unpunished outrages, but the
security for princes and magistrates also become tyrants; and so wise men set
prince and up laws to provide security for both princes and people. Therefore*
people I think there is no worse example in a kingdom than to make a law

78ʳ and not observe it, and so much the worse∥when it is not observed
To scorn the by him who made it. The example of James III King of Scots
law is hateful
to the people shows this, who with his nobles and commons ordered by law that
Scottish laws neither he nor any succeeding king could ever decide questions of making war or concluding peace, or indeed of marrying his children or setting taxes or tribute, without the consent of his barons. Nevertheless when James later saw that such a law was against his own

78ᵛ interest he was∥unwilling to observe it any longer, but instead governed everything according to his own lights, saying that he was king to give laws to all others, and not to take them from anyone. This bad example of the prince gave rise to such hatred among his barons that they immediately gathered an army, made his son their head (although against his will) and began to rage furiously against all those who took the king's side. Finally, when the king

79ʳ saw the great∥danger, he sent to his barons to talk peace, but they insisted upon his yielding royal authority as a precondition to any pact or agreement. But James judging that that was the worst that

James King of could happen decided first to try his fortune and fight them, and
Scotland killed so he was killed* among his own people.

John King of England, though he usurped the throne, would
John deposed have been tolerated if he had not violated the laws of the land, which
79ᵛ provoked the nobles together with the commons to drive him∥from the throne. Therefore princes should know* that they begin to lose their state at that hour when they begin to break the laws and change ancient customs and usages under which men have lived for a long time. And when they are deprived of their state, should they ever become so prudent as to know with what ease kingdoms are held by those who take wise counsel, their loss would become greater,

and they would condemn themselves to a greater punishment //
than they were condemned by others: for it is much easier to be
loved by the good than by the bad; better to obey the laws than
command them, since the one is full of danger, and the other is
safe.

80^r
It is easier to
be loved by the
good than by
the bad

In addition to scorn for the laws, greed for people's property
also gives rise commonly to hatred. This greed is mother of all
vices, and he who is possessed by it cannot stand long, for a kingdom
is like a natural // body in which the prince is the head: just as the
head ought to take only its proportional nourishment so that the
other members do not become anemic, nor give so much to one
member that the others cannot be nourished (as happens in the
dropsical), so the prince ought not to arrogate so much to himself,
nor give so much to his familiars that the others suffer, for just as
the body cannot live long in such an unregulated state, so such a
kingdom will not be able to stand long. Men // risk all hazards to
acquire property, and even more so to conserve what they acquire.
A man* easily forgets the injuries done to his father or his brother,
because they were not constantly necessary to him, but the need
of property comes every day and therefore every day he remembers
his seized goods, with mortal hate for him who took them, and
determines to take revenge whenever the occasion comes; and
therefore that prince who is avaricious by nature and rapacious of //
other people's property is never secure anywhere as the example
of King Rufus* of England shows: he was killed while hunting
amongst his nobles by an arrow shot by a base man who fled and got
away without being pursued by anyone. In fact he would have
been rewarded if he had been recognized, for when the people
heard of the king's death, they made great fires, rang bells throughout the land, and rejoiced at his // death in their fashion just as they
would have done at the coronation of another, thanking God who
had thus liberated the people and the kingdom from such a tyrant.
Such princes who for any reason are hated by their people are safe
neither in peacetime nor in war, for in peace their subjects conspire
against them in secret, and in war when their own force is not
sufficient they become open enemies and go over to the enemy.

To be greedy
for property
generates
hatred
The king is like
a natural body
80^v

John King of England, among his other // vices (he had many),
was avaricious and most rapacious for the people's property and
harassed them every day with new kinds of taxes, sparing neither
the religious orders nor anyone else, so that he came to be hated
by all. Some of the barons conspired against him, and seeing that

131

they could not overcome him, ran for help to Philip King of France,
asking Louis his son for assistance in driving John out, promising

83ʳ to make him king in his stead. When Louis came, all ran⫻to him, and
John, fleeing to the northern part of the kingdom for succor, was

The impiety poisoned in the monastery of Swineshead* by a monk who, thinking
of a monk to do something pleasing to God and to his land, drank also of the
King John wine mixed with poison so that the king would not suspect any evil,
poisoned
Richard II and so both fell to earth dead.
deprived of life   This avarice and nothing else divested Richard II of both his

83ᵛ kingdom and his life, for after the death of⫻Duke John of Lancaster
his brother, he seized his property, defrauding Henry his son without cause. This bad example of avarice caused his own people to
have a bad opinion of him, fearing that if they did not use force to
prevent it in time, the same thing would happen to their children
after their deaths: and therefore with Henry Duke of Lancaster

84ʳ as their leader, they plotted against him. ⫻Because of this he retired
to Flint Castle, abandoned by all his own, and was taken alone,
imprisoned, and after he had renounced the throne he was put
to death in prison. Such is the force of this vice in making a prince
hated by the masses. These then are the things which principally
give rise to general hate for a prince, and on account of which
princes often lose their state, as happened to Vortigerius with the
fall and destruction of the entire British dynasty.

84ᵛ   *Alph:* I⫻remember reading in histories that this kingdom was also
possessed by the Danes.
  Steph: Yes it is true, for knowing that the English had divided
the kingdom, and that they were also divided amongst themselves,
one making war on the other, the Danes made continual raids like
thieves, and then engaged themselves in the pay of the King of
Northumbria against the other English princes until they were
sufficiently versed in the secrets of the realm, and knew its great

85ʳ weakness⫻caused by the civil discords; whereupon they assaulted
first one then another until they had the whole which they possessed

The Danes for thirty years until the reign of their King Canute. He thought he
held sway in was safe there after so long and, not suspecting such a thing, was
England poisoned in Lambeth house* on the bank of the Thames opposite
Westminster, whence arose another alteration; for the English, re-
membering that in all the time they were governed by the Danes they

85ᵛ were without favor, ⫻regard or influence, but ill treated and scorned,
thought the time had now come to take full vengeance on such
ungrateful people and drive them out of the kingdom; and quickly

choosing King Alfred the son of Ethelred they immediately and
furiously turned on the Danes, killing them wherever they found
them scattered throughout the realm, without respect of age or
sex. Greater cruelty has never been seen: even //the English women
who were married to Danes conspired against their husbands and
killed them either in their beds with steel or elsewhere with poison.
So that of the many there had been, none remained alive except a
very few who escaped to the continent.

Alph: I do not marvel at all at the cruelty of the English when the
causes which moved them to it are considered, for it is an extreme
grief to men of any nation or province //to see other men, foreigners, possess those honors, offices and dignities which in past times
their fathers or predecessors enjoyed, and to see their own children
deprived of them without cause, as unworthy.

Steph: It is quite true, and reason supports them in such a case,
for in every age some of their predecessors, their ancestors long dead,
have lost life or property in the service of their country's honor,
advantage or interest, and reason //does not permit nor can the
nature of man patiently suffer unknown foreigners to enjoy the
fruits of other men's labor. In this matter King Stephen* of England
used discretion and considered the dangers which often befall those
princes who show themselves wanting in affection and favor towards
their subjects, for such lack of favor is a sure sign that the prince does
not love and trust them since he gives //honors and offices to foreigners. Stephen therefore used the counsel of Englishmen in all the
affairs that had to do with the governing of England, and preferred
only Englishmen to the offices and honors of the realm. Although
he had continually with him many honored persons both French
and Norman because he was Duke of Normandy, nonetheless he
did not prefer them to honors in England, judging Hannibal's
example relevant, who after the long //war with the Romans said
that it would be to the good of all that Romans govern Rome and
Carthaginians Carthage. So Stephen wanted Englishmen in
England and Normans in Normandy, and by this means there was a
continual fraternal love between the English and Normans, and he,
though he was French (the name of which is hated by the English),
ruled until his natural death. //

And the prince who does otherwise will find those dangers which
the aforesaid Canute found, unless he is continually in arms like the
Spaniard in Milan and Naples, and he will end as the Danes in England. After the Danes, the Normans, led by William, a spirited

Cruelty of the English 86ʳ

The courage of the women

86ᵛ

87ʳ

The prudence of Stephen

87ᵛ

88ʳ Saying of Hannibal

88ᵛ

133

and powerful man, seized their opportunity, conquered the king-
89ʳ dom, and sought to extinguish the name //of the English as the Danes
had tried to do but with a stronger hand.

Alph: What occasion was it that he took?

Steph: The discord that then was between King Harold and
Tostig* his brother. For although he had great valor and strength,
if he had not taken his opportunity he would never have shown
his virtue.

Alph: Those men are truly wise who recognize those opportunities.

89ᵛ *Steph:* So they are, and few men know this: the safest way is to //
encounter opportunity straight on for she is a changeable woman:
in front her head is full of hair, by which a man can easily hold her,
but behind she is bald. William of Normandy knew how to take
her in time, for finding the two brothers then divided and Harold
not yet secure in the kingdom it was easy to crush him, since nothing
is more advantageous to an enemy than the discord of his adversary,
90ʳ and nothing more harmful to those who //should be friends. For
so enemies gain the opportunity to attack and the possibility of
winning, so the aid and favor of disunity opens the way to the
enemy's good fortune and one's own ruin. Thus an enemy should
always foment disunity as did Philip* father of Alexander in Greece
among those republics where he caused such discords and seditions
and kept them so occupied with bloody wars against their own
90ᵛ people, always aiding //the weaker side, that finally he forced the
one and the other, the victorious and the conquered, to submit to
the hard slavery of his rule. The cause of this was that the Thebans
called him into Greece against the Athenians. The Thebans nursed
such hidden animosities that no citizen was able to tolerate the
greatness of another, and they preferred to choose Philip a
foreigner for their captain than any citizen, which was the cause of
91ʳ the ruin //of all Greece after. For after Philip had conquered the
other cities he turned against those which had made him captain
and, though he had achieved his victories with the help of their
forces, he occupied and sacked them all, sparing neither temples nor
those houses where he had been received with such honor and
courtesy, but after he had thus preyed on those he had led as well as
91ᵛ on those others against whom he was called and had sold all their
wives and children, //he returned to Macedonia.

Alph: Doubtless a prince cannot have better occasion to occupy
a city or a kingdom than to be called to the defense of one faction

Margin notes:
It is a great virtue to take the offered opportunity

William the Norman

Philip

The Thebans

The ingratitude of Philip

within it, or to take such a task upon himself during such discord. For so great is the force of discord among enemies who seek the destruction of one another that they do not think of the destruction that foreign armies bring. This discord made Philip great and destroyed⫽all Greece.

Discord destroyed Greece

92ʳ

Octavius Augustus, taking the occasion of the lascivious and sensual life of Mark Antony in Egypt with Cleopatra, gained victory and a prosperous reign. The discord between the Emperor* of Constantinople and certain princes of his realm favored by the despots of Serbia and Bulgaria was the cause of the greatness of the Ottoman dynasty and the expansion of the kingdom of the Turks. The Emperor called in 15,000 horse⫽against his enemies and with their aid he conquered the enemy, but gave occasion to Amir* their ruler to aspire to his throne, and to that of all Greece. After a short time there Amir knew the countryside well and marched against the princes with a great army under pretext of revenging the injuries done the emperor. He not only beat them in battle, but also took possession of part of the emperor's territory.⫽Not many years passed before his successors little by little made themselves masters of the whole, and today they have so enlarged their confines on the European side that if the bounty of God does not quickly put it in the hearts of the Christian princes to oppose them not many years will pass till they will be made lords of the remainder to the dishonor and perpetual slavery of Christendom, through the discord of its princes.

Lascivious life of Mark Antony

Discord between the Emperor of Constantinople [and the princes]

92ᵛ

93ʳ

The discord of Christendom has augmented the Mohammedan empire

The discord and jealousy⫽which arose amongst the confederates* against the Venetians (when all Italy and other princes conspired against them) not only caused their recovery of all the dominion they had lost, but was the reason that they, taking this opportunity, made themselves lords of the domains of others. And to these I shall add an example of our own. Henry VII, being in France, learned of the discord between Richard III and his barons because of his cruelty.⫽In order to usurp the crown, Richard had his two nephews killed, to whom he had been appointed protector by their father. He had accused his own mother of lewdness; and he was trying still to kill his wife. These and other tyrannical acts had earned him the hate of all. Henry, with the help of some friends, came into the kingdom and encountered Richard's army near the town of Barnet* ten miles from London, crushed it and killed him,⫽carrying the dead body all bloody to London, bound like a calf on a vile nag: a truly wretched display, but nonetheless not inappropriate to his life.

93ᵛ

Henry VII

94ʳ

Cruelty of Richard

Richard's death

94ᵛ

135

These various examples show how dangerous discord within a kingdom or province is, when there is an armed enemy without. The discord of the barons has placed this realm in great danger

95ʳ many times, danger little short of //complete destruction and the obliteration of the name of the English.

Alph: Whence arose such discord between King Harold and

The cause of the discord between King Harold and his brother Tostig Tostig his brother?

Steph: From envy of rule, for when he did not obtain the ranks and honors he sought, he immediately turned in hate against the king his brother, making him enemies wherever he could, first

King Harold of Norway arousing the Scots, and then going to King Harold* of Norway and

95ᵛ promising him great things, such as that //through him he could easily take possession of the whole realm of England. So Harold of Norway, believing that Tostig had many friends and that all the rest of what he said was true, came a few days later with 150 ships and arrived at the port now called Newcastle. And there he waited several days for the friends of Tostig but not one ever came. Nevertheless he decided to try his fortune with his own men (the number

96ʳ being great) and encountered the army of //Harold of England

Death of King Harold of Norway near the river Derwent not far from Stamford where his army was broken and defeated, and he was killed along with Tostig for being so rash* as to undertake an endeavor on the word of men deprived

Do not believe the words of refugees of their country, who very often speak things remote from the truth to return to their country or to avenge themselves on their enemies. They think that everyone will befriend them, and they deceive themselves, so that between that which they believe and

96ᵛ those arguments which //they know how to use for their purposes, they often fill ambitious princes with hope of undertaking exploits which later make them consume a treasury in vain, or even bring about their downfall.

Of this old books are full of examples, and there are also many modern examples before our eyes. He who considers the present wars in Tuscany will see that they do not proceed from anything but the industry of the exiles of Florence, Salerno, Naples and other

97ʳ cities of Italy. //They have convinced the Most Christian King

Cause of the wars in Tuscany that through them and their friends he could take possession of

The valorous Henry of France Tuscany and then in time of all Italy. The valorous and magnanimous prince believed them because men easily believe that

Men readily believe that which they desire which they desire, and he also had reason for hope because of the division among the princes of Italy, so that he made a very great expenditure and the final result of it will be as God wills.

But for the most part those who rely on the ⫽promises or friends 97ᵛ
of such men deceive themselves for they, to maintain the war and
to keep themselves in good opinion, say many things which they
cannot produce, and their friends who are in warm houses forget
the exiles and will not place their lives or property in danger for
the service or pleasure of those whose cause is uncertain and dubious.

Alph: Reason requires that everything be done for friends, without regard for property, or life itself, when ⫽the thing they ask is 98ʳ
just and honest.

Steph: Yes, but experience is against reason in this matter. All Men follow
run after fortune, and few care about unfortunate friends. When fortune
fortune leaves someone, his friends no longer know him. Therefore
it is a foolish thing for a prince to trust them or their friends for
very often they are left disgraced and empty-handed, or even wholly
ruined, as was Harold of Norway ⫽who lost 22,000 men as well as 98ᵛ
his own life through excessive credulity.

Thus William Duke of Normandy took the port of Hastings The Duke of
12 miles south of Dover with fifty* ships and landed his men there. Normandy
Harold, who was still in the northern part of the kingdom where England
he had joined battle with the King of Norway, was greatly
troubled when he heard the news, ⫽for a great part of his soldiers 99ʳ
had been killed in the battle against the Norwegians, others had been
wounded and the remainder had fled with the booty already taken
from the enemy so that he found himself in great danger, lacking
soldiers. Nevertheless, he went with all speed to London, and having
collected an army, came to battle with William, Duke of Normandy.
But after a long battle he was killed, together with 25,000 others. King Harold
This battle greatly weakened the forces of the ⫽English, and took 99ᵛ
all their flower of youth, so that William, after such a victory, went
on to London without hindrance and was crowned, promising the The Duke of
English many things in a fine speech, and telling them they might crowned in
expect all good from him, as from a father. But his deeds were all London
the reverse, for, having fortified himself with his Normans against The extinction
the natives, and having a fleet for protection against external enemies, of the royal line
he took precautions first against all those of the ⫽royal line, and 100ʳ
others who by title or power could aspire to the crown. He deprived
others of offices and dignities, which he gave to the Normans; he
oppressed the people with new tributes and taxes every day, sparing Cruelty
neither sacred things nor profane; and he held the nobility in no
honor, so that it seemed to all that he sought the ruin of the kingdom.
Many fled, some to Scotland, some to Flanders, and others to

100^v Denmark, procuring him enemies without and //inciting the people within to revolt. William* saw by the frequent revolts that the spirit of the English was completely alienated from him, realized

Fortresses he could no longer trust them, and decided to restrain them more narrowly. He built four fortresses in different parts of the kingdom, took all arms away from the English, and forbade them to leave their houses after eight at night with many other kinds of harsh slavery, so that he was shown to be, in all his proceedings, an enemy or

101^r destroyer rather //than a defender or father, and without doubt if his life had not ended he would have completely extinguished their name.

Alph: But new princes* and particularly those who acquire a territory by force cannot avoid many acts of cruelty, surely, for in the conquest of territory it is necessary to kill the people, destroy the countryside, burn the houses and inflict countless other injuries for which the prince will acquire the common hatred of the multi-

101^v tude; //and having injured them in this way he can no longer trust

Mercy is them but must depend upon his own. Mercy and liberality will not
useless when help him: to practice them would bring him ruin instead, for* a
injuries are
still remembered former injury is not erased with current liberality or mercy: revenge is merely deferred till the time affords good occasion.

102^r Therefore once a prince //has aroused hatred (even justly), he would be fooling himself if, having then tried to erase it with mercy, he trusted his people. There is no way to maintain a province or

Things gained kingdom acquired by arms except by the same arms, until the inju-
by arms must
be maintained ries done by the prince are forgotten in the course of time, which
by arms mitigates all sorrows. Thus it seems to me that William, wishing to

102^v keep what he had acquired, //adopted the safest and best course.

Steph: Not in this only, but in all his other actions he showed great prudence and took always the safe way,* without concern for being thought avaricious or cruel, for he laid hands on those who by reason or title could aspire to the crown and extinguished them all, as well as others whom, by reason of their influence or the favor of

103^r the people, he judged capable of attacking him. //

Alph: This is a more common practice among all princes than divine law permits.

Steph: Our purpose at present is not to show what a prince is permitted to do and what he is not permitted to do, but only to show by what ways and means a prince can maintain or lose his state. Consequently, I say that he who does otherwise will meet countless dangers, will himself be in a continual state of fear (which

is worse than death itself), and will always be in danger*⫽of losing 103ᵛ
his state and life while those live who have been despoiled or
defrauded of it, as the misfortunes of Henry VI show: because of Idle compassion
idle compassion he did not seek to make himself safe from Edward is harmful
IV when he had him in his hands but let him escape, because of which
he afterwards was deprived of state and life. A new prince (I am
not speaking of hereditary princes) who leaves anyone alive or at
liberty who has any legal claim to his domain⫽nourishes a serpent 104ʳ
in his bosom, as did Louis of France:* when the ambition of the Proverb
Venetians* had made him sole judge of Italy and lord of the third The error of
part of it, he placed a comrade, the King of Spain, in the kingdom Louis
of Naples, so that those who were discontented with his rule had a
place to go to complain and an instrument to effect their revenge;
and this pattern is manifested also by Henry VII who out of compassion let⫽Edward* son of the Duke of Clarence live imprisoned, 104ᵛ
though he had a claim to the throne. The people and the barons,
finding no other way to revolt, pretended to have with them this The peril of
Edward, under whose colors they assembled a large army, and not Henry VII
without peril was it put down by Henry. Because of this he was Death of
finally forced to protect himself against young innocent Edward, Edward, son
to take from his hands every occasion for further revolt. Richard of the Duke
Duke of York⫽(later Richard III) plotted many ways of getting the 105ʳ
crown, but none succeeded while his nephews and wards, the sons
of his brother Edward IV, lived: and therefore he tyrannically ordered Richard made
the death of the innocents entrusted to him as to a father's protec- himself safe
tion, and having thus quenched the royal line, the crown came from his
to him without opposition. And as⫽the above have reigned through 105ᵛ nephews
knowing how to protect themselves against those who could hurt tyrannically
them, so Sultan Bayazid* Emperor of the Turks lost his empire Bayazid lost
and his life through idle compassion for his impious son Selym, his life through
and so that you will better understand I will tell you the story. idle compassion
    This Selym was of a cruel and ambitious nature, a great dissem-
bler. Fearing lest one of his brothers succeed to the empire after
the death of their father, he⫽thought to take it by force while his 106ʳ
father lived, and proceeded in this way: under pretext of going to The impiety
Hungary to take up residence in his possessions,* he assembled a of Selym
large army and once on the march turned toward Adrianopole
where Bayazid his father was, expecting to find him sleeping; but
he had been informed of his son's wicked plan, was prepared, and
attacked him not far from Adrianopole, where they joined a most
cruel battle in which⫽Selym lost 35,000 men and barely saved 106ᵛ

The father victorious over the son

himself by flight. Notwithstanding this horrible filial treason, the father not only pardoned Selym but called him to Constantinople giving him a safe conduct, promising to make him general of an army to be sent against Sultan Ahamat his other son, who was then rebelling in Anatolia.

107ʳ   Selym answered his father that he would do everything //he wished, but that he feared Corcuth his other brother would be made emperor while he was in Anatolia. His father said that he might be of good cheer, for there was no doubt whatsoever that Selym alone

Words alone did not satisfy him

would actually succeed him. But words without deeds did not satisfy Selym. He did not wish to leave Constantinople before he was assured of the empire. Therefore Bayazid, seeing how importu-

107ᵛ   nate //he was, and being also counseled by certain pashas,* friends

Selym made emperor

of Selym, renounced the empire in his favor, made him emperor, and, thinking to live a private life, left Constantinople for Dimetoka where he had a palace. Now after the departure of Bayazid, Emperor Selym assembled an army to oppose Ahamat his brother, and

108ʳ   when he was ready to set out a great //suspicion arose in him that in his absence his father would return to Constantinople and make himself emperor again: so to still this fear he had him poisoned

Selym had his father poisoned

before he left. Thus Selym, in return for the mercy and compassion his father had shown in pardoning him when he deserved not one but a thousand deaths, took his father's life for no reason but mere

108ᵛ   suspicion, after he had willingly made him emperor. And so, now // instructed by the misfortune of his father, who did not try to protect himself when he could, Selym decided no longer to trust brother,

The cruelty of Selym to reign securely

nephew, or anyone else of royal blood. Therefore he first killed Ahamat his brother, then five of his nephews, and finally his brother Corcuth, and in this way reigned with felicity and Turkish honor.

109ʳ   *Alph:* You have placed your English examples in the proper context, //for surely they are more Turkish than Christian.

Steph: I do not praise them,* on the contrary I say that it would be better for Christians to live privately than to reign with such cruelty. But such a trick is sure to work, and one doesn't want to

Proverb

trust those who can strike back: William made himself safe this way, and afterwards made himself safe from every incipient revolt

109ᵛ   of the masses with the fortresses he built; //and these, too, were to his purpose.

Fortresses make princes less respected

Alph: Using cruelty is indeed to the purpose: it makes a prince more bold, more violent, less concerned about offending his subjects, and gives him greater occasion each day to become more cruel.

140

Steph: I do not blame such cruelty when a prince is all but forced to do it, in order to maintain his state.

Alph: Nor can I praise it in any case, since mercy avails much more than cruelty.

Steph: //You should know that where mercy is effective, he is 110^r
more than severe who will practise the contrary. But where it cannot avail, it is necessary to imitate the good surgeon, who does not use the iron and the fire unless the medicine, either because of its The knife is
weakness or the greatness of the wound, cannot work. And thus necessary when
in this case it would not be beyond the scope of our argument, which medicine does
now concerns the government of William, to show how and in not work
what cases //cruelty and mercy help or harm those princes who use 110^v
them. Cruelty is a vice which gives rise to a certain amount of infamy, but no danger: provided it is not done out of greed for property. Nonetheless the prince ought to be compassionate and merciful and not cruel, unless compelled by the wickedness of men; Note well
and when he is cruel he should show that he is constrained to be so against his will, because justice requires cruelty, or because he is a new prince faced with many //situations in which he must be 111^r
crueler than other princes.

The present example of William shows the great occasions that he had for cruelty, in view of the continuous revolts and plots and traps that were laid to catch him. Nonetheless he conquered his enemies, pacified the revolts, transformed the kingdom, gave it The harsh
laws and honors, and left it to his successors in peace and trust: government of
and he did so by employing cruelty which was without doubt more William
praiseworthy than that harmful compassion and mercy of Richard // 111^v
II and Henry VI, who through their ill-considered mercy lost many The harmful
places and cities in France and Scotland which their predecessors mercy of
had gained, and gave occasion to their subjects to scorn them and to Henry VI
plot against them, whereby both of them lost their states and their lives. Thus* a prince should not be concerned about the infamy of cruelty, if he holds his subjects united and in their place, because by making a few examples he will be more merciful than //those who, 112^r
by not putting one person to death, let revolts or other disorders occur which give rise to murders and rapine. These hurt everyone, whereas an execution ordered by the prince hurts only the individual.

Alph: In William's case, cruelty was more useful and helpful than mercy because he was, as you have said, a new prince who had gained the kingdom by arms, and had no means other than //arms 112^v
to maintain it.

Cambyses   *Steph:* Cruelty* helped Cambyses, who spared no one when he
Sulla   won a victory. Sulla likewise showed how cruelty to those who are
besieged and then conquered is often useful, for others, fearing the
Tamerlan   same cruelty, submit without resistance, as did all the territories
where Attila and Tamerlan went, for fear of their cruelty. But such
113^r men did not seek to be loved: it was enough for them simply //to
be feared.

It is good* that a prince be feared as well as loved; but (since it is
hard for fear and love to coexist for long) when he must lack one, it
is safer to be feared than loved, for generally men are inconstant,
desirous of change, dissembling, greedy for gain, and completely
It is safer to   corrupt: while they see an advantage they are servants and slaves,
be only feared   they offer life and blood when there is no need; but when danger
113^v comes //they remove to a distance. Therefore he who bases his
strategy only on the love of his subjects will be betrayed in time of
danger. Men put themselves in danger more for their positions and
from fear than from love. Love is held as a bond of obligation, which,
men being wicked, is broken on every occasion at their pleasure.
But fear is held by terror, which never abandons a person, and thus
114^r to be feared is not harmful, provided that one abstains from the //
property of the subjects, for when the prince is greedy for property
and displays cruelty to obtain it, he acquires fear and hate, which is a
most dangerous thing. Therefore I should prefer a prince to pro-
It is less   ceed against blood with all rigor (when he has proper justification)
dangerous to   rather than show the slightest desire for property. Men forget more
proceed against
blood   quickly the death of a father than the loss of patrimony: the father
than against   was born to die, but the patrimony must sustain his children.
property
114^v *Alph:* You would say //that, having cause, he can proceed
against blood. I believe that this is no cruelty, but justice. A prince
can even punish people in certain cases (the parents or children of
Henry   rebels, for example) on suspicion without manifest proof, as Henry
imprisoned
Courtenay for   did with Courtenay,* who was imprisoned though innocent because
an offense   of the offense imputed to his father. A prince can justly do this when
imputed to his
father   he has an eye to the common peace of his subjects rather than to his
115^r private //advantage or particular revenge.

Steph: And as far as the military is concerned,* it should not
Severity is   trouble the prince to be held cruel, for he who has to govern a
necessary in
war   multitude without such a reputation cannot hold an army united
Hannibal   and in military discipline. Among the notable deeds of Hannibal is
numbered this, that having to wage war in foreign lands with a
vast army composed of men of many races, dissension among the

troops or against the leader never arose, either in good // times or 115ᵛ
bad; and this came of nothing if not his cruelty, which together
with his other virtues made him always revered and terrible in the
eyes of his soldiers: and without cruelty, all of his other virtues
(even though they were many) would not have sufficed to produce
such effect.

On the other hand it is seen that the excessive mercy of Scipio
was the reason that his armies rebelled* in Spain: he gave them more
license than was consonant with military // discipline; and therefore 116ʳ
he was reproved by Fabius Maximus* in the senate and called The mercy of
corrupter of the Roman military, and further, when the Locrians, Scipio is
allies of the Romans, were offended by one of his lieutenants, not harmful
only did they get no satisfaction from Scipio, but he did not even
punish the lieutenant's insolence. This came of Scipio's excessive
laxness, and for it he was called to the judgment of the
senate.

Alph: This example of cruelty you allege of Hannibal is unique
among all the other captains who ever lived. // But considering the 116ᵛ
end you will see that the kindness of Scipio was worth more in the
hearts of his soldiers than the cruelty of Hannibal, which, although
it availed to hold an army together when they were far from the
enemy (where their disunity would have had no effect), nevertheless
when troops are in battle order near the enemy the kindness of the
captain is better: he begs his soldiers in vain to fight valorously
then, if he was inhuman and cruel before; // and this is seen in 117ʳ
Hannibal's case: although he ordered his army against Scipio with
great wisdom at Carthage, he was nonetheless defeated, and his
fierceness was of no avail in keeping his soldiers in order, for without
doubt kindness avails more than severity in times of danger.

Steph: Now this may be said of the military, but let us turn to
civil government, and we will see that in certain places and among
certain people cruelty is more useful and necessary than mercy in
peace as well as in // war, and that in other regions the opposite is 117ᵛ
true, and therefore in deciding to use the one or the other one must
consider the place, the time and the people. Without cruelty the Without
Turkish empire would have fallen, and this is so because all the cruelty the
authority is so bound to the person of the sovereign that every Turkish empire
other prince of his kingdom expects to have his head cut off for any would have
whim that comes into the sovereign's head; // because they are all 118ʳ
his slaves, he shuffles offices and dignities about as he wishes,
without any other consideration.

But if a prince of France or England proceeded in this manner he would fall immediately. Still, cruelty is worth more than mercy to him who has to govern and hold in terror a number of slaves or servants who dare not rise against him, like Darius, Alexander, and
118ᵛ the present Turk. But the Romans* and other Christian princes // have under their rule subjects and not servants. The Roman plebs

The barons of England participate in the state with the king

had almost equal power with the Senate, and the barons of England and France participate in the state with the king, and they have privileges and authority with the people, so that such severity cannot be employed to the full, nor can they be managed with cruelty.

The people are subject to the barons

Alph: What authority have the English barons with the people?

Steph: The people are by the ancient law subject in certain ways
119ʳ to the barons,* // for they lease their holdings and houses to the people without rent, requiring them in return to render certain services so many times a year, and to go to war only under them or at their command and many like services, definite obligations to which the people are bound by oath, so that if the prince practiced such cruelty, the barons would lead the people against him. Thus it
119ᵛ is seen that in this kingdom hereditary // kings or others who have come to power peacefully have had more fruitful results with love and kindness than others have had with fierceness and cruelty.

Alph: This is true of many emperors besides the kings of England,

Julius Caesar the clement

as Alexander, Cyrus and Caesar, who shared a temple in Rome with the goddess Clementia, when he was alive, for he never left
120ʳ undone any work that could be required of a kind and // merciful

The kindness of Camillus

prince. And Camillus attained a similar reputation for his kindness, as anyone who has read Livy knows.*

When he was with the Roman army around the city of the Faliscans, there came a schoolmaster under pretence of taking an outing with some noble children of the city. Thinking to gratify Camillus and the Roman people, he led them all into the camp before Camillus and presented them to him and said that for the sake of
120ᵛ these children the city would surrender. Camillus not only // refused this gift, but made the master undress, bound his hands, and gave each of the children a rod, and had them escort him (while giving him a good thrashing) back to the city. When the citizens heard of this, the humanity and integrity of Camillus so pleased them that they decided to surrender the city without resistance. Thus one sees that sometimes the humane and pious display has
121ʳ more force in the hearts of men than a fierce // and cruel act. History

is full of examples in which a display of kindness, pity, chastity or generosity has gained entry in provinces and kingdoms to which neither arms, instruments of war, nor any other human force have been able to gain entry. All the strength of Rome was not sufficient to drive Pyrrhus from Italy, but the generosity of Fabricius was; he left when Fabricius informed him of an offer made by one of his servants to poison him. All//the victories of Scipio would not have given him such a reputation as one instance of chastity, in which he returned a young beautiful wife untouched to her husband. The fame of that deed made all of Spain friendly to him.

The generosity of Fabricius

121ᵛ

The chastity of Scipia

Steph: These examples you adduce are rare and quite out of date for our times and he who did as Fabricius or Camillus would be considered to have little experience, for I say, as regards mercy and cruelty, that it helps a//prince to seem sometimes cruel, provided that his mind is not dominated by cruelty, so that afterwards, when he shows himself kind in secret, he can do it comfortably. For mercy ought in any case to vanquish cruelty, otherwise the prince will not resemble God, of whom he is the living image. The Holy Scriptures call God merciful* and just, putting mercy first.

122ʳ

Mercy ought to vanquish cruelty

Alph: So you would conclude that the prince//ought to be rather merciful than fierce?

122ᵛ

Steph: Yes, he should always be compassionate and kind in spirit, but not so kind that he be unable to practice cruelty as well, when the occasion arises. It is good to have the reputation of a merciful prince, provided that greater trouble does not follow from it than from the contrary. So you have my opinion concerning mercy that a prince should practice it, but likewise employ the methods of William, Duke of Normandy, in//subjugating the kingdom, extinguishing seditions, pacifying rebellions, and leaving the kingdom in faith and peace to his successors.

123ʳ

Alph: In my opinion, it would be safer for the prince to proceed contrary to William's practice: he should be kind, merciful, generous and the rest, and should prefer to reign rather in the hearts of men than in fortresses of stone.

Steph: You should know that he who has gained a realm or a province by force of arms//has one way to hold it, and he who has gained one through favor of friends, hereditary laws or by matrimony must take a different course to keep his state. The basis of this latter course should be mercy, affability and generosity (this, especially, penetrates the hearts of men, however hard). These qualities bring the prince reputation and fame at the outset, open the

123ᵛ

Generosity breaks gates of iron

6-2

124ʳ way to being loved and obeyed, and are necessary for a prince who wishes to gain the love of a foreign people. Alexander, //Caesar, King Alphonso of Naples and King Stephen of England gained *Generous princes* kingdoms by these qualities and held them. For truly* it is not *The qualities* very difficult for a new prince who has come in by way of friend-*by which* ship to hold his kingdom, when he is safe from those of royal blood. *princes maintain* *their states* This is the greatest danger that can befall the ruler of any kingdom, 124ᵛ for then he lives in constant fear, and is never //safe. Men naturally desire change. But by making himself safe from those of royal blood, the prince takes all occasion of effecting such innovation from the nobles, and also from the people of following them, for men are never aroused without at least a semblance of truth.

The presence of the prince has great force Then it is a great help for the prince to go to live in a new pos-session. His presence alone is of great efficacy in restraining the 125ʳ appetites of the //seditious and frightens them from doing that which their appetites desire. And being there,* he can spot disorders quickly and put them right, but being absent he hears of them when they are great and there is no longer a remedy.

The presence of the prince restrains the avarice of ministers who make a practice of fleecing the poor. The latter are content to have a ready way to complain to the prince; if they are well-intentioned it 125ᵛ gives them the more reason //to love him, and if they are not, to fear him. And if by chance foreign enemies think to attack the state, they will have greater caution: so that living in his new state the prince can very easily keep it. Provided that he does not change their laws, nor oppress them with new taxes or duties, he *Duties of* will in a short time become well established in the principality.

the prince He should have particular care to hold his barons united, avoid 126ʳ //disorders from the beginning before they become strong, administer justice to all equally without favoritism (for that gives rise to envy), reward the virtuous and punish the wicked, show himself easy going, kind and affable to all, listen willingly to the complaints of the poor, and so doing in a short time he will acquire reputation and will be more secure than a hereditary prince. King Stephen of England maintained himself safely by these means although he was 126ᵛ French //(whom the English hate) and usurped the kingdom as well. But among all the qualities there is none of greater force in *Affability* gaining fame and reputation with a people than to listen to the *acquires great* complaints and supplications of the poor and avenge their injuries. *reputation* Infinite examples confirm this in history, of which I shall adduce several.

According to Scripture Absalom,* son of King David, used to   Absalom
place himself in the entrance hall of his father's royal palace in the
morning, and whomever he saw come for audience with the king
he //kindly called to him and listened to him with great compassion.   127ʳ
Although he did not do this with a sincere heart, it nonetheless
brought him into such favor and repute with the people that all
Israel rebelled from his father, listening to him. The same is seen in
Solomon and Octavius Augustus, who often sat on tribunals in   Octavius
person to hear the causes of their people, for which as well as for
their great kindness they gained the love and trust of their people
and were safe among them. // Just as Henry VIII was not inferior   127ᵛ
to any prince of his day in the strength of his body and in his wit   The affability
(when he used it well), so in this virtue of affability he surpassed all   of Henry VIII
others. Truly he gave his people great opportunity to conspire
against him when he began the rape of the spiritual property and the
overthrow of the monasteries, and particularly in the counties of
Lincoln and York for people there were more opposed //to his   128ʳ
opinions than all others in the kingdom. He became utterly enraged
at them for their frequent revolts and conspiracies against him and
treated them very cruelly, killing some and confiscating the property
of others for the slightest transgressions. And on the other hand,
the gentlemen who followed the king's party (knowing he was
angry with the people) mercilessly threw them out of their holdings
and took their property unjustly and //illegally; so that the poor   128ᵛ
countryfolk became desperate, being every day oppressed with new
injuries.

It happened that one of these poor old men* began a trip with
his wife and children to the court to complain of injuries done him
by a neighboring knight. Henry, who by chance was returning from
the hunt, spied this poor man on his knees at a distance, all ragged
and full of mud, //bridled his horse in the middle of a ring of many   129ʳ
nobles, listened with great kindness to all that the man wanted to
say, and then, speaking kindly and with a merry countenance told
him to be of good cheer and take comfort, 'for I', said the king,
'will defend my simple sheep from the greed of the wolves, and
avenge their injuries', and so graciously commanded that the poor
man be given money for his return home and dismissed him. And
afterwards, when the king investigated //the suit of the poor   129ᵛ
countrymen and found the said gentlemen at fault, he first made them
make restitution to those poor people, and then he had them
hanged by the neck at their own gates; and when news was spread

throughout the country how he had listened so kindly to the complaint of a poor man, giving him justice and avenging his injuries, he acquired great love and trust among the people who before hated 130ʳ him because he had usurped⫽religious property. They lifted their hands to the heavens, thanking God for giving them such a king who listened to the complaints of the poor and gave them justice, and thus afterwards they were always most obedient and loyal.

Likewise, in the beginning of his reign in another singular episode, Henry gained the minds and hearts of his people, who were then greatly oppressed by the law* which Henry VII his 130ᵛ father⫽made, which was that anyone who was found to have violated the laws of the realm had to pay the penalty prescribed by the laws regardless of the antiquity of the statute; and the king placed two judges and many informers in each county to accuse such offenders, so that in a short time he had collected a large sum of money, as men of every condition were accused every day by these 131ʳ informers,⫽who were too intent on their own profit and accused the innocent as well as the guilty. Because of this the people murmured against the cruelty of such a law, and flocked to Henry VIII after his father's death, demanding the revocation* of the bad law and the restoration of property unjustly taken by the avaricious ministers. But the king, judging that it would not do for him to restore all the property confiscated under the old law, found a way 131ᵛ to pacify the fury of the people⫽and even gratify them. For, knowing how the people hated the judges and informers (who were too severe in judgments and sentences), he commanded that the judges and informers be called to judgment and then condemned to death or to a variety of other penalties; some had their noses

How Henry satisfied the people cut off, some their ears, some their tongues and others were branded on the forehead. By this means the people were satisfied and most 132ʳ happy with the king who effected their⫽revenge on the evil ministers, and thus he enjoyed their money without any murmurs or other trouble.

Alph: There is nothing that gains the prince the hearts of his people more than seeming to favor those they love, and to hate those they hate.

Greatness of spirit *Steph:* In addition to the things mentioned above, a prince gains reputation by showing greatness, strength and gravity of spirit 132ᵛ in all he does, and an irrevocability⫽of opinion and judgment in his relations with his private subjects. No one will dare to fool or dupe a prince who enjoys such a reputation and is well respected.

And against one who is so reputed plots cannot be easily made, and great security results from that. In his other actions* the prince should seem pitying, kind, affable, merciful, generous, and observant of trust.

Alph: These qualities are very praiseworthy but somewhat hard for a prince to observe.

Steph: It is quite true, //nor do the conditions of kingship allow 133ʳ them to be entirely observed; and even if a prince always observed them, it would bring him more harm than good, and therefore it suffices if the prince is prudent enough to know how to escape the infamy of the contrary vices, when he has to use them, and to avoid those vices which will lose him his state, such as greed for the property of his subjects, violation of the ancient laws, and disregard for the nobles and men of merit. And as for*//being held merciful, 133ᵛ generous and observant of faith, I commend them most highly provided that to observe them does not bring more danger than good. The contrary of these sometimes are of great help to the man who uses them, particularly when he works them in artfully.

Pope* Alexander VI was in his time the great master of this art,   Pope Alexander hiding an ambitious endeavor with a veil of piety, and without doubt such deception often was of greater use//than the simple 134ʳ truth: for he who deals honestly with the wicked and the crafty will fail as did Henry VI. A new prince especially cannot observe all the things by which men are held good, even if he wants to, since it is often necessary, to maintain his state, to act contrary to mercy, religion and faith. Therefore his character must be such that he can change what he does//like the wind according to the variety 134ᵛ of fortune while what he says seems full of faith, mercy and charity,   The counsel of for these semblances gain him great reputation with the multitude,   a politic man and a people marks more the effects of the eyes and of the tongue than those of the hand; and if, perchance, the deeds of a prince are not wholly consonant with his words and his public image, this will be imputed to the errors of his ministers and not//to the king, 135ʳ as is seen in the example of Henry VIII mentioned above.

I have digressed thus to respond to your questions, and now nothing remains for me to say on this subject, having shown how William subjugated the realm of England and left it in trust to his successors until the coming of the powerful and most merciful Philip, son of the Emperor Charles V. This I do not call//change or 135ᵛ alteration in the kingdom, but legitimate succession, confirmed by all orders, for the restoration of religion, the honor of the kingdom

and benefit of the people, as augured by the noble blood of the
Praise of the
blood of the
most noble
house of Austria unconquered seed of the most powerful Germany and of that most
happy house of the glorious Emperor Charles, which his own excel-
lence and valor promise to confirm. Who does not know the greatness conjoined //with virtue of Emperor Frederick* III Duke of
Austria, to begin no further back, who with the patience of Fabius
together with incomparable wisdom restored almost completely
the Christian religion which had fallen before him. The great
Maximilian his son, who knows not how much piety, goodness
and valor was in him, and what honorable exploits he made in
Brabant, Flanders and Italy, and what zeal //he always had for
religion, and towards all virtuous men? I do not speak of Philip
his son, because he was stopped by cruel death before he had time to
show great works, worthy of this most noble blood, but we have
Charles V his father,* who at only 18 was made emperor and mon-
arch of the world, whose name makes the Turks pale, and the
Moors, and all the enemies of Christianity //fear the good fortune
which God gave him. Therefore the Ottoman great lord and
emperor of the Turks used to say that he did not fear Charles but
his fortune. His grandeur is a greater ornament to the empire than
the empire is to him; and like the sun, the great rays of his most
valorous exploits have illuminated the old and the new world: and
even more clearly than the sun, for its splendor yields to night, and
his will never yield //at all.
And what may we then hope of the great soul of Philip his
son conjoined with such religion, piety and mercy? Lions do not
bring forth rabbits, nor eagles doves, but lions produce lions and
eagles hatch out eagles. Therefore it has pleased the great God that
he be given sovereignty over so many provinces and kingdoms;
not advanced by chance, or crime, like many other princes, but
brought forth in this age in justice by the highest //divine providence
so that Christianity after such dark clouds would have the bright
light of the sun, and the Christian people, after such long and cruel
wars, would enjoy the precious and inestimable joy of peace so
much desired and longed for by everyone. Peace, called the daughter
of God, nurse of nature, conservatrix of the human race, sower of
virtue, and mother of adundance. No voice is more pleasing to
men's //ears than the name of peace, nor is there anything which
is desired more, or which is enjoyed with such delight, because
there is no happiness or content in any heart where there is no peace.
Therefore he who takes peace from men takes the sun from the

world and life from the creatures. But Philip is the man who
is ordained to restore the one and the other, and to that end wields
the sword of such great kingdoms in his right hand, placed there by
the Supreme Mover⫽so that with its power he can as the mighty 139ʳ
lion humble proud tigers, encounter the vicious wolves, punish
the disturbers of the Christian concord, as a most merciful father
reward the virtuous, defend the innocent, and maintain his subjects
in peace, which is all that the heart of this great-souled man seeks, The innate
desires and longs for. I tell you this and I know it is so. This love goodness of
and great zeal for the common⫽good and Christian benefit 139ᵛ
moved him by honorable means of holy matrimony to rule over the
powerful realm of England as a most pious father. And by this*
his kingdoms and his power in these parts are now consolidated,
and he has become without dispute the arbiter of peace and war of Arbiter of
all Christendom, a name truly most worthy of the blood of Austria world
and suitable to the sincerity of religion, piety, and⫽mercy of his controversy
sublime mind. 140ʳ

Alph: The immortal God grant that he use his authority and power
for the honor of God, and, as you have said, for the peace and
tranquillity of all Christendom.

Steph: We also pray for this continually, with hands raised to the
heavens, and we pray that the highest giver of all good things give
him, together with happy rule, the execution of all his holy desires.
But listen, Signor Alphonso, the hour is six. The Duke of Norfolk*
awaits – let us go to dinner. 140ᵛ

NOTES

II^r. 1–6: In England it was customary to list Philip's title to England before his title to Spain (see *Ven. Cal.* vi, Pt. 1, 412). Philip's own preference was for the order Rainsford follows here.

II^v. 9. *Antonio*: Antoninus Pius (A.D. 86–161).

III^r. 9. *chiaressa del sole*: Probably a reference to the restoration of the Catholic religion. 9. *pace*: The short lived Truce of Vaucelles was signed on 5 February 1556.

6^v. 1 *va circondando*: The details of Plato's travels were given in early lives by Apuleius, Diogenes Laertius and Olympiodorus, and repeated in Ficino's *Vita Platonis* which accompanied the various printings of his edition of Plato's works. 2. *Archita*: Archytas of Tarentum was a follower of Pythagoras. This account of men who travelled for knowledge emphasizes the secret oral teachings of the hermetic tradition. Pythagoras, Archytas, Plato, the Brahmans, the Gymnosophists and Apollonius were thought in the Renaissance to be links in a chain of oral teaching (the *prisca theologia*) revealed to Hermes Trismegistus before the time of Moses (see Frances Yates, *Giordano Bruno and the Hermetic Tradition* [London, 1964], *passim* and D. P. Walker, *The Ancient Theology* [London, 1972]). Gardiner's point in invoking this tradition seems to be that political knowledge also has its dangers and its secrets. The idea of politics (particularly Machiavellian politics) as a secret tradition in some ways parallel to the hermetic tradition was subsequently developed (seventeenth century) by Gabriel Naudé (*Apologie pour les grands hommes soupçonnez de magie*), Arnold Clapmar (*De arcanis rerumpublicarum*) and others. 4. *Apolonio*: Apollonius of Tyana was a first century (A.D.) Neopythagorean sage and wonderworker. The details of his travels are to be found in Philostratus' life of him. 7. *scithi*: Philostratus denies (Loeb Classical Library ed., 1. 35) that Apollonius ever visited the Scythians, though he admits other writers have alleged it.

7^r. 2. *secreti di nativita*: An allusion to the fact that Iarchas was considered an avatar or incarnation of King Ganges.

7^v. 6–7. *authorità (la qual mostra l'houmo)*: 'Magistratus virum indicat', M. P. Tilley, *A Dictionary of Proverbs in England in the Sixteenth and Seventeenth Centuries* (1950), A 402.

10^v. 6. *Bruto*: Gardiner follows Polydore Vergil's adaptation of Eusebius on the period from the coming of Brutus to the Roman conquest. Polydore considered Brutus mythical, and gives Eusebius' account with skepticism. Gardiner ignores Polydore's reservations. (See *Anglicae historiae libri XXVI*, Basle, 1534, p. 16.)

11^r. 6. *Aetio*: cf. *Angl. hist.* p. 48. Polydore cites Gildas.

12^r. 6. *Cadavaladro*: cf. *Angl. hist.* pp. 77–8.

14^r. 7. *Il testo*: 'Porro Brittani principes, cum viderent tantam tempestatem a Scotis aeque ut a Pictis hostibus multo ferocissimis, crudelissimisque impendere ... statuerunt sibi aliquem unum regem optandum. Itaque habito confestim concilio, plures iudicabant, id decus deferendum Vortigerio, quod esset vir inter viros, autoritate, nobilitate, virtute summus' (*Angl. hist.* p. 52).

16^r. 5–17^v. 6. *Gli vengono* ... *non l'annullano*: Gardiner's discussion of reputation is based upon Machiavelli's account of how men are chosen for public office in popular governments (*Disc.* III: 34):

Dico, adunque, come il popolo nel suo distribuire va dietro a quello che si dice d'uno per publica voce e fama, quando per sue opere note non lo conosce altrimenti; o per presunzione o opinione che si ha di lui. Le quale due cose sono causate o da' padri di quelli tali che, per essere stati grandi uomini e valenti nella città, si crede che i figliuoli debbeno essere simili a loro, infino a tanto che per le opere di quegli non s'intenda il contrario; o la è causata dai modi che tiene quello di che si parla. I modi migliori che si possino sono: avere compagnia di uomini gravi, di buoni costumi, e riputati savi da ciascuno. E perchè nessuno indizio si può avere maggiore d'un uomo, che le compagnie con quali egli usa; meritamente uno che usa con compagnie oneste, acquista buono nome, perchè è impossibile che non abbia qualche similitudine di quelle. O veramente si acquista questa publica fama per qualche azione istraordinaria e notabile, ancora che privata, la quale ti sia riuscita onorevolmente. E di tutte a tre queste cose che danno nel principio buona riputazione ad uno, nessuna la dà maggiore che questa ultima: perchè quella prima de' parenti e de' padri è sì fallace, che gli uomini vi vanno a rilento; ed in poco si consuma, quando la virtù propria di colui che ha a essere giudicato non l'accompagna. La seconda, che ti fa conoscere per via delle pratiche tue, è meglio della prima, ma è molto inferiore alla terza; perchè, infino a tanto che non si vede qualche segno che nasca da te, sta la riputazione tua fondata in su l'opinione, la quale è facilissima a cancellarla. Ma quella terza, essendo principiata e fondata in sul fatto ed in su la opera tua, ti dà nel principio tanto nome, che bisogna bene che operi poi molte cose contrarie a questa, volendo annullarla.

Machiavelli is quoted by permission of the Giunti Publishing Group in the Mazzoni and Casella edition, *Tutte le opere* (Florence, 1929, repr. with additions 1969).

18^v. 4–6. *Dove...la fortuna vale poco*: Cf. *Prince* XXV, 'fortuna...dimostra la su potenzia dove non è ordinata virtù a resisterle'.

19^r. 4. *come dice la istoria*: 'Ad extremum bonae principum parti suis opibus diffisae in mentem venit, et regi cum primis, Saxones Anglos fama rei militaris illustres accersire' (*Angl. hist.* p. 52). Gardiner changes *diffisae* to *diffisus*. In his version, the king acts on his own authority, in the face of the advice of his barons.

20ᵛ. 3. *Lotrecchio*: Odet de Foix, seigneur de Lautrec (d. 1528) commanded the French forces at the siege of Naples in the campaign of 1528. Lautrec was aided by the fleet of Andrea Doria, which blockaded the harbor. But the French did not pay the fleet, and Andrea Doria abruptly switched to the Imperial side. The siege was not immediately lifted, but its effectiveness was broken. Lautrec died on 16 August.

21ᵛ. 4 ff. *era un cavallo*: The fable is not in Polydore.

23ᵛ. 6–7. *perchè . . . disobedienti*: Cf. *Prince* xii, 'perchè le sono disunite, ambiziose, sanza disciplina, infidele'. 8–24ʳ. 1. *Tengino . . . houmini*: 'Non timore di Dio, non fede con gli uomini' (*Prince* xii).

24ʳ. 3–5. *Et tutto l'amore . . . basta di vivere*: 'La cagione . . . è che le non hanno altro amore nè altra cagione che le tenga in campo, che un poco di stipendio; il quale non è sufficiente a fare che voglino morire per te' (*Prince* xii).

24ᵛ. 2–3. *Francesco . . . Henrico . . . Henrico*: François I, Henry VIII, Henri II.

25ᵛ. 2. *Fabio . . . Varrone*: Fabius Maximus Cunctator avoided battle with Hannibal as a conscious strategy. Varro was commander at Cannae, where Hannibal won with fewer troops. See Polybius iii: 107–18; Livy xxii: 43–9.

26ʳ. 3. *mercinarii soldati*: In 1549, a rising against the use of the *Book of Common Prayer* was put down with the aid of German and Italian mercenaries. The rising in Norfolk (Kett's Rebellion) was put down in the same year. See J. D. Mackie, *The Earlier Tudors 1485–1558* (Oxford, 1952), pp. 489 ff., and F. W. Russell's *Kett's Rebellion* (London, 1859), pp. 91, 121, 141. Also S. T. Bindoff, *Ket's Rebellion, 1549* (London, 1949); F. Rose-Troup, *Western Rebellion of 1549* (London, 1913).

27ʳ. 2–3. *gli venitiani . . . havevanno acquistati*: '[i viniziani] in una giornata perderono, quello che in ottocento anni, con tanta fatica, avevano acquistato' (*Prince* xii). The reference is to the decisive battle of Vailà, which the Venetians lost to the French in 1509. 5–8. *I carthaginesi . . . proprii cittadini*: '[I cartaginesi] furono per essere oppressi da' loro soldati mercinarii, finita la prima guerra con li Romani, ancora che e' Cartaginesi avessino, per capi, loro proprii cittadini' (*Prince* xii). 8–27ᵛ. 3. *Che altra cosa . . . vi messe dentro*: 'Lo imperadore di Constantinopoli, per opporsi alli suoi vicini, misse in Grecia diecimila Turchi; li quali, finita la guerra, non se volsono partire; il che fu principio della servitù di Grecia' (*Prince* xiii). John Cantacuzene appealed to Orchan, the Emir of Bithynia, for aid, and the troops sent by the latter in 1353 established a Turkish presence in Europe. 3–5. *I milanese . . . li suoi patroni*: 'E' Milanesi . . . soldorno Francesco Sforza contro a' Viniziani; il quale, superati gli inimici a Caravaggio si congiunse con loro per opprimere e' Milanesi suoi patroni' (*Prince* xii). Sforza defeated the Venetians near Caravaggio in 1448, and then turned upon the Milanese, whom he conquered in 1450.

28ʳ. 2–28ᵛ. 5. *per non monstrarsi . . . officii del regno*: This passage is composed of several short borrowings from Polydore.

Hos rex benigne accepit, sedesque in Cantia ad habitandum assignavit
(p. 52) . . . Hengistus, vir summo ingenio, summaque prudentia, cognita
regis mente, qui iam totus in Anglorum virtute acquiescebat, ac patriae
ubertate perspecta, protinus secum cogitare coepit, quibus dolis, aut
artibus regnum sibi atque suis in insula sensim pararet. . . . Deinde
nititur regi persuadere, maiorem militum manum ex Germania esse
ducendam, ut eo praesidio insula munita hosti terrorem, suis quietem
praebeat . . . Igitur continuo ingens hominum multitudo in Britanniam
commigravit, simulque prout tradunt, adducta est filia Hengisti nomine
Ronix, forma eleganti, ad pertentandum Vortigerii animum, quia quo ille
vitio laboraret, satis Anglus cognorat (p. 53) . . . At postquam affinitas
Saxonibus Anglis cum rege intercesserat, Ronix eius uxor suos in summa
gratia apud virum ponere, illis in primis honores deferendos curare (p. 54).

29^r. 3–29^v. 7. *Il proverbio dice* . . . *aiuterà tal ruina*:
E detto che Tito Livio ha tutti e' sopradetti disordini, conchiude dicendo:
'Adeo obcaecat animos fortuna, cum vim suam ingruentem refringi non
vult' . . . Fa bene la fortuna questo, che la elegge un uomo, quando la
voglia condurre cose grandi, che sia di tanto spirito e di tanta virtù, che ei
conosca quelle occasioni che la gli porge. Così medesimamente, quando
la voglia condurre grandi rovine, ella vi prepone uomini che aiutino
quella rovina (*Disc.* II: 29).
Cf. Livy V: 37. I.

30^v. 6–31^r. 4. *Alcuni affirmano* . . . *nove sedie et habitationi*:
Sunt, qui scribant Saxones non accitos a rege, sed fortuito in insulam
pervenisse, causamque transeundi eiusmodi referant. Sane apud Anglos
Saxones regionis Germaniae gentem bellicosissimam, mos erat, ut cum
multitudo hominum eousque crevisset, ut non facile eam patria alere
posset, iussu principum, optimos quosque ad bellum gerendum iuvenes
sorte eligerent, qui novas sedes quaerendi, bellandique causa, finibus
educerentur (*Angl. hist.* pp. 52–3).

32^v. 5–8. *le guerre* . . . *Cesare*: 'L'una [guerra] è fatta per ambizione de'
principi o delle republiche, che cercano di propagare lo imperio; come
furono le guerre che fece Alessandro Magno, e quelle che fecero i Romani'
(*Disc.* II: 8).

33^r. 5–6. *i gothi et vandale* . . . *saporiti frutti*: 'furono alletati dalla dolcezza
delle frutte e del vino d'Italia, delle quali mancavono in Francia' (*Disc.* II: 8).
And cf. Livy V: 33. 2.

33^v. 5. *grand mine d'oro*: Cf. Livy XXVIII: 3.

34^r. 1–35^r. 6. *Queste tal sorte* . . . *fattola lor sedie*:
Le quali guerre sono pericolose, ma non cacciano al tutto gli abitatori
d'una provincia; perchè e' basta, al vincitore, solo la ubbidienza de'
popoli e il più delle volte gli lascia vivere con le loro leggi, e sempre con
le loro case, e ne' loro beni. L'altra generazione di guerra è quando uno
popolo intero con tutte le sue famiglie se lieva d'uno luogo, necessitato
o dalla fame o dalla guerra, e va a cercare nuova sede e nuova provincia;

non per commandarla, come quegli di sopra, ma per possederla tutta particularmente, e cacciarne o ammazzare gli abitatore antichi di quella. Questa guerra è crudelissima e paventosissima. E di queste guerre ragiona Sallustio nel fine dell'Iugurtino, quando dice che, vinto Iugurta, si sentì il moto de' Franciosi che venivano in Italia: dove ei dice che il Popolo romano con tutte le altre genti combattè solamente per chi dovesse comandare, ma con i Franciosi combattè sempre per la salute di ciascuno. Perchè a un principe o a una republica, che assalta una provincia, basta spengere solo coloro che comandano; ma a queste populazioni conviene spengere ciascuno, perchè vogliono vivere di quello che altri viveva. I Romani ebbero tre di queste guerre pericolosissime. La prima fu quella quando Roma fu presa, la quale fu occupato da quei Franciosi che avevano tolto, come di sopra si disse, la Lombardia a' Toscani, e fattone loro sedia (*Disc.* II: 8).

36^r. 5–37^v. 4. *i maurisii* . . . *per via d'amicitia et confederati*: The passage is borrowed entirely from *Disc.* II: 8, but Machiavelli's order has been changed,[1] and some of Machiavelli's discussion has been omitted:

la necessità nasce o dalla fame, o da una guerra ed oppressione che ne' paesi propri è loro fatta; talchè e' son constretti cercare nuove terre. E questi tali, o e' sono gran numero; ed allora con violenza entrano ne' paesi d'altrui, ammazzano gli abitatori, posseggono i loro beni, fanno uno nuovo regno, mutano il nome della provincia: come fece Moisè, e quelli popoli che occuparono lo Imperio romano . . . come è la Lombardia, che si chiamava Gallia Cisalpina: la Francia si chiamava Gallia Transalpina, ed ora è nominata da' Franchi, chè così si chiamovono quelli popoli che la occuparono: la Schiavonia si chiamava Illiria; l'Ungheria, Pannonia . . . Moisè ancora chiamò Giudea quella parte di Soria occupata da lui. . . . ne voglio addurre lo essempio de' Maurusii, popoli anticamente in Soria: i quali, sentendo venire i popoli ebraici, e giudicando non potere loro resistere, pensarono essere meglio salvare loro medesimi, e lasciare il paese proprio, che, per volere salvare quello, perdere ancora loro; e levatisi con loro famiglie, se ne andarono in Africa, dove posero la loro sedia, cacciando via quelli abitatori che in quegli luoghi trovarono . . . Ma quando quegli che sono costretti abbandonare la loro patria non sono molti, non sono sì pericolosi come quelli di che si è ragionato; perchè non possono usare tanta violenza, ma conviene loro con arte occupare qualche luogo, e, occupatolo, mantenervisi per via d'amici e di confederati.

There are several differences between the text and its source that require comment: in considering these and other departures from Machiavelli it is well to keep in mind that variation may have occurred in three ways. Gardiner did not always follow his Machiavelli exactly, but made alterations and omissions for the sake of relevance and brevity, and thus authorial intention accounts for many of the variations. The translator doubtless

---

[1] In such cases I have arranged short passages within a chapter in the order in which Gardiner quotes them.

introduced further changes unintentionally: Rainsford tried to use Machiavelli's exact words whenever he could, but Gardiner's English did not permit a complete return to Machiavelli's Italian, and many of the errors may have arisen from the translator's desire to be faithful to Machiavelli's text as well as Gardiner's which did not always say the same thing. Finally, there is always the possibility of scribal error. It is not always possible to distinguish the three sources of variation. In this passage it may have been Rainsford or the scribe who skipped a line at 37^r: 5 in which the subject changes from the conquerors ('come fece Moisè') to the conquered provinces ('come è la Lombardia') thus creating a grammatical confusion. It is worth noting that the common kind of scribal omission of a line would have yielded something slightly different: the scribe's eye, passing from the first *come* to the second, would pass over all the intervening material, not part of it. The translator, on the other hand, wishing to use as much Machiavelli as Gardiner's compression would allow, could more easily have made this error, thinking that since *come fece* and *come è* were grammatically parallel, Moses, the Gauls and the province of Lombardy must also be parallel. Likewise the failure of parallelism ('amicitia et confederati') that ends the passage may be the work of the translator faced with Gardiner's English, which may have been 'by means of friendship and confederation' or something similar (compare the Walker trans. 'make alliances and form confederations') and Machiavelli's 'per via d'amici et di confederati'. A third variation, in which the present text omits the lines in which Machiavelli states that a small number of migrants is not so dangerous as a large number strikes me as authorial, for it accords with the summary offered on 39^r: 3–4: 'sel nomero è grande o picolo, il pericolo è sempre grande'. When Machiavelli says that a small number is not so dangerous, he means that the bloodshed consequent upon such migrations is less: he does not mean that there is no danger of the migrants eventually dominating the natives: in fact his example of the small band of Trojans who settled in Italy, maintained themselves by friendly means, and finally dominated the country shows that the reverse is true. Gardiner saw that Machiavelli's statement was slightly misleading and changed it. The contemporary application of his argument – that even a small number of Spanish settlers would be intolerable to the English – required this careful modification of Machiavelli.

The ultimate source for the expulsion of the Moors is Procopius, *De Bello Vandalico* IV: 10.

41^v. 4–42^r. 2. *Et quanto . . . l'armi d'altrui*:
Concludo, adunque, che, sanza avere arme proprie, nessuno principato è sicuro; anzi è tutto obligato al fortuna, non avendo virtù che nelle avversità con fede lo difenda. E fu sempre opinione e sentenzia degli uomini savi 'quod nihil sit tam infirmum aut instabile quam fama potentiae non sua vi nixa' (*Prince* XIII).
Machiavelli quotes Tacitus, *Annals* XIII: 19.

42^r. 2–42^v. 4. *Percio* . . . *proprii sogetti*:
Debbe, adunque, uno principe non avere altro obietto nè altro pensiero, nè prendere cosa alcuna per sua arte, fuora della guerra e ordini e disciplina di essa; perchè quella è sola arte che si espetta a chi comanda; ed è di tanta virtù, che non solamente mantiene quelli che sono nati principi, ma molte volte fa gli uomini di privata fortuna salire a quel grado; e, per adverso, si vede che e' principi, quando hanno pensato più alle delicatezze che alle armi, hanno perso lo stato loro (*Prince* xiv).

42^r. 7. *Agatocle*: Agathocles, Tyrant of Syracuse 317–289 B.C. His rise to power is discussed in *Prince* viii and *Disc.* ii: 13, iii: 6, where even Machiavelli approaches a tone of moral condemnation. Gardiner ignores the moral question.

43^r. 2–43^v. 3. *il principe* . . . *disagi*: Again, the order of Machiavelli's ideas has been reversed:
Debbe, pertanto, mai levare el pensiero da questo esercizio della guerra, e nella pace vi si debbe più esercitare che nella guerra . . . debbe stare sempre in sulle cacce, e mediante quelle assuefare el corpo a' disagi: e parte imparare la natura de' siti, e conoscere come surgono e' monti, come imboccano le valle, come iacciono e' piani, ed intendere la natura, de' fiumi e de' paduli . . . debbe il principe leggere le istorie, e in quelle considerare le azioni degli uomini eccellenti; vedere come si sono governati nelle guerre; esaminare le cagioni delle vittorie e perdite loro, per potere queste fuggire, e quelle imitare (*Prince* xiv).
In rendering 'queste fuggire, e quelle imitare' both B and E make nonsense of the passage: E is redundant and B reverses the sense. The confusion may have been caused by the English text, for the order would naturally be reversed in English ('imitate the former and fly the latter' instead of 'fly the latter and imitate the former'). The translator copied the first part of the antithesis correctly from Machiavelli ('fuggire questo') then improperly emended *imitare* to *evitare* under the influence of the English text, which put avoiding losses second. However the error arose, it is clear that the variation from Machiavelli to E to B is sequential, for E differs from Machiavelli only in the substitution of *evitare* for *imitare*, whereas B, in an unsuccessful emendation of E, retains neither of Machiavelli's verbs.

50^v. 4. *assalto lo potentissimo regno di Francia*: In 1513, Henry VIII invaded France. The French took flight at the Battle of the Spurs, and Thérouanne and Tournai fell shortly afterwards. cf. *Disc.* i: 21.

51^r. 2. *morte di Jacomo lor re*: In the war between France and England in 1513, James IV (1473–1513) took the side of the French. He fell at the Battle of Flodden (9 September) in which the Scots were beaten decisively by the English, commanded by the Earl of Surrey.

53^r. 4–54^r. 3. *Nella citta di Yorcka* . . . *minima parte d'essi*:
Erat Eboraci vetus ac opulentissimum xenodochium, id est, domus hospitalis, divo Leonardo dedicata, ubi mendici et inopes homines hospitio accipiebantur curabanturque aegroti. Hinc domui tam sanctae

tota ea provincia pietatis causa, numerum quendam frumenti ut frugum omnium primitias, qui pauperibus usui esset, quotannis contribuebat, quem quidem frumenti numerum agrorum cultores persuasu quorundam Varuicensis factionis principum, velut fama erat, dare primo recusant, argumentantes id quod dabatur, non pauperibus, sed divitibus loci praefectis esse (*Angl. hist.* p. 509).
The remainder of Gardiner's account of the incident follows Polydore loosely. However Polydore places the incident in the reign of Edward IV, not Henry VI.

54^v. 8–55^r. 1. *diece mila huomini*: Polydore's figure is fifteen thousand (p. 509).

56^v. 7. *il tumolto delli popoli di Linconia*: The revolts of 1536, which included the Pilgrimage of Grace, were not limited to Lincolnshire, but involved Northumberland, Durham, Cumberland, Westmorland, Lancashire, and especially Yorkshire. See M. H. and R. Dodds, *The Pilgrimage of Grace* (London, 1915) and C. S. L. Davies, 'The Pilgrimage of Grace Reconsidered', *Past and Present*, XLI (1968), 54–76. Gardiner's claim that the revolts were stirred up by the nobility is not borne out by the evidence, though gentry and nobility did participate.

57^v. 2. *Giovanni Caddo*: Jack Cade, leader of the insurgents of 1450, in the reign of Henry VI. *Giovanni Strava*: Jack Straw, one of the leaders of the Great Revolt of 1381 in the reign of Richard II. 4. *Ketto*: Robert Kett, see note to 26^r. 3.

60^r. 8 ff. *altro tumolto qual Stravo era capitano*: This follows Polydore, pp. 397, 399. Polydore's version lacks the pithy saying 60^v. 5–7. *dicevano . . . scortigarebbe anche*:

> Itaque tributum in capita singula utriusque sexus hominum, qui id aetatis essent, quam iurisconsulti legitimam vocant, impositum est, ut singuli numos singulos argenteos, quos grossos dicunt, solverent. Et hoc pauperum fuit onus. Divitibus vero ac sacerdotibus amplior pecunia, ut par erat, imperata est. Haec exactio cum nova et insolita tum intolerabilis, ita plebis animum vulneravit, ut posteaquam pauperes qui solvendo non erant passim conquerentes diras voces in autores tanti facinoris iactarunt, et nihil se eo modo proficere viderunt, arma demum capienda statuentes, iamiam mortes et manus ubique exactoribus intentarint (p. 397).

61^v. margin. *Gli defetti del popolo nascono del principe*: Cf. *Disc.* III: 29 (title): 'Che gli peccati de' popoli nascono dai principi.'

62^v. 7. *Ezechias*: II Kings 20: 1–11; Isa. 38: 1–20.

63^r. 5. *Salomone*: Prov. 21: 1.

63^v. 2. *David*: I Sam. 26: 11. 8. *Paulo*: Rom. 13: 1–3.

64^r. 1–2. *in un altro luogo*: Eph. 6: 5–8.

65^r. 4. *io faro la vendetta*: Deut. 32: 5; Rom. 12: 20.

67^{v}5–72^r. 8. *Edouardo . . . amazzato*: Gardiner's account of Edward II paraphrases *Angl. hist.* pp. 341–54.

73^r. 7–74^r. 7. *fanno l'nimico.* ... *l'amazzo tutti*:
[il minacciare e il ingiurare] non tolgono forze al nimico; ma l'una lo fa
più cauto, l'altra gli fa avere maggiore odio contro di te, e pensare con
maggiore industria di offenderti ... Di che ne seguì già uno essemplo
notabile in Asia: dove Gabade, capitano de' Persi, essendo stato a campo
a Amida più tempo, ed avendo deliberato, stracco dal tedio della ossidione,
partirsi; levandosi già con il campo, quegli della terra, venuti tutti in su
le mura, insuperbiti della vittoria, non perdonarono a nessuna qualità
d'ingiuria, vituperando, accusando, e rimproverando la viltà e la pol-
troneria del nimico. Da che Gabade irritato, mutò consiglio; e ritornato
alla ossidione tanta fu la indegnazione, che in pochi giorni gli prese e
saccheggiò (*Disc.* ii: 26).

73^v. 6. *Gabide*: Cobades took Amida in 503 A.D. See Procopius, *Bell.*
Pers. i, 7: 12–29; Ammianus Marcellinus xix, 1 ff.

75^r. 4–5. *fece una legge*: There is no statute of Edward VI dealing with this
question.

76^v. 6. *il dispregiare le leggi*: Machiavelli warns against this in *Prince* i,
ii, iii and *Disc.* iii: 5. 7. *Empedocles*: The saying is not from Empedocles,
and I have not found it elsewhere.

77^r. 6. *Solone*: Actually Heraclitus is responsible for this remark:
'μάχεσθαι χρὴ τὸν δῆμον ὑπὲρ τοῦ νόμου ὅκωσπερ τείχεος' (Diogenes
Laertius ix, 2; Kirk and Raven, no. 252). 'The people must fight on behalf
of the law as though for the city wall.'

77^v. 6–78^r. 2. *Pero credo* ... *da chi l'ha fatto*: 'Perchè io non credo che sia
cosa di più cattivo essemplo in una republica, che fare una legge e non la
osservare; e tanto più, quanto la non è osservata da chi l'ha fatta' (*Disc.* i:
45).

79^r. 5. *amazzato nel mezo di suoi*: James III (1451–88) was thrown from his
horse and murdered at the Battle of Sauchieburn.

79^v. 1–80^r. 5. *Sapino* ... *l'altro di sicurtà*:
Sappino adunque i principi, come a quella ora ei cominciano a perdere
lo stato che cominciano a rompere le leggi, e quelle consuetudini che
sono antiche, e sotto le quali lungo tempo gli uomini sono vivuti. E se,
privati che ei sono dello stato, ei diventassono mai tanto prudenti che ei
conoscessono con quanta facilità i principati si tenghino da coloro che
saviamente si consigliano; dorebbe molto più loro tale perdita, ed a
maggiore pena si condannerebbono, che da altri fossono condannati.
Perchè egli è molto più facile essere amato dai buoni che dai cattivi, ed
ubidire alle leggi che volere comandare loro (*Disc.* iii: 5).

81^r. 3–6. *L'huomo dismentiga* ... *beni tolti*:
gli uomini sdimenticano più presto la morte del padre che la perdita del
patrimonio (*Prince* xvii). Le cose che hanno in se utilità, quando l'uomo
n'è privo, non le dimentica mai, ed ogni minima necessità te ne fa
ricordare; e perchè le necessità vengono ogni giorno, tu te ne ricordi
ogni giorno (*Disc.* iii: 23).

81ᵛ. 2. *Rufo*: William Rufus (reigned 1087–1100) was killed, probably accidentally, by Walter Tirel. Cf. *Angl. hist.* pp. 174–5.

83ʳ. 2–3. *Suinshedo*: John had an attack of dysentery at Swineshead, and died several days later at Newark (1216). Gardiner follows *Angl. hist.* p. 283.

85ʳ. 5. *Lambeth*: Canute died at Shaftesbury in 1035, not at Lambeth.

87ʳ. 4. *Stephano*: reigned 1135–54. His reign is discussed by Polydore, pp. 196–206.

89ʳ. 3. *Haraldo re, et Tosto*: Harold II was chosen king January 1066. Tostig enlisted the support of Harold of Norway, and their armies were defeated at Stamford Bridge on 25 September. On 29 September, William landed. Gardiner loosely follows *Angl. hist.* pp. 141–3.

90ʳ. 5. *Philippo*: In 346 B.C. the Thebans called upon Philip to help them in their war with the Phocians. He destroyed Phocis, and this led to other successes in Greece. The Athenians and the Thebans combined against him, and were defeated at Chaeronea in 338. He is discussed, though more briefly, in *Prince* XII.

92ʳ. 4–5. *imperator di Constantinopoli*: See 27ᵛ. 2–3 n. and *Prince* XIII. And compare Peter Ashton, *A Shorte Treatise Upon the Turkes Chronicles* (1546), fols. iiiʳ–viʳ.

92ᵛ. 2: *Amurato*. Amir, the Emir of Ionia.

93ᵛ. 1–2. *confederati contra i venitiani*: The League of Cambrai began to disintegrate after the victory at Vailà (see 27ʳ. 2 n.). Pope Julius II had allied himself with the Emperor and the King of France against Venice, but his real aim was to free Italy from foreign influence, and therefore after Vailà he became reconciled with Venice (1510) and Venetian power again increased.

94ʳ. 7. *Bernetto*: Bosworth is correct. The Battle of Barnet (1471) was waged by Edward IV against the Earl of Warwick.

95ʳ. 8. *Haraldo re di Norvegia*: see 89ʳ. 3 n.

96ʳ. 4–96ᵛ. 4. *Per esser . . . roina*:
Debbesi considerare, pertanto, quanto sia vana e la fede e le promesse di quelli che si truovano privi della loro patria . . . E quanto alle vane promesse e speranze, egli è tanta la voglia estrema che è in loro di ritornare in casa, che ei credono naturalmente molte cose che sono false, e molte a arte ne aggiungano: talchè, tra quello che ei credono e quello che ei dicono di credere, ti riempino di speranza talmente che, fondatoti in su quella, o tu fai una spesa in vano o tu fai una impresa dove tu rovini (*Disc.* II: 31).

98ᵛ. 3. *cinquanta*: Polydore's figure is thirty (p. 143).

100ᵛ. 1. *Guilhelmo*: William's repressive measures are discussed in *Angl. hist.* p. 148.

101ʳ. 3–5. *in vero . . . crudelita*: 'al principe nuovo è impossibile fuggire il nome del crudele, per essere li stati nuovi pieni di pericoli' (*Prince* XVII).

101ᵛ. 3–5. *perchè . . . clementia nuova*: 'mai le ingiurie vecchie furono cancellate da' beneficii nuovi' (*Disc.* III: 4).

102ᵛ. 3-6. *piglio . . . li spense tutti*: Cf. 'a possederli securamente basta avere spenta la linea del principe che li dominava' (*Prince* III). Machiavelli is referring to new possessions not accustomed to free government.

103ʳ. 9-103ᵛ. 2. *sempre in pericolo . . . defraudati di quello*: 'si può avvertire ogni principe, che non viva mai sicuro del suo principato, finchè vivono coloro che ne sono stati spogliati' (*Disc.* III: 4).

104ʳ. 1-6. *come fece . . . lor odii*:
El re Luigi fu messo in Italia dalla ambizione de' Viniziani. . . [I Viniziani] feciono signore, el re, del terzo di Italia. . . [Luigi] per volere il regno di Napoli, lo divise con il re di Spagna; e dove lui era, prima, arbitro d'Italia, e' vi misse uno compagno, a cio che gli ambiziosi di quella provincia e malcontenti di lui avessino dove ricorrere (*Prince* III).
2. *l'ambitione deli venitiani*: The Venetians signed a treaty with Louis XII in 1499, under the terms of which they were to receive Cremona and the Ghiradadda. 4. *il re di Spagna*: Ferdinand of Aragon, who signed the Treaty of Granada with Louis in 1500, dividing the territory of Naples.

104ᵛ. 1. *Edouardo*: Edward, Earl of Warwick (1475-99) was beheaded 1499.

105ᵛ. 2-108ᵛ. 5. *cosi sulthan Paiaxit . . . honore turchesco*: Gardiner's Turkish history comes from Paolo Giovio, probably by way of Peter Ashton's English version, *A Short Treatise upon the Turkes Chronicles* (1546). The account of Bayazid and Selym is found on fols. 53ʳ-77ᵛ in that work. Gardiner follows the order of events in Ashton's version closely, but his account is shortened, and differs in several details. Gardiner gives the number of troops Selym lost in his first battle with Bayazid, and Giovio gives no number. In listing the relatives Selym killed, Gardiner says he killed his brother Ahamat first. Giovio *mentions* the death of Ahamat first, but later puts it last in chronological sequence. Gardiner also puts the number of nephews killed at five, whereas Giovio gives no number. 105ᵛ. 2. *Paiaxit*: Bayazid II (1446-1512). 4. *Selym*: Selym I (1467-1520).

106ʳ. 3. *un stato di vivere*: In Samandria. 5. *dove era Paiaxit*: (Ashton fols. 53ʳ-54ʳ) Bayazid was *en route* to Constantinople fearing Selym would take it, and their forces met in battle near Adrianople.

107ᵛ. 1-2. *alcuni bassi*: Mustapha Pasha threatened Bayazid with death if he did not renounce his title (Ashton fols. 59ʳ⁻ᵛ).

109ʳ. 3-6. *io non li lodo . . . offenderlo*:
Sono questi modi crudelissimi, e nimici d'ogni vivere, non solamente cristiano, ma umano; e debbegli qualunque uomo fuggire, e volere piuttosto vivere privato, che re con tanta rovina degli uomini; nondimeno, colui che non vuole pigliare quella prima via del bene, quando si voglia mantenere, conviene che entri in questo male (*Disc.* I: 26).
Questi modi referred, in Machiavelli, to the cruelty of Philip of Macedon.

109ʳ. 7. *fortrezze*: Compare Machiavelli's opinion in *Prince* XX.

111ᵛ. 5-112ʳ. 4. *Per tanto . . . particolare*:
Debbe, pertanto, uno principe non si curare della infamia di crudele, per tenere li sudditi suoi uniti e in fede; perchè con pochissimi esempi,

sarà più pietoso che quelli e' quali, per troppa pietà, lascino seguire e' disordini, di che ne nasca occisioni o rapine; perchè queste sogliono offendere una universalità intera, e quelle esecuzioni che vengono dal principe offendono uno particulare (*Prince* xvii).

112ᵛ. 2. *la crudeltà*: Cambyses, King of the Medes and Persians (d. 522 B.C.), among his other acts of cruelty, had his brother put to death. 3. *Silla*: Lucius Cornelius Sulla (138–78 B.C.). The reference is to the proscriptions of 81 B.C., in the first year of Sulla's dictatorship. 4. *è piu volte utile*: Cruelty, not Sulla, is the intended subject. The sentence is incorrect as it stands, but it is clear that Sulla's example is offered to show the utility of cruelty. 6–7. *Attila . . . Tamerlanes*: Both, of course, famous for cruelty. Attila, King of the Huns (c. 406–453 A.D.); Tamerlan, Tartar conqueror (1336–1405).

113ʳ. 2–114ʳ. 8. *e buono . . . i figlioli*:
Nasce da questo una disputa: s'egli è meglio essere amato che temuto, o e converso. Rispondesi che si vorebbe essere l'uno e altro; ma perchè egli è difficile accozzarli insieme, è molto più sicuro essere temuto che amato, quando si abbia a mancare dell'uno de' dua. Perchè degli uomini si può dire questo generalmente: che sieno ingrati, volubili, simulatori e dissimulatori, fuggitori de' pericoli, cupidi di guadagno; e mentre fai loro bene, sono tutti tua, offeronti el sangue, la roba, la vita, e' figliuoli, come di sopra dissi, quando il bisogno è discosto; ma, quando ti si apressa, e' si rivoltano. E quel principe che si è tutto fondato in sulle parole loro, trovandosi nudo di altre preparazioni, rovina; perchè le amicizie che si acquistano col prezzo, e non con grandezza e nobiltà di animo, si meritano, ma le non si hanno, e a' tempi non si possono spendere. E gli uomini hanno meno respetto a offendere uno che si facci amare, che uno che si facci temere; perchè l'amore è tenuto da uno vinculo di obligo, il quale, per essere gli uomini tristi, da ogni occasione di propria utilità è rotto; ma il timore è tenuta da una paura di pena che non ti abbandona mai.

Debbe nondimanco el principe farsi temere in modo che, se non acquista lo amore, che fugga l'odio; perchè può bene stare insieme essere temuto, e non odiato; il che farà sempre, quando si astenga dalla roba de' sua cittadini e de' sua sudditi, e dalle donne loro. E quando pure li bisognasse procedere contro al sangue di alcuno, farlo quando vi sia iustificazione conveniente e causa manifesta; ma sopra tutto, astenersi dalla roba d'altri; perchè gli uomini sdimenticano più presto la morte del padre che la perdita del patrimonio (*Prince* xvii).

114ᵛ. 5. *Cortineo*: Edward Courtenay, Earl of Devon (1526–56) was imprisoned in the Tower from 1538 until 1553. His father, the Marquis of Exeter, had been executed in 1539 as an aspirant to the Crown. Gardiner was in the Tower during the reign of Edward VI, and became a friend to the young Courtenay. He favored a match between Courtenay and Mary until Mary made known her preference for Philip of Spain. Courtenay was implicated, along with Elizabeth, in Wyatt's Rebellion in 1554, and Gardiner was accused of shielding him from prosecution.

115ʳ. 2–116ʳ. 6. *et quanto . . . in giuditio*:

Ma quando el principe è con gli eserciti e ha in governo moltitudine di soldati, allora al tutto è necessario non si curare del nome del crudele; perchè, sanza questo nome, non si tenne mai esercito unito ne disposta ad alcuna fazione. Intra le mirabili azioni di Annibale si connumera questa, che, avendo uno esercito grossissimo, misto di infiniti generazioni di uomini, condotto a militare in terre aliene, non vi surgessi mai alcuna dissensione, ne infra loro nè contro al principe, così nella cattiva come nella sua buona fortuna. Il che non potè nascere da altro che da quella sua inumana crudeltà; la quale, insieme con infinite sua virtù, lo fece sempre, nel cospetto de' suoi soldati, venerando e terribile; e, sanza quella, a fare quello effetto le altre sua virtù non li bastavanno . . . E che sia vero che l'altre sua virtù non sarebbano bastate, si può considerare in Scipione, rarissimo non solamente ne' tempi sua, ma in tutta la memoria delle cose che si sanno: dal quale gli eserciti suoi in Ispagna si ribellorono; il che non nacque da altro che dalla troppa sua pietà, la quale aveva data a' suoi soldati più licenzia che alla disciplina militare si conveniva. La qual cosa li fu da Fabio Massimo in senato rimproverata, e chiamato da lui corruttore della romana milizia. E' Locrensi, sendo stati da uno legato di Scipione destrutti, non furono da lui vendicati, ne la insolenzia di quello legato corretta, nascendo tutto da quella sua natura facile (*Prince* xvii).

And compare Machiavelli's treatment of the same figures in *Disc.* iii: 21.

115ᵛ. 7. *ribellorno suoi esserciti*: The rebellion took place in 206 B.C. See Livy xxviii: 24–9.

116ʳ. 2. *Fabio massimo*: In 205, Scipio had recaptured Locri. When complaints of the cruelty of Scipio's lieutenant there reached Rome, Fabius attacked Scipio in the Senate. See Livy xxix: 19, 21. Alphonso makes the point, which is in neither of Machiavelli's discussions of Scipio and Hannibal, that Scipio won (fol. 117ʳ).

118ʳ. 7. *I romani et altri principi christiani hanno in governo subditi, et non servi*: Gardiner's discussion of this distinction between those who can be ruled by cruelty and those who must be handled with kindness is based on *Disc.* iii: 19:

o che tu hai a reggere uomini che ti sono per l'ordinario compagni, o uomini che ti sono sempre suggetti. Quando ti sono compagni, non si può interamente usare la pena . . . e perchè la plebe romana aveva in Roma equale imperio con la Nobiltà, non poteva uno, che ne diventava principe a tempo, con crudeltà e rozzezza maneggiarla.

But note the difference: for Machiavelli the distinction is between comrades, who must be treated well, and subjects, who can be handled roughly; Gardiner draws the line between subjects and slaves. Machiavelli is contrasting republics and monarchies; Gardiner contrasts the limited monarchies of England and France with the despotism of the Turk.

118^v. 7–8. *soggetto ali baroni*: Gardiner gives an extremely anachronistic account of the function of the peerage, both in regard to rent and military service. On the military survivals of feudalism see Lindsay Boyton, *The Elizabethan Militia, 1558–1638* (London, 1967), pp. 31–3.

120^r. 2–121^v. 4. *che non vede* . . . *al suo marito*: The account of the discomfiture of the schoolmaster is based, ultimately, on Livy v: 27. The siege of Falerii occurred in 394 B.C. The Roman general was Marcus Furius Camillus (fl. 396–365 B.C.). The story of Fabricius and Pyrrhus is to be found in Livy, *Periocha* XIII and Plutarch, *Pyrrhus* XXI. The incident took place in 278 B.C. The final example of humanity, that of Scipio's return of the wife of a local chief during the campaign against New Carthage, is from Livy XXVI: 50. But Gardiner's immediate source was, without doubt, *Disc.* III: 20, which contains all three examples:

Essendo Cammillo con lo essercito intorno alla città de' Falisci, e quella assediando, uno maestro di scuola de' più nobili fanciulli di quella città, pensando di gratificarsi Cammillo ed il popolo romano sotto colore di esercizio uscendo con quegli fuora della terra, gli condusse tutti nel campo innanzi a Cammillo, e presentandogli, disse, come, mediante loro, quella terra si darebbe nelle sue mani. Il quale presente non solamente non fu accettato da Cammillo; ma, fatto spogliare quel maestro, e legatogli le mani di dietro, e dato a ciascuno di quegli fanciulli una verga in mano, lo fece da quegli con di molte battiture accompagnare nella terra. La quale cosa intesa da quegli cittadini, piacque tanto loro la umanità ed integrità di Cammillo, che, sanza volere più diffendersi, diliberarono di darli la terra. Dove è da considerare, con questo vero essemplo, quanto qualche volta possa più negli animi degli uomini uno atto umano e pieno di carità, che un atto feroce e violento; e come molte volte quelle provincie e quelle città che le armi, gl'instrumenti bellici ed ogni altra umana forza non ha potuto aprire, uno essemplo di umanità e di pietà, di castità, o di liberalità, ha aperte. Di che ne sono nelle istorie, oltre a questo, molti altri essempli. E vedesi come l'armi romane non potevano cacciare Pirro d'Italia, e ne lo cacciò la liberalità di Fabrizio, quando gli manifestò l'offerta che aveva fatta ai Romani quello suo familiare, di avvelenarlo. Vedesi ancora, come a Scipione Affricano non dette tanta riputazione in Ispagna la espugnazione di Cartagine Nuova, quanto gli dette quello essemplo di castità, di avere renduto la moglie, giovane, bella, ed intatta, al suo marito; la fama della quale azione gli fece amica tutta la Ispagna (*Disc.* III: 20).

122^r. 6. *misericordioso et giusto*: Perhaps Exodus 34: 6–7 is meant: 'A God merciful and gracious . . . but who will by no means clear the guilty.'

124^r. 3–6. *in vero* . . . *sangue reale*: Cf.:

Dico, pertanto, che questi stati, quali acquistandosi si aggiungono a uno stato antiquo di quello che acquista, o e' sono della medesima provincia e della medesima lingua, o non sono. Quando e' sieno, è facilità grande a tenerli, massime quando non sieno usi a vivere liberi; e a possederli

NOTES

securamente basta avere spenta la linea del principe che li dominava (*Prince* III).

125ʳ. 3–125ᵛ. 6. *Et sendovi* . . . *nel principato*:
standovi, si veggono nascere e' disordini, e presto vi puoi rimediare; non vi stando, s'intendono quando e' sono grandi, e che non vi è più remedio. Non è, oltre di questo, la provincia spogliata da' tuoi officiali; satisfannosi e' sudditi del ricorso propinquo al principe; donde hanno più cagione di amarlo, volendo essere buoni, e, volendo essere altrimenti, di temerlo. . . . [debbe] non alterare nè lor legge nè loro dazii; talmente che in brevissimo tempo diventa, con loro principato antiquo, tutto uno corpo (*Prince* III).

'Antico nel principato' in the Gardiner text is an unusual locution: what has happened is that the adjective 'antico' which refers in Machiavelli to the prince's original possessions has been transferred to the prince himself. Machiavelli's meaning is that the new state will soon become one with the old ('antiquo') while the Gardiner–Rainsford version means that the prince will soon become well-established ('antico') in the new territory. The shift probably originated through Gardiner's desire to avoid the final phrase 'tutto uno corpo'; he wished to offer Philip advice on establishing himself in England, but surely did not want England, the new possession, to become 'tutto uno corpo' with Spain. If Gardiner wrote something like 'the new prince will soon become well-established' Rainsford would have found something that looked like that in Machiavelli ('diventa, con loro principato antiquo') and offered his own 'venerà antico nel principato' as a reading that preserved Machiavelli's words and Gardiner's meaning.

126ᵛ. 7. *Absalon*: II Sam. 15: 2–6.
128ᵛ. 4. *questi poveri homini*: See 56ᵛ: 7n. for the Lincoln and York revolts. This incident is not recorded elsewhere.
130ʳ. 7. *la leggi*: 11 H. VII c. 3, probably.
131ʳ. 5. *per rivocare quella iniqua legge*: 1 H. VIII c. 6 repealed 11 H. VII c. 3.
132ᵛ. 4–133ʳ. 6. *in altre attioni* . . . *il stato*:
E io so che ciascuna confesserà che sarebbe laudabilissima cosa in uno principe trovarsi, di tutte le soprascritte qualità, ma perchè li non si possono avere nè interamente osservare, per le condizioni umane che non lo consentono, gli è necessario essere tanto prudente che sappia fuggire l'infamia di quelli vizii che li torrebbano lo stato (*Prince* XV).
133ʳ. 8–134ᵛ. 5. *quanto d'esser* . . . *delle mani*:
A uno principe, adunque, non è necessario avere in fatto tutte le soprascritte qualità, ma è bene necessario parere di averle . . . come parere pietoso, fedele, umano, intero, religioso, ed essere; ma stare in modo edificato con l'animo, che, bisognando non essere, tu possa e sappi mutare el contrario . . . Alessandro VI non fece mai altro, non pensò mai ad altro, che a ingannare uomini: e sempre trovò subietto da poterlo fare. E non fu mai uomo che avessi magiore efficacia in asseverare, e

166

con magiore giuramenti affermassi una cosa, che la osservassi meno: nondimeno sempre li succederono gli inganni ad votum, perchè conosceva bene questa parte del mondo ... Sendo, dunque, uno principe necessitato sapere bene usare la bestia, debbe di quelle pigliare la golpe e il lione; perchè il lione non si difende da' lacci, la golpe non si difende da' lupi ... E hassi ad intendere questo, che uno principe, e massime uno principe nuovo, non può osservare tutte quelle cose per le quali gli uomini sono tenuti buoni, sendo spesso necessitato, per mantenere lo stato, operare contro alla fede, contro alla carità, contro alla umanità, contro alla religione. E però bisogna che egli abbia uno animo disposto a volgersi secondo ch'e'venti della fortuna e le variazioni delle cose li comandano ... Debbe, adunque, avere uno principe gran cura che non gli esca mai di bocca una cosa che non sia piena delle soprascritte cinque qualità; e paia, a vederlo e udirlo, tutto pietà, tutto fede, tutto integrità, tutto umanità, tutto religione. E non è cosa più necessaria a parere di avere che questa ultima qualità. E gli uomini, in universali, iudicano più agli occhi che alle mani (*Prince* xvIII).

Gardiner has rearranged the sequence.

133^v. 6. *Alessandro papa sesto*: Rodrigo Borgia (1431–1503, Pope from 1492).

136^r. 1. *Federico*: Frederick III (1415–93).

136^v. 6. *padre*: This is a mistake: Charles was the son of Philip I and the father of Philip II.

139^v. 3–5. *per loquale ... la christianità*: 'Regni (in questi parti)' may refer to England and the Netherlands. Philip was made sovereign of the Netherlands on 26 October 1555.

140^v. 1–2: *Il duca di Norforchia*: Probably Thomas Howard, 4th Duke of Norfolk (b. 1536). See intro. p. 3.

INDEX

Numbers in roman type refer to pages. Numbers in italic type refer to folios in the text of the *Ragionamento* and in the translation.